THE
SEARCH
FOR MYSELF

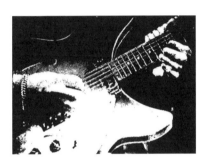

THE
SEARCH
FOR MYSELF

Mike Pender

British Library Cataloguing-in-Publication Data
A catalogue record for this book is available from the British Library.

ISBN: 978-0-9931213-0-2

Published worldwide by Genuine Article Books, Malpas, Cheshire *(Prop: M. Prendergast).*

Produced by Poppleton Publishing Services, York.

Printed by TPH Printing www.theprintinghouseuk.com.

For Michael, Stephanie, Nathan and Alexander

...and for John Wayne,
without whose original search
this book might never
have been written

Acknowledgements

I would like to thank everyone who has helped me write this book, especially Tony Sherwood, Bill Kenwright, Frank O'Connor, Ann and Roger Askey, Sylvia Beaumont, Gill and Geoff Westwood, Margaret Brown, Roger Dopson, Spencer Leigh, Sam Leach, Pete Dolan, Tony West, Horst Fascher, Bob Wooler, Ron Musker and Sam Erskine.

In particular, I would like thank Richard Mahoney, who first suggested to me that I should write my life story, and who helped me put it all together. Also David Parker and George Groom-White for their assistance in getting it ready for publication.

Last but by no means least, I would like to thank my wife, May, for her support throughout what has been an exciting, but at times difficult and emotional journey.

Mike Pender
September 2014

Foreword by
Bill Kenwright, CBE

You had to be there...Liverpool 1961. Everyone had their favourite band – Rory and his Hurricanes topped a lot of lists at first, before the Beatles conquered everyone who had come before. Gerry was always considered to have a great, indefatigable voice. The Big Three had the connoisseurs drooling, and Billy J. had the looks. But my favourite band was not in the Eppie empire.

Mike, John, Tony and Chris started out as a four-piece and later backed Johnny Sandon. But soon their supreme musicianship and unbeatable harmonies dictated that they backed no one but themselves. Their path to stardom was probably a little quieter, a little less showy than the rest – but when it hit, it bit big. They were truly superstars of their era – recording hit after hit and creating some of the greatest pop music classics of all time. They had potentially career-threatening changes in personnel as they climbed the ladder to international success, but they retained, above everything else, their pivotal vocal mastery. And that was especially prevalent in the impeccable vocals of Mike Pender.

Mike and I shared another love, apart from the rhythm & blues that was the musical source of all things Liverpool in those days: our love for the Merseyside team that played in blue. Do I have to mention their name? No – but I will: Everton Football Club. In particular, and alongside tens of thousands of Bluenoses, we shared an adoration for one particular player – Alex Young, 'the Golden Vision'.

I will never forget a freezing Friday night at the County Ground, Stockport, where much to the dismay of Evertonians, Alex Young made his debut for Stockport County only a few months after leaving his beloved Everton. County were one of the first clubs to play on Friday evenings in those days, so many Evertonians made the journey to salute their idol. I found myself cheering alongside another of my heroes, Mike Pender of the Searchers, sitting nearby.

I can remember, as clearly as if it was yesterday, that Mike approached me and introduced himself, and said his wife May was a *Coronation Street* fan. Maybe he was simply being kind, but I was dumbstruck. Until this day, 'Needles And Pins' remains probably my all-time favourite record of the Mersey beat era. And there, standing in front of me, was the guy who had been hugely responsible for its success, saying that he knew *me*!

That night was the start of a friendship that has lasted for more than four decades. Mike now has his own Searchers, and I am the Chairman of Everton Football Club. But I am pretty convinced that we are the same two Evertonians that met on that cold night. Certainly, our relationship has never changed. Whenever we meet, Mike will always ask about my mum, and I will always ask about May. Then we will talk Everton.

I was saddened when Mike and John parted, but was pretty thrilled when, soon after, Mike's new band appeared for me at a function. And there he was, looking and sounding better than ever – and Mike always was the best-looking kid on the block!

Life's had many ups and downs for Mike and May, particularly over the last few years, as I am sure you will read in this book. But I know that their roots, their near and dear ones, and their own personal togetherness, have helped them through.

And then there is the music. For Mike, there has always been the music – and he is a musician to his fingertips. A great guitarist and a supreme vocalist whose legend will always be around. Simply put on your record player a scratchy 'Don't Throw Your Love Away', then go to 'Goodbye My Love', and finish with the immortal 'Needles And Pins', and you will be in the presence of three of the greatest pop anthems that this country has ever known, sung by one of its greatest proponents. And, yes, if you want to follow that with Johnny Keating's 'Z Cars Theme', Mike and I wont mind at all. Respect, Mike.

Your fan Bill – your friend Bill.

Contents

Contents

Introduction

I have thought many times about writing my autobiography, to literally set the record straight, not only about my time both with and after the Searchers, but to corrcct the many myths and legends that have grown up over the years.

I believe that, as the founder member of the group who brought in Tony and Chris, now is the right time to publish a book – after the 50th anniversary of the group's very first single and No. 1 hit, 'Sweets For My Sweet'. However, I did take a bit of persuading. Now I'd like to set the record straight after seeing other claims made by other sources. As someone who was there from the beginning, I hope this book provides the first authentic history of a group that was proud to be widely regarded as second only to the Beatles in 1964.

In 2010, a big fan of the classic '60s Searchers and of my post-1986 group, Mike Pender's Searchers, a guy that I'd never met before, Richard Mahoney, arranged a meeting with me in my dressing room at Birmingham's Symphony Hall, before a *Solid Silver '60s* show.

Like many other Searchers and MPS fans, he had read various books and articles about the group and was very unhappy about how many of these publications were biased against me and did not acknowledge the role that I played as lead guitarist and lead vocalist for so many years, in the good times and the bad.

He was also aware that the true story of my departure from the group in December 1985 had never been told, which was also the cause of the legal battles that were waged in later years in the High Court. I was happy to accept Richard's kind offer to help me tell my story, with assistance from my many friends, colleagues and fellow musicians.

You will read how important my family life has been to me

and how I have other interests apart from music – there are many.

Now in my early 70s, I still enjoy performing with MPS, and the fans certainly appreciate our gigs, although over the last ten years or so there have been many solo gigs with friends from the '60s, including Dave Berry, Brian Poole and Tony Crane and Bill Kinsley of the Merseybeats.

I still have a large collection of guitars – 18 at the last count – including my beloved 12-string Rickenbackers.

The *Hearts In Their Eyes* box set, released recently, includes many tracks on which I provided the lead on guitar and vocals. It is a fitting musical tribute to the group in the 1962-85 period, and also a very appropriate tribute to those Searchers sadly no longer with us – my once great friend Tony Jackson, Chris Curtis, and not forgetting Joe (Tony) West, our original bass player, and our vocalist from our pre-fame days, Johnny Sandon (Billy Beck).

CHAPTER 1

Memories –
Where It All Started

'Life's had many ups and downs for Mike and May, particularly over the past few years, as I am sure you will read in this book. But I know that their roots, their near and dear ones, and their own personal togetherness, has helped them through. And then there is the music. For Mike, there has always been the music – and he is a musician to his fingertips.' — Bill Kenwright, CBE.

I was born in 1941 in Bootle, a suburb of Liverpool, and the war was raging all around us, as the city was particularly badly hit. Ever since my early childhood days, I had been fascinated by Western movies. That was the start of something big, but I had no inkling of it at the time. All will become clear.

It's not easy for anyone to remember events far back in the depths of their memories when they were just a few years old, but I vividly recall when, as an eight-year-old, every Saturday afternoon I went to my local cinema, the Commodore, known to me and my pals as the 'Commie'. History was made the day years later when, in 1957, aged sixteen, I went to the Regent Cinema in Liverpool Road, Crosby, Liverpool. A new cowboy film, *The Searchers*, starring John Wayne was showing and I was dying to see the movie, mostly because it was cowboys versus Indians.

At the time, and after leaving school with my brains in my feet, it was my fingers that would start me on a journey that would take me beyond my wildest dreams. As lead singer of the

Searchers, I enjoyed a career as a singer-guitarist that took me to the top of the pops and beyond. But the years of success as a performer from an early age and the vagaries of the lifestyle and relationships took their toll, and I decided I wanted a less stressful lifestyle. I opted out, but little did I know what animosity and back-biting it would bring in the aftermath.

As the instigator of the regular group, which, as well as going to the cinema, was already delving into pop music fame, I had no hesitation, when waiting for the bus home that day, of suggesting 'Searchers' as the name of our proposed musical group. I think three people were there that day – John McNally, Big Ron Woodbridge and myself. I am certain about those three, but there could have been one or two more. The only 'Searchers' ever heard of before that fateful sunny afternoon in 1957 were John Wayne and Jeffrey Hunter, who spent much of the film searching for a young Natalie Wood, who had been captured by Comanche Indians. This film also inspired my later idol, Buddy Holly, who picked up the phrase 'That'll be the day', which is repeated several times in the film by John Wayne. Buddy recorded his new song, which was to become an all-time classic. The Regent Cinema in Crosby first opened in 1920, but closed as a cinema in 1968 to become a venue for bingo, and, later, it was used as a sports hall by a local school.

In the early years, I would practise playing guitar over and over in my mother's front parlour until the skin on the ends of my fingers would harden and turn black – which actually made it easier to play.

Then, John McNally and I met for the first time. Even from those early days, memories seem to be stretched. Frank Allen states in one of his books that John had a skiffle group, which I apparently joined. When taking up music and meeting other friends, contrary to what has been said or written, I was *never* influenced by skiffle. If McNally had a skiffle group, it must have been before I met him. In those early days, we were probably as close as we would ever be. We would get together, mostly at his house, to play instrumentals.

After John McNally and I helped Joe West learn to play

bass guitar, the original and first real, performing line-up of the Searchers was complete. This line-up appears on our earliest known photo (drummer Joe Kennedy is unfortunately out of shot). Our uniform was red sweaters, black slacks, white shirts and pale blue ties. It broke up when our Watkins Dominator amp – which is also in the photo – was stolen. Joe had bought the amp for John and myself, but decided he didn't want to carry on.

After months of just hanging around, I lost touch with John. Then someone, probably the Dolan boys, told me John was in Walton Hospital awaiting a serious operation. So now it was just me and my Club 60.

I found Tony Jackson at the Cross Keys pub and we became good friends. The members of the next Searchers phase were myself and John McNally on guitars and Tony Jackson vocals (more about Tony later, and about how our friendship developed). Tony then learnt to play bass and we played as a trio. This was roughly about 1959.

Chris Curtis joined later on drums, and after I had brought the four of us together – Tony, Chris, John and myself – we performed as that line-up for a while, with Chris and his extrovert personality being the frontman, although Tony and I did our fair share of vocals. I preferred playing lead guitar, of course.

The four of us were pretty close in those early days, and 'then we were five' when Johnny Sandon – real name Bill Beck – later joined as our vocalist. The idea was suggested to us by Cavern deejay Bob Wooler, who, after us playing many gigs in and around Liverpool, told us we would sound better with a lead vocalist. We then became known as Johnny Sandon & The Searchers.

I must make it clear at this point – because it has been written otherwise – that Johnny Sandon did not join us until *after* Tony, Chris, John and I were established as the Searchers: a fact confirmed by Tony, Chris, myself and many others including Mersey beat concert promoter Sam Leach.

In his excellent book, *The Rocking City*, Sam describes how he met up with us on April Fool's Day 1960, just before a big show he was putting on at St George's Hall. A couple of hours before the show was due to start, he recalls he saw 'a group of four lads offering to play for nothing. I admired the initiative of those four fresh faces before me, and let them in for free... Before long I was booking them regularly behind Johnny Sandon... I thought at the time they would go far and I wasn't wrong... The world got to know them as the Searchers, a really great bunch of lads, especially Tony, their version of John Lennon.' I think he meant Chris, however this important quote confirms that we were a group of four before Johnny Sandon joined us.

Interviewed in 1993 by *Record Collector*'s Alan Clayson, Tony Jackson explained that Chris initially assumed lead vocals from behind the drum kit, but 'it was felt we'd stand a better chance with a guy out front with a real good voice.' That person was Bill Beck. 'He was basically country & western, Johnny Cash, Jim Reeves, all that sort of thing, so we drifted into that kind of market. We got a residency at a pub by Liverpool football ground called the Sandon, and as Billy sounded like Johnny Cash, we rechristened him Johnny Sandon.'

This version of events was also corroborated by Chris. When he was asked by interviewer Spencer Leigh in 1998 whether Johnny Sandon was the lead singer when he joined the Searchers, Chris replied, 'No, he joined not long after me. He had a marvellous voice, and later on I recorded him independently for Pye Records: *(sings)* "Your lips on mine are soft as dew" – you know the Brook Benton song, "So Many Ways" – and he did it brilliantly. God knows what happened to the tapes.'

Johnny left the band in February 1962, hoping to become a solo artist and comedian. We were a bit despondent at first to lose him, but it turned out to be a blessing in disguise. We realised we didn't actually need Johnny's voice, and that we had become very capable vocalists ourselves. Chris, Tony and I shared all the vocals from then on, and the local fans loved us. Chris would get rapturous applause for his version of 'Stand By Me', while Tony and I would harmonise on 'Listen To Me'. By this time, my confidence had grown to the extent I was singing songs right across the board. 'Take Good Care Of My Baby' comes to mind, which was a favourite with all our fans, especially the girls – and one girl in particular: the lovely Miss Doyle.

Not long before he passed away, aged 72, on 11 November 2010, Joe West sent me a copy of the historic photo he had found of 'some young pop stars', as he described the original Searchers line-up – Joe Kennedy, Joe West, John McNally, and Mike Pender, with the infamous amplifier that was later stolen. In his note, Joe asked me to autograph the photo, which, with the other autographs, has become a very important and rare item of Searchers memorabilia.

Joe died at his home in Hightown, Merseyside. The headline in the *Liverpool Echo* was 'Searchers Legend Dies in His Sleep'. Obviously, our friendship went back a very long way – he always referred to me as 'Mick', which hardly anybody else does. Joe attended St Mary's College in Crosby and had a successful career as a show-business agent, establishing Tony West Entertainments in 1976. He was a lifelong fan of Liverpool Football Club and was a personal friend of Bill Shankly. Very regrettably, in recent times we had met only at funerals – those for Tony Jackson, Chris Curtis, and for my son, Nathan, who had died young in tragic circumstances, but Joe had remained a close friend of John McNally. He was an extremely nice man and his passing took away yet another strong link with Liverpool and the original Searchers.

As already mentioned, it wasn't until I met up with Chris Crummey (Curtis) in Bootle, in 1959, that the final line-up was brought together. The line-up of Pender, McNally, Jackson and Curtis were the Searchers signed by Pye Records in March 1963. When we hear the No. 1 records on the radio nowadays, those are the four people who are featured. Frank Allen joined the band later, after our three No. 1 hits.

Whether or not the original line-up will ever be inducted into the Rock and Roll Hall of Fame remains to be seen. Two of those awards would, very regrettably, be posthumous. It has to be said that these are the four young men that made history on both sides of the Atlantic, and in many people's opinion were second only to those other four famous Liverpudlians. Fifty years on, it also has to be said that, although there are still two original members of that nostalgically famous group still playing music today, albeit not together, anything relative to those four original members will always be a tribute group, and must be taken in tribute form only. As someone once said, 'It is only the original that stands the test of time, anything that follows is a copy.' But what a test it turned out to be, and what a way to make a living!

CHAPTER 2

Early Years – The War

I enjoyed many happy and adventurous hours travelling the length and breadth of the country trainspotting.

Someone said to me, 'Never forget your roots.' How can I? Going back to my childhood and the post-world-war years, another of my fond memories is that of my mother sitting me on the side of the brown sink in the kitchen, washing my hair and combing it into a side parting – a style that I would keep until leaving school (well, almost).

The scary war years were no longer in full flow, and I can remember playing with the other kids in the bombed-out buildings and corner shops. It had been a living hell. Liverpool city – and my home area of Bootle in particular – were hit by thousands of tonnes of high-explosive bombs and thousands of incendiaries dropped by the German Luftwaffe on seven consecutive nights between 1 May and 8 May 1941, shortly after I was born.

People remember the Nazi propagandist Lord Haw Haw addressing a radio message to the people of Bootle, saying, 'The kisses on your windows won't help you.' That was a reference to the tape stuck across windows in an attempt to stop the glass shattering in bomb raids. So I was told. Bootle is close to the docks and was the location of many large factories, such as the Bryant & May matchworks, which was totally destroyed in the bombing. When I was just a few years old, me and the other boys would sometimes find coins on the bombed-out sites where the local shops had been. There were halfpennies, threepenny bits, tanners (as we called the sixpenny-piece) and – on a good day – half-crowns. I can't remember if I ever told my parents.

I vividly remember one night hearing a loud bang and running out next morning to find a huge crater in the road where a plane had crashed, quite near our house, past the 'subby' (subway). Me and the other kids spent hours in the hole looking for 'bollies' (ball bearings).

People often refer to their parents as 'mum' and 'dad'. Well, the 'dad' applied, but as a child growing up, I used the very Northern 'mam'. Very few children used 'mum', and even at school-leaving age, it was always 'mother', never 'mum'. In truth, I suppose (to me anyway), it was always a posh way of referring to your mother. My wife May tells me she always referred to her mother as 'mum', even though at the time, she didn't live a million miles from me. Like many Scousers, I can still hear those words, 'me mam and dad'.

I have lots of fond memories of St John's Road, Bootle, a town regrettably made infamous many years later by the murder of James Bulger. We were a family of four – mother Elizabeth, father John, and my older sister by five years, Maureen. At that time, most fathers in Bootle worked at the docks, probably five minutes' walk from our house at 98 St John's Road, while most mothers, I seem to remember, worked at Littlewood's or Vernons Pools.

My mother and father were of Irish descent, as were many people from our patch, and our family was known as 'the Penders'. At school, I was known as 'Micky Pender'. As a child, I was taken to the old Prendergast family house in Ireland, at Oldcastle, County Meath. This was an adventure for me every school summer holiday up to the age of seven or eight. I remember the journey well: steam train from Liverpool to Holyhead, ferry to Dublin, and steam train to Oldcastle. On arriving at Oldcastle station, we would be met by our relations in a pony and trap. I always enjoyed those train journeys. In later years, I enjoyed many happy and even more adventurous hours, travelling the length and breadth of the country trainspotting with my old school pal and lifelong friend, Peter Dolan.

Looking back and remembering those friends of my youth, as a young (not so innocent) boy, my favourite place was 9 Malcolm Street, just around the corner from our house in St John's Road. The Dolan boys lived there: Peter, and his twin brother Brian. I would be round there many an evening and Saturday morning, playing and messing about with their boxer dog, Butch. The three of us attended St Winefride's Secondary Modern School until Brian won a scholarship to St Mary's College.

The other house I used to go to, now and then, was around another corner, where the Ashton boys, Billy and Arthur, lived. It was Arthur Ashton who would introduce me to Big Ron Woodbridge in 1956/57, when as young teenagers we were into Buddy Holly and Elvis.

Big Ron, as his name suggests, was much taller than any of us, and with his long sideburns he was an early Elvis lookalike. One of the things I remember most was his belt, with its huge buckle and studs. Ron never made it to the final group stage with us, as by then he'd gone his own way, but one of his best performances (of the few we did) and the one I will always remember was a gig at the Convivial pub on the dock road, not far from my Granny Pender's (as I called her), where Pete Dolan, Bob Fazackerley and I would sometimes play darts. It was around Christmastime and there was a roaring coal fire blazing away in the bar that night. As the bar was jam-packed, the only space where we could perform was in front of the fire hearth. Ron lost a few pounds that night – I don't mean from his wallet!

The Monaghan boys, Pat and James, were also around, and in the next road lived Bob Fazackerley, who I got to know a bit later – more about him will emerge. But it was the Dolan boys I was closest to, and Peter would become my best pal throughout my life.

Looking back to my childhood, like most youngsters today, I loved playing football. Many a night would find me outside my house, playing football with a tennis ball until quite late, with the aid of a gas street lamp. All the local lads played football, and they called me 'Greedy Pender' because I would

---

County Borough of Bootle.

EDUCATION COMMITTEE.

BOYS' *Department,*

ST. WINEFRIDE'S SEC. MODERN *School,*

Bootle 20th March *195* 6

<u>To whom it may concern</u>

<u>MICHAEL PRENDERGAST</u> is a boy of average ability and attainment.

As House Captain, he has carried out his duties in a conscientious and satisfactory manner.

Quiet in manner, he will make a loyal and industrious worker.

Regular and punctual in attendance, he leaves school with an excellent character.

Y. Nevin

Headmaster.

---

hold on to the ball as long as I could, dribbling past opponents and then going back and doing it all again and again to the same players.

Sport was to stand me in good stead in my later school years, as it made up somewhat for my inadequacy on the academic side. In fact, football made me quite popular in and around the neighbourhood in those early days. If there was any kind of match arranged, especially when played in nearby King's Park, there would be several knocks on our front door, with cries of 'Make sure Mick Pender is playing!' Most kids with the name Michael would get called 'Mick', but I was also known as 'Pender'. People living close by always referred to us as 'the Penders', even though our family name was Prendergast.

I left school at the age of fifteen with no qualifications and was given an average report signed by the headmaster, Mr Toolin, and the deputy head, Mr Nevin. I remember Mr Toolin well, a very distinguished man, but I was just a name to him, as were most boys. However, in my senior years, when I became the Lionel Messi of St Winefride's School, he took more notice and made me captain of one of the school's four houses, which were Merton, Balliol, Pembroke and Oriel. Mine was Merton House.

So, academically, I did not measure up to others, but my sporting ability – mostly football – got me through. I was good enough to play for Bootle Schoolboys – another adventure for me, as this would take me to places like Oldham, Salford and Preston to play against their schoolboy teams.

Looking back to those halcyon days, the most memorable game has to be the one against Liverpool Schoolboys at Anfield. Many of my mates, including Pete Dolan, were standing on the Kop to cheer us on, but Liverpool Schoolboys won the game, 3-2 This was the *W.R. Williams Cup Final*, played every year at Anfield. After the game, both Liverpool and Everton FC would sign up most of the players from both sides. This was not binding, of course, and your dad had to sign the form that you were given. Actually, I can't remember my dad signing it.

I still have my losers' medal from that night and can still hear Pete Dolan and friends shouting out 'C'mon Mick!' as they cheered us on. One thing I would say about that game is that we had a very good team that included two English International Schoolboys – Jackie Carvin, who later signed for West Bromwich Albion, and a lad from Bootle Technical College whose name I can't remember. But I have to admit the Liverpool team were a notch above us. That night will live long in my memory and I will always remember the confidence given to me by my sports teachers at St Winefride's, Gerry Rogan and Matt Rooney (no relation to Wayne).

Schooldays came to an end, of course, and on we went to the more serious side of our lives. My first job was office boy with a major shipping company, Rea's Tugs, delivering mail and official business letters to the big shipping companies in Liverpool city centre. I travelled on the overhead railway, known as the 'Dockers' Umbrella', which ran from Gladstone Dock to Dingle Dock, a distance of about 20 miles. I enjoyed that job, but soon realised it was just a stepping stone to something else.

Here's my philosophy on life. Money and music were something of a motivation for me in those early days. It's a true saying that we stand or fall by our decisions in life, as many an older person will tell you. This applies to any aspect of life, to any joint venture or partnership – and that includes marriage. Everything has a start, a middle, and an end, but I didn't have any big ideas of becoming a pop star, or forming a pop group. I was not a child prodigy, and I didn't get into music until I was fifteen or sixteen years old.

My childhood years were spent dreaming of being a cowboy, like Hopalong Cassidy. Then I woke one morning feeling stupid and with a head full of ideas. I quickly realised I needed to get into something else – trainspotting! – and I had some great years doing that. Next, I wanted to be a footballer and obviously play for the Blues (no, not Chelsea – Everton, of course, the team that my father took me and my best mate Peter Dolan to see as young boys).

Then, out of mixed emotions, I heard Elvis Presley singing 'Heartbreak Hotel' and saw Buddy Holly and the Crickets at the Philharmonic Hall, and my direction changed. At first just for fun in spare time, I found deep excitement just to have a guitar and stand in front of Mam and Dad's wardrobe mirror. Martin Luther King said, 'I have a dream', and that's all it was. I had come to believe I would be working at Birchall's Printers (my last place of work). Music was just for enjoyment, for pretending, not something for making into a career.

After leaving Rea's Shipping Company and after the monthly payments for my Hofner Club 60 guitar had finished, I found myself at a loose end and my mother would constantly remind me about finding another job. But I was really into the guitar by now, trying to learn Arthur Smith's 'Guitar Boogie' – this being the original a few years before Bert Weedon's 'Guitar Boogie Shuffle'. I would play the Arthur Smith record over and over again until I could play along with it note for note.

After a few months, and with my mother now becoming concerned, I answered an advert in the *Liverpool Echo* from a company that wanted floor-layers, offering excellent wages. The company was John Fiddies Ltd. I got the job and made a good friend there, young Dougie Tartt, a lovely lad from a lovely family. Doug and myself made a lot of money from laying floors, using Marley tiles – thermoplastic tiles – and woodblock flooring. We had a great time: music, parties and guitars. After seeing my Club 60 guitar, Doug bought himself one, but a sunburst one as he didn't want to copy. I will always remember those days with Doug and his family.

But I was getting itchy feet again, and when one day I had a disagreement with Mr Fiddies, I said goodbye to Doug and floor-laying. I was on to my third job before I realised what became my real aim in life. My dad's brother, Uncle Mike, heard about my departure from Fiddies Ltd and told my dad he could put a good word in for me where he worked, at Birchall's Printers in Liverpool city centre.

So, I joined their bookbinding department and really enjoyed my time there, making many friends before I eventually left after my first trip to Hamburg. Despite my deep-seated desire, even when I temporarily left Birchall's to go to the Star-Club, I somehow knew I would be going back to what was a big company in Liverpool at the time, and my job would still be there after my 'Hamburg experience', as my boss, Charlie put it. But the Star-Club decided for me, and, as the story of my life unfolds, you will see that music has served me well ever since.

CHAPTER 3

Birth of the Searchers – Buddy Holly Live

My first memory of seeing a guitar was when I came across one lying around at my grandmother's house.

Like the road to fame, St John's Road is a very long road, running from Kirkdale in Liverpool to Bootle. My early life during the war years, and after, was in a close-knit community and my closest childhood (and later) friends were just a stone's throw from my house: Peter and Brian Dolan, James and Patrick Monaghan, Arthur Ashton (cousin of William Ashton, better known later as Billy J. Kramer), Bob Fazackerley, Dave Rimmer and Luke Snow. Peter and Bob were my trainspotting buddies, and only Arthur Ashton came anywhere near being musically talented among all my friends at that time.

Before I met John McNally, I would learn songs by Hank Williams, Faron Young, also known as ('The Young Sheriff'), Jimmie Rodgers' 'Honeycomb' and 'Kisses Sweeter Than Wine', and Frankie Laine's 'Hey Joe!'. Then Guy Mitchell came on the scene when I was about twelve years old. I remember learning the B-side of one of his early hits, a song called 'Wise Man Or A Fool'. At parties at our house, for whatever reason, my mother would embarrass me by getting me to sing that song for everyone. I guess you could say it was my party piece – my first public performances!

I knew about Lonnie Donegan and skiffle, but I *didn't play it* and I *wasn't influenced by it* – unless you think Westerns and cowboy music was early skiffle. As I've mentioned, one of the several intriguing myths trotted out over the years is that I was.

Before I saw the *Searchers* film starring John Wayne, there were no groups as such, just teenagers hanging about on street corners, some playing skiffle music, others playing American Western music, but I do remember a lot of washboards would go missing from back kitchens in those early days.

My first memory of seeing a guitar was when I came across one lying around at my grandmother's house, where I used to go every Sunday with my sister Maureen, after our mother had dressed us up in our Sunday best. In those days, around where I lived you would always hear Hank Williams singing 'Your Cheatin' Heart' or 'Lovesick Blues'. I remember going to see the movie *High Noon* three times. Gary Cooper, who looked old when he was young, was the star of the film, but I also loved the haunting theme song sung by Frankie Lane.

My early influence from Western or cowboy music broke out when I heard Elvis sing 'Heartbreak Hotel'. I was also lucky enough to go to Buddy Holly's concert on 20 March 1958 at the Philharmonic Hall in Liverpool. Before that concert, I was influenced by many of the American rock'n'roll stars, although Holly was then No. 1 for me. When I found out Buddy was not only coming to the UK, but was to headline a show at the Philharmonic, I just knew I had to be there for that very special night! It was so special that everything changed that night, and I vividly remember feeling the hairs on the back of my neck tingle with excitement when he walked onstage. That night will live long in my memory.

Luckily for me, I went to the second show: the first house was not a sell-out, due to poor publicity. There were also technical problems with Buddy's amplifier, which delayed the performance for quite some time. Hundreds of fans, including myself and other future entertainers like Jimmy Tarbuck were kept waiting outside the hall in pouring rain, waiting for the late-running first show to finish. The wait was more than worthwhile, and Buddy and the Crickets soon had the audience jiving in the aisles, despite the best efforts of the theatre staff.

They blasted out their early hits, with Buddy kneeling on the stage with his Fender Stratocaster held high over his head, and Joe Mauldin climbing up and spinning his double bass. What struck me was that they had so little gear on the stage – just a guitar, double bass, a small drum kit...and the most enormous amplifier I had ever seen. But when they started playing, the sound was unbelievable – it filled the whole theatre. Buddy's vocals were something else, as was his Fender guitar-playing. Everyone just went berserk.

Although I didn't realise it at the time, in those days most – if not all – vocal acts used the in-house PA system. Today, nearly all bands travel with their own sound system (or tour promoters insist on putting in their own systems), to guarantee a good, all-round sound. As they finally left the stage, Jerry Allison threw his drumsticks into the audience.

If you ask me who started the Mersey beat explosion, I would put it down to Buddy Holly and the Crickets. There were youngsters like myself there that night who would later be part of the Swinging Blue Jeans, Faron's Flamingos and many other bands. It all seemed to grow from that concert. Buddy's huge influence on the future Beatles is also well-documented. As the Quarrymen, their first-ever recording was 'That'll Be The Day'. All of a sudden, everyone was starting groups and they were all doing Buddy's stuff.

On my way home after the concert, I dreamt of having a Fender Stratocaster like Buddy. However, at that time, Fender Strats were not available in this country. Even if they had been available, the price would have put it out of my reach. But I still loved my Hofner Club 60 – another guitar I wish I still had today among the many I have owned and played. I gave it to my good friend at Birchall's, Jackie Eaton, soon after I bought the Burns Tri-Sonic.

Musically, events began to shape up. John McNally and I lived in the same road. I had my mates and John had his, but guitars brought us together, and as teenagers we both knew the Dolan twins, who would play some part in our lives. Both lads and a certain Chris Crummey (later Chris Curtis) all attended the same secondary school as me – St Winefride's – but being from Liverpool, John attended a different school, Major Street Secondary Modern.

We would get together in our front parlours or on street corners, and I suppose we were mainly an instrumental duo/ group to start with. I would learn all the popular instrumentals and John would back me with the chords. Our favourites at that time were Duane Eddy's '3.30 Blues', 'Guitar Boogie' by Arthur Smith, 'Sleep Walk' by Santo & Johnny, and later 'Walk Don't Run' by the Ventures. Some of these were on old 78s.

In the early days with Westie (Joe West), I thought we should have the American look and I was influenced greatly by the American stars of the time: Elvis, Ricky Nelson and James Dean all seemed to wear red sweaters or cardigans in their publicity photos. John and I both had Hofner Club 60 guitars – the same colour, blonde – which were great-looking guitars, and, from memory, I believe we were the only local group to have them in the 1957-58 period. I seem to remember that we both got them round about the same time. I cant remember if my parents paid the monthly instalments, or whether I paid them. As I had my first job by then, I think I probably did.

John and I saw a lot of each other at that time and we sounded pretty good playing together. We were both totally self-taught and I remember John being so impressed with my guitar-playing that he got his mother to sign on the dotted line (HP – hire purchase) for a Futurama/Strat-lookalike guitar with a tremolo arm from Hessy's music shop, where most Liverpool groups bought their guitars. When John's mother found out that I was playing it, she went ballistic and made him take it back to the shop! Shortly after that came the incident when our Watkins Dominator amp was stolen and John and I were back to square one. I lost touch with him after that, and we both went our separate ways until fate later brought us back together.

CHAPTER 4

And So It Began

Some months after the break-up, I heard that John McNally had been taken to Walton Hospital for a major operation. So then I had no guitar connection – I was on my own with my Hofner Club 60.

What could I do? I took it upon myself to go to the Cross Keys pub in Liverpool city centre with my guitar, to try to meet up with other guitarists. I had heard about the pub because live music was played there on Saturday nights, and you could get up onstage and sing with the resident band. As I was not a vocalist at the time, I actually had second thoughts about going to see what it was all about. I knew where the pub was, near the Liverpool Stadium, here I had been a few times to see the wrestling. So, off I went on that Saturday night, little knowing I was about to find the third famous Searcher.

As I got there, I could hear someone belting out an Elvis song. I didn't pay much attention to who was singing, as the place was so packed you could hardly see the stage, or what passed for a stage – it was more of a platform really. I can't remember what drink I ordered, but it was probably 'brown mixed', as that was what all my mates drank.

This was my first meeting with Tony Jackson. I remember him looking very distinctive, with a tanned face, black hair and long sideburns. Talk came easy to us as we had something in common: music. During the evening, I found out he was married to Margaret, who was there with him that night. I asked Tony if we could start up a group, with him as the vocalist and John and me backing him. I never thought about a bass player, as we were so used to playing without one in pubs or on street corners, and even though we had taken the time to teach Joe West to play bass before our first little group had broken up, I didn't think we really needed one to get started again.

Tony was so keen when I told him about John and myself – although I hadn't seen John for a while – that he invited me to his house, which was quite a way from were I lived. Even so, the next day I caught the bus to Wavertree and found 23 Ritson Street where Tony lived, and what felt like the road to success began again.

In those early days, Tony and I found we had a lot in common – we both loved Everton Football Club and went to all the home games. Also, we both loved Buddy Holly, and when I took my guitar to his house, Tony would ask me to play 'Peggy Sue' over and over again. We both really loved that song. Tony's favourite Buddy song was 'Listen To Me'.

By this time, I was in contact with John McNally again. He had left hospital and was convalescing. Eventually, the three of us got together, sometimes with Norman McGarry, a friend of Tony's who played drums. Norman never became part of the band; he was just someone Tony knew and who would rehearse with us.

We had some good parties at Tony's house. Tony and Margaret didn't have any children, so they loved having parties. At one of these, Margaret said to me, 'Mike, Tony is so glad he has met you.' A close friendship between Tony and myself soon developed, and with John now recovered, the three of us would start rehearsing mostly Elvis songs with a couple of instrumentals thrown in.

I remember Tony and me going to C&A, a large department store in Liverpool, to buy some kind of uniform for the three of us, as we had our first gig coming up at a club in Garston near Liverpool. We ended up buying three what we called 'lumberjack jackets' – not ideal stage wear, but it was all we could afford at the time. I thought they looked great. Strangely, I can remember only that one gig we played in Garston with just the three of us: Tony singing, and John and myself on guitars.

Tony soon learnt how to play bass guitar, after I had convinced him it was the best way forward. He picked it up quickly when he realised each bass note had to match each chord that we played. He was brilliant – I never thought he would be able to play and sing so well. He even made his own guitar!

So there we were, the three of us, not knowing what fate had in store. When I think back about how I met Tony, and then my later chance meeting with Chris Crummey on that Saturday morning in Stanley Road, Bootle as he got off the bus, it was as though it had all been planned. Fate again. Good times ahead. And so it began.

Of course, I already knew Chris from when we both attended St Winefride's. When he and some other brainy lads won a scholarship to St Mary's College, I thought nothing of it and carried on with my football and trainspotting, and meeting my many friends at school. So here we were and here it was, 1959-60. Although I didn't know it at the time, I had brought together a major group of four young people who would later be rated second only to the Beatles.

The four of us rehearsed at Chris's house. Seeing as he was the drummer, his parents did not object – although their neighbours probably did! We learned ten or twelve songs including 'Bad Boy' (me), 'Stand By Me' (Chris), 'Wondrous Place' (Chris), 'What'd I Say' (Chris), 'Glad All Over' (me), 'Listen To Me' (Tony and I), 'When My Blue Moon Turns To Gold Again' (me) – a special request from Cavern deejay Bob Wooler – and the instrumental '3.30 Blues', among others. After lots of practice, John and I had now become proficient players.

One of the first gigs we played before Johnny Sandon joined us was in early 1960 at the Reo, an old cinema in Longmoor Lane, Fazakerley, not far from the Aintree Institute and the Orrell Park Ballroom. In those days, we had to get to gigs on the bus, hauling our guitars, amplifiers and drums up and down the stairs. We weren't too popular with the bus company, but we had quite a few laughs! At the time, we sometimes made as much as £2.50 a week each (£2.10.0 in old money, which in those days wasn't bad).

John and I travelled to the Reo by bus and met Chris and Tony there. Never mind the screaming girlie fans who were so visual in those early days, it was the blokes who gave us most bother. A punch-up outside afterwards, as we were leaving, was the main reason why I remember that gig so vividly. As we appealed so much to the young girls in the audience, a group of nasties decided to give us a hard time, which resulted in fisticuffs. But we gave as good as we got, and, apart from a few bruises and scraped knuckles, we held our own until the bouncers broke it up.

As young lads, we could handle most situations – especially Tony. Many's the time a fight would start during or after some of our early gigs played in our home city. The fights were mostly started by jealous boyfriends or just jealous blokes who couldn't stand their girlfriends, or just girls in general, wanting to touch us or befriend us. Sometimes, a whole dance hall would erupt in a swearing punch-up, with the bouncers trying to keep the peace and restore order.

One night, sad to say, I actually instigated such a fracas. It happened at the Civil Service Club, quite an upmarket place compared to the Cavern or the Iron Door. My girlfriend May was with us that night, as was Tony Jackson's girlfriend, Ella. I was up on stage singing (I can't remember what the song was), when I caught sight of a guy dancing with May. Now, to be fair, he had already asked me if he could dance with 'my girlfriend', but being a jealous guy myself, I thought he was holding her just a bit too close. I immediately stopped the band and jumped off the stage, to the astonishment of the audience. I went straight for this guy, and the next minute there was pandemonium – people wrestling and fighting and chairs being thrown. I'm laughing to myself as I write this, because, when all the trouble started Tony Jackson started singing, 'C'mon everybody, throw your chair...', mimicking the Chubby Checker song, 'Let's Twist Again'. But seriously, the first thing I did was get May out of the way as quickly as I could. Order was restored after about fifteen minutes and we carried on with the show. I seem to remember there was a problem getting paid that night. I got the blame of course, but I wouldn't fancy doing it today.

We played a lot of gigs in Liverpool including the Casbah, Orrell Park Ballroom, Litherland Town Hall and St John's Hall, Bootle, where we first saw the Beatles when Stuart Sutcliffe was the bass player. Our most important gigs were at the Cavern and the Iron Door, which became our second home, and the guy who owned it, Les Ackerley, became our manager.

Whenever we played a lunchtime session at the Cavern or the Iron Door, I could always find someone to clock me in at Birchall's – a very far cry from today. Although I knew nothing of it at the time, my boss Charlie was turning a blind eye. I took advantage really, as I knew he was a good friend of my Uncle Mike, who was the union boss. Charlie must have liked me because, as already mentioned, when we got the offer to play at the Star-Club in Hamburg, he told me to go and that my job would still be there when I got back. By this time, Chris and Tony had packed in their jobs and they would come and stand outside Birchall's, shouting, 'Come on Mike, it's time to leave!' Embarrassing or what? So there I was: decision time.

CHAPTER 5

Rocking the Iron Door (And Other Cellars)

The emerging names of the Swinging '60s began to emerge slowly.

The Iron Door played a major role in our rise to fame and fortune – and not just ours, because other big names played their first gigs there as well. Geoff Hogarth and Harry Ormesher had opened the Iron Door Club on 9 April 1960 in a butter-packing warehouse in Temple Street, a narrow side alley in Liverpool's city centre just a few minutes' walk from the Cavern. Take a walk down Temple Street and you'll see a large plaque on the wall where the club was sited at No. 13, now almost in the middle of posh offices and the inevitable car parks. For those with satnavs, the site is at L2 5HR, where some of the old warehouses still stand.

There was always keen competition between these two clubs, which were the best-known of the rock'n'roll 'sweat cellars' in the early 1960s. Both had their roots in the Liverpool jazz scene. In fact, the Iron Door was also known as the Liverpool Jazz Society and the Storyville Jazz Club up to 1962. While the Cavern was a well-established jazz venue up to 1960-61, the Iron Door was the first to offer evening sessions exclusively for rock'n'roll. We played the Cavern a few times in our early days and it was there where I first met the lovely Miss Doyle, who I would later get to know very well indeed.

One night, George Harrison, Pete Dolan and I walked all the way from the Cavern to the Pier Head bus terminus – a tidy distance when carrying a guitar. It was one of the few times I was able to converse with George. He was a lovely lad and easy to talk to. He caught the last bus to Woolton, and Pete and I caught the No. 16 home to Bootle.

The emerging names of the Swinging '60s began to emerge slowly. Just twelve months after the Iron Door Club opened, we made our Cavern Club debut on Wednesday, 5 April 1961 with our lead vocalist, Johnny Sandon, followed by a lunchtime session on 14 June. Johnny had joined us in September the preceding year. Our first appearance with the Beatles was at their 'Guest Night' on Wednesday, 26 July. The Four Jays were also on the bill. We performed again with the Beatles on the night of Wednesday, 6 September with Ian & The Zodiacs. Gerry & The Pacemakers had played the lunchtime session that day. They were regulars at the Cavern, as were the Merseybeats and the Swinging Blue Genes (the 'Genes' was later changed to 'Jeans').

We found the Iron Door was certainly much bigger – and rather more salubrious – than the Cavern. The club's authorised capacity was between 1,600 and 1,950. In the early 1960s, Temple Street, just off the main thoroughfare of Dale Street, was scary: very narrow and lined on both sides by tall warehouses, and dimly lit at night. Steps up to the front door led first to the cloakroom and coffee bar. A flight of slatted wooden stairs went down to the club itself, a very large room with a low ceiling. Two pillars supported the roof, and the stage was along the far wall, but not much higher than the floor. We would be literally face-to-face with our audience. Paintings of African tribal masks, shields and spears harking back to the club's jazz origins hung on the walls, and bench-style seating was lined up opposite the stage, against the wall and beneath the stairs.

The club attracted well over 2,000 punters to a famous *'Rock Around The Clock'* all-night session on 11 March 1961, and 22 bouncers were on duty that night. The overriding aroma at the club was said to have been like 'the smell of steamed hot dogs and sweat'. Bacon sandwiches were also very popular, especially at all-nighters.

A sixteen-year-old Priscilla White (*aka* Cilla Black)

performed many times at the club, and was also the cloakroom assistant at the Cavern. In a recent conversation, she recalled those all-nighters at the Iron Door, which would start at 8.00 p.m. and finish at 8.00 a.m. the following morning: 'We'd all be tumbling out and pinching bottles of milk off doorsteps, because we'd been singing all night.'

The Beatles' former road manager, Tony Bramwell, remembers seeing us in action one night at the club with Johnny Sandon – in some ways, we were his backing band: 'When Johnny left the stage for a break, Chris Curtis would sing "What'd I Say", standing up to play the drums.' Chris had grown his hair very long – which was unusual in Liverpool at that time – and he wore leather trousers, so we became well-known as the band with the long-haired drummer. That was a party piece. Chris repeated it at the *NME* Poll Winners concert at Wembley Empire Pool in 1964, when we were voted second only to the Beatles. You can watch that unique performance on YouTube. Another of Chris's showstoppers was his version of Del Shannon's 'Runaway'.

Johnny Sandon had a rich voice ideal for Jim Reeves/ Johnny Cash country songs, so we attracted the jazz and country music crowd, especially at lunchtime sessions. Brian Epstein supposedly attended one of these sessions at the Cavern, although I didn't actually see him. It is important for me to point out here – and contradict – stories that I've read about our behaviour: although the five of us had visited the Grapes pub before the session, *no one* was drunk. I remember Johnny tripping over some guitar or microphone leads on the very cramped stage. Mr Epstein passed on the chance to sign us, but he did make an unsuccessful bid to sign us two years later, which was vetoed by our manager, Tito Burns.

Talking of Eppy reminds me of the one occasion when the Searchers topped the bill over the Beatles. I was still working at Birchall's and couldn't wait to get home that night, little knowing who would be on the bill with us. We were starting to make a name for ourselves locally, and that night at St John's Hall, Bootle we came face-to-face with the band then known as the Silver Beetles. They were clearly paying homage to the great

Buddy Holly and his band, the Crickets.

I remember that night well, as all five Beatles were sitting on the floor – there were no chairs or settees in those days. I thought they looked great in their black leathers, with matching cowboy boots. Obviously, I wasn't the only one who loved cowboys. They told us they had just returned from Hamburg and were a bit nervous about their second gig back on English soil.

When they went onstage, the place erupted, as the young audience had never seen anything like it before. I can honestly say the boys really knocked me out. I noticed one wasn't plugged in and was pretending to play an old Framus 6-string guitar – but what a voice that guy had, especially singing Little Richard songs.

In February 1962, Johnny Sandon suddenly decided to leave us to join the Remo Four. But, with Johnny gone, we quickly realised we had never really needed him in the first place. It had only been a 'confidence thing', and Bob Wooler's advice at the time had put it into our heads that we would be more appealing with a frontman. I don't want to take anything away from Johnny, who had a great voice and was a lovely lad and great friend, but, truth to tell, we had good voices within the group but lacked the confidence to use them. That changed after our Star-Club gigs, when we learned we could sing with the best of them.

Time went by, and we were enjoying a great following at the Iron Door Club, which soon became our second home. We asked the club's co-owner, Geoff Hogarth, to manage us, but he was already Freddie Starr's manager. Soon after that, Les Ackerley took Geoff's place and also effectively became our manger for the next few months.

Around May or June 1962, Horst Fascher, booking agent for Hamburg's Star-Club, saw us at the Cavern with Johnny Kidd & The Pirates. That resulted in us joining the Mersey beat procession to Hamburg in October of that year. Actually, we all had to borrow money to go over there, but, like the Beatles, we really learned our trade at the Star-Club and became a really good band. The Iron Door did us proud on our return from Hamburg, putting on a special night for us, billed as *'The Homecoming of the Searchers'*. So, the Iron Door was now officially our 'home'.

The '60s scene was gaining pace and the record industry was on the move. After the Beatles achieved national fame in late '62/early '63, for the first time every record company began showing considerable interest in other Liverpool groups. So, the Searchers went on to record, and, in January or February 1963, behind locked doors, we recorded an 11-track demo tape at the Iron Door. In addition to 'Sweets For My Sweet', we also cut crowd-pleasing classics like 'Maybellene', 'Let's Stomp', 'Sweet Little Sixteen' and our own version of the traditional Liverpool folk song, 'Maggie Mae'. A Chris Curtis composition called 'Darling Do You Miss Me' was also included. We later recorded it as 'I'll Be Missing You' for the *Sounds Like Searchers* LP and the B-side of 'When You Walk In The Room'. Basically, all the tracks were from our current stage repertoire.

The only surviving acetate was originally in Tony Jackson's private collection. He sold it to Trojan Records, who in turn passed it on to Sanctuary, who controlled our Pye catalogue. They eventually released a remastered version on their Castle label in 2002, on the CD *The Iron Door Sessions*.

Our manager, Les Ackerley, arranged for acetates of the tapes to be sent to several of the major record companies in London. Pye Records producer Tony Hatch was impressed enough by what he heard to make the journey from London to see us at the Iron Door. This paved the way for our first-ever recording session in London and immediate (well, almost) success with 'Sweets For My Sweet'. Not a great deal needed to be added to our recording of the song as a demo track.

We were due to return to the Star-Club in June 1963, but were able to buy ourselves out of that contract. The New Iron Door Club, as it was restyled, was still described as 'The Home of the Searchers'. After 'Sweets For My Sweet' went to No. 1, we did one more gig at the Iron Door, with people queuing down the street to get in.

The club was open seven nights a week, plus Sunday afternoons, and it was famous – or infamous – for the toughness of its bouncers. One early press advert for the club specified

'No Weirdoes, Beatniks or Teddy Boys'. Chief bouncers from early 1961, and throughout 1962, were brothers Jim and Ben Evans, who hailed from Scotland Road and had a fearsome reputation

When we first played there, it could be quite rowdy sometimes. The Undertakers' lead guitarist, Chris Huston, has been quoted as saying that the club 'could be a dangerous place'. The club management tried to set the tone early on by introducing a formal membership system with unique membership cards. Sadly, the Iron Door was to have a life of only four years – from 1960 to 1964 – but during that time the cream of Mersey beat groups and singers performed there. That long honours list includes the Searchers, the Beatles, Gerry & The Pacemakers, Billy J. Kramer, Freddie Starr & The Midnighters, the Mojos, the Big Three (who developed from Cass & The Casanovas), the Remo Four, the Undertakers, Rory Storm & The Wild Ones, Cilla Black, Kingsize Taylor & The Dominoes, Beryl Marsden and Faron's Flamingos.

In a recent feature article in the *Daily Express*, Freddie Starr discussed his early career as a pop star before he turned to comedy, but for some reason he omitted to mention the Iron Door. Freddie, whose real name is Fred Fowell, dyed his blond hair black to give more authenticity to his Elvis impressions at the club.

In my opinion, the Iron Door could certainly claim to be the birthplace of 'Scouse Rock' and should not be eclipsed by the Cavern in the history of Mersey beat. Compared to the Cavern, little documentation is available on the Iron Door. Geoff Hogarth and Les Ackerley are among the unjustly forgotten heroes of Mersey beat history. Everyone who was anyone in the Liverpool and Merseyside music scene in the '60s played the Iron Door. For the 12-hour all-nighter sessions, twelve groups and solo performers would each do a one-hour set. Flushed with success from signing the Beatles, Brian Epstein came to the Iron Door to see Priscilla White belt out 'Fever' and other big ballads, and promptly signed her too, complete with new name.

After the Iron Door closed in 1964, it became the Pyramid Club, but that closed in the early '70s and was later demolished to make room for a car park. Years later, an Iron Door reunion gig was organised for 3 September 2004 by Geoff Hogarth at another well-known venue in Liverpool, the Olympia in West Derby Road, which was the Locarno in its '60s heyday. On the bill with Mike Pender's Searchers were the Undertakers, Kingsize Taylor & The Dominoes, Lee Curtis, Faron's Flamingos, Johnny Rocco, Karl Terry & The Cruisers, Nicky Crouch's Mojos, the Taylor Maids and the Del Renos. I dropped in my versions of 'My Girl', 'Hold Me', 'Games People Play' and 'You Got It', and the show closed with storming performances of 'Johnny B. Goode' and 'Rockin' All Over the World'.

In his otherwise excellent book on Liverpool's key role in the history of popular music, *Liverpool: Wondrous Place – Music from Cavern to Cream*, Paul Du Noyer makes only four passing references to the Iron Door Club, but devotes many pages to the Cavern. He does, however, say some very nice things about Chris, Tony, John, Frank and myself:

'The Searchers are in many ways the connoisseur's Mersey beat band, and, in their prime, made music that sparkles like champagne.'

'While they were at their peak...the Searchers laid down some tracks that are as durable and influential as any in rock history.'

'It was the Searchers' sound that was so special – the radiant, chiming twin guitars above all...'

'The Pender and McNally vocal harmonies survived the replacement of bassman Tony Jackson with Frank Allen, while the founders, Pender and McNally, continued to blend their two guitars to shimmering effect.'

Thanks, Paul, I like your style!

Mersey beat expert and author Spencer Leigh gives an incredibly detailed day-to-day account of the Cavern's history in his admirable book, *The Cavern – The Most Famous Club in the World*, which also covers the 'new' Cavern. Our appearances at the Cavern are all in there[1], along with all the other bands from

---

[1] See *Appendix II* for a list of our Cavern appearances.

Merseyside, from all over the country and from abroad who also played there in the '60s and '70s, and after that time at the new premises. Again, as with Mr Du Noyer's book, the Iron Door Club gets very few mentions.

Not long a ago, on 17 October 2012, BBC Radio 2 broadcast a documentary about the Casbah Coffee Club, described by some as the 'birthplace of Mersey beat'. The club was in the basement of the house in Liverpool owned by Pete Best's mother, Mona, who owned and ran it as a private members' club. The documentary was presented by Pete, who was of course the original drummer of the Beatles. First opened in 1959, the Casbah has recently been awarded blue plaque status. It was a unique rock'n'roll venue, as the majority of Liverpool clubs at that time had their roots firmly in jazz, folk or country music.

CHAPTER 6

Stargazing in Hamburg

And then we were on our way to Hamburg – another adventure starting in my life.

So, from the spring of 1962, we had begun an exciting adventure but did not know where it would lead us or what heartache it would cause us. Our last gig with Johnny Sandon was on 28 February 1962 at the Cavern. His first gig at the Cavern with the Remo Four was on 17 October 1962.

In May, back as a foursome, fate placed us at the Cavern, where a certain Mr Horst Fascher from Hamburg was recruiting bands for the opening of what was to become the world-famous Star-Club. Horst was accompanied by Ted 'Kingsize' Taylor's road manager, John Fanning, a guy I had known from my schooldays at St Winefride's. I have no doubt Mr Fanning put in a good word for us that night: Horst confirmed it to me when I met him at the Star-Club's 50th anniversary show in April 2012.

Horst and John liked the band and asked us if we would also be interested in playing at the Star-Club. Tony and Chris had already given up their jobs and eagerly said 'Yes'. I remember thinking, *It's decision time*, as I was still working at Birchall's. John was also working full-time, so it took a little persuasion from Chris and Tony. After our performance, Johnny Kidd's guitarist, who I didn't know, commented on my playing of Duane Eddy's '3.30 Blues', one of two instrumentals we still featured in our set. I realised later it was Mick Green who had made the comment. He was to become a revered guitarist in later years, both with Johnny Kidd and in his own right.

At the end of September, we packed and got ready to travel to Hamburg for our four weeks of gigs at the Star-Club. I was used to long train journeys, having already done ambitious overnight trips to Dundee and Perth as a mad twelve-year-old trainspotter, with my friends Pete Dolan and Alun Davies. Actually, looking back, we had many great adventures travelling the length and breadth of this once-great country. I say 'once-great', as, after two World Wars (and the terrorist threat we all live with today) the ideals our fathers and grandfathers went to war for seem to be as far away as ever.

But things were different then: I was a young boy, and trainspotting was a distant memory. I was leaving the two loves of my life, Miss Doyle, the sweetest girl in Liverpool, and my home city itself. Miss Doyle was near to tears on that late September morning in 1962 and I knew in my heart how much I loved that girl. That first month at the Star-Club was a long time when you are in love. Tony Jackson was still my mentor at that time and we were very close friends. I can still remember Tony's words: 'Don't worry, May. I'll look after him.'

And then we were on our way to Hamburg – another adventure starting in my life. Being used to trains, I had worked out all the train times with Chris before we left Liverpool, as we had quite a few connections to make before we reached Hamburg. When anyone asked any questions about times of arrival, Chris would say, 'Ask Beeching.' This was his pet name for me on that journey, referring back to my trainspotting days and to the infamous Dr Beeching, the Tory Transport Minister who closed down many branch and secondary lines throughout the UK in the '60s.

It was a very long journey, but we had many laughs and a also few hairy moments, such as trying to convince the taxi driver at Euston Station to take the four of us – and Chris's drum kit – to Liverpool Street Station for the journey to Harwich. I remember it vividly, as I paid for the taxi, but it was amazing what you could pack into those old hackney cabs. I think, on reflection, any one of us would have paid for the taxi – it really was a case of 'one for all and all for one'. I also remember that we travelled on the 'Hook Continental' to Harwich – trainspotting again.

We took the ferry to the Hook of Holland and travelled on by train through Holland into Germany. When we finally arrived in Hamburg, we had travelled for almost two days with hardly any sleep. It was no picnic when we had had to stop at the German border while our passports and luggage was checked. I recall Tony saying to me, as the security guards passed through the train, 'Here come the Gestapo' – and they really did look like those guys you see in war movies! I thought it was great: the uniforms, the jackboots; only the swastikas were missing.

I also thought the train we were on was a joy to behold: the kind you see in films like *Murder on the Orient Express*. You will probably have gathered by now that I am something of a romantic. It has been in my make-up since I was a child, dreaming of being one of those Western heroes. Travelling was no joyride either, though. I've already mentioned that Chris had to take his drum kit – how times have changed. Horst Fascher had stipulated that only the 'back line' (amplifiers) and PA (microphones) would be provided – we had to bring everything else with us.

I can't remember if Horst was at the station to meet us, but we duly arrived at the Star-Club and were taken to our hotel – or rather guest house, or the German version of the YMCA. Our accommodation at the Pacific Hotel was just about bearable, but this was a whole new venture for us and we soon realised how lucky we were to be at the Star-Club, rubbing shoulders with legends like Ray Charles and Jerry Lee Lewis, as well as our contemporaries from Liverpool. The world was opening up and Hamburg was a magical time for us. We met our rock'n'roll heroes – well, most of them.

But it was also a lonely time for me, and from the first week I missed my Liverpool beauty, Miss Doyle. Although we were relatively young, I knew I would marry that sweet girl – although not quite so soon, as it turned out, but that's another story.

In those days, Hamburg was much like Liverpool: both

busy seaports that had been heavily bombed in the war. There were many bomb sites near to the Star-Club, and you could certainly say that Hamburg was 'a city that never slept'.

One afternoon in the Star-Club, we were going over a new song when who should come strolling in, but one of my real heroes, Jerry Lee Lewis. I was gobsmacked Here was a rock'n'roll god, casual as you like, asking me if I knew the guitar intro to his latest record, 'How's My Ex Treating You' – which I didn't. You have to remember that we were four youngish lads from Liverpool who'd just given up their day jobs to enter a new world. Before I could even answer his question, Jerry was seated at the piano playing. If only he'd played 'Whole Lot Of Shakin' Going On', we could have busked it with him. 'How's My Ex Treating You' was not as popular as Jerry thought it was.

Bill Haley & His Comets arrived the following week and the audiences went crazy. Bill was not a great favourite of mine, but the Germans loved him. When I met him, I wondered if that kiss curl was a stick-on one, but I never got to find out. One night, during Bill's performance, a drunken German guy threw an ice cream onto the stage. Horst Fascher immediately frogmarched him out of the club and I can only imagine what the guy looked like after Horst had finished with him. He was very good to us though. 'Nice English boys,' he would say, but if you didn't obey the Star-Club rules, you would see the other side of him.

Some members of certain groups did cause problems, and when you look at the many groups that appeared at the club, someone was bound to step out of line. Horst spoke very good English and reminded me of a boxer (which we found out later he really was!) – square chin, short and muscular – and he would sort out anyone who did not toe the line. I have met him several times since over the years, and Mike Pender's Searchers were invited to perform at the Star-Club's 50th anniversary show in April 2012. But back then, fifty years earlier, the Searchers were just a fill-in group to work around the big American stars.

One man stood out: Ray Charles was really something else, and must have cost a fortune at the time. The club would open at 4.00 p.m. and close at 4.00 a.m., the last spot being 3.00 a.m. We played the last spot often – there was no getting round it, everyone had to share.

The basic schedule was: four groups from England would come and stay for a month, while every other week the boss, Manfred Weissleder, would bring in a big name from America. The English groups had to perform for three separate hours a night, three shows each. The money was great – my wages when I left Liverpool to travel to Hamburg were £10 a week – and that was with overtime. At the Star-Club, it was £50 a week – not much in today's money, but it was a lot in 1962-63.

It was hard but enjoyable work in those early days in Hamburg. Chris and Tony would go their own way, while John and I would stick together most of the time, entertaining ourselves with the football machine in the bar next to the Star-Club. When we weren't sleeping, we'd be rehearsing new songs – not original stuff, self-penned, because none of us thought we could write songs. It was more a case of: find an old song already recorded and make it your own, like we did with 'Sweets For My Sweet', recorded originally by the Drifters. After we played the last spot, we would walk to our hotel at 4.30 a.m. with the city's lights still shining brightly.

Discipline was strong: and we couldn't really leave the confines of the club. By the time we had done our last spot, we were so tired that we slept most of the day, so the time would pass pretty quickly. But not for a certain young lady waiting back in Liverpool. Needless to say, I was desperate to get home after that first month at the Star-Club.

After recording the now-famous demo/acetate at the Iron Door in January 1963, we were committed again to the Star-Club, this time for two months Things had started to happen quickly while we were in Hamburg. Our manager, Les Ackerley, had started the ball rolling, and when we got back to Liverpool after our success at the Star-Club, we did that rough recording session at the Iron Door. Publicity became important and in December we were featured on the front cover of the *Mersey Beat* newspaper, thanks to its owner and editor, Bill Harry.

'THE SEARCHERS.'
MR. C. CRUMMEY.
30, FLORIDA STREET
BOOTLE 20.
LPOOL, LANCASHIRE.
ENGLAND.

MR. HORST FASCHER.
20, GROSSE FREIHEIT.
HAMBURG 4.

Dear Sir,

We wish to convey our thanks to everyone at the Star Blub for making our last season there such a pleasant and successful one.

The Searchers now definitely wish to return for the two months of ÷ February & March 1963. We also wish to know if you can increase our pay. If this is possible, could you please make a new contract for us (with same conditions, i.e for transport & playing time etc) and send it by post to us. Hoping you can, and thanking you once again, I remain,

Yours faithfully.

P.P. THE SEARCHERS.

"THE SEARCHERS"
c/o MR C CRUMMEY
30, FLORIDA ST
BOOTLE 20
LIVERPOOL.
ENGLAND.

MR MANFRED HEISSLEDER K.G.,
39. GROSSE - FREIHEIT.
HAMBURG - ST PAULI.

Dear Sir,

I have today received your contract for the 1st February – 1st march, which I thank you for

In my letter to mr. Fascher requesting a new contract for the Searches, I asked if it was possible to increase our salary. I would now like the Searchers to be paid 400 Dm per week each. If the increase can be paid please send a letter in agreement, or a new contract including the new salary. Hoping you can and apologising for any inconvenience caused, I remain.

Yours faithfully.

P.P. THE SEARCHERS

We returned to the Star-Club, performing there throughout February and March. I remember it well, especially the weather. Hamburg was snowed under and it was freezing-cold. I had been back to Birchall's after our first trip to Hamburg, to thank my boss, Charlie, for his offer of my job still being there for me, but he understood what was happening and wished me all the best, as did all my workmates. Miss Doyle was near to tears when I told her the band was returning to Hamburg – we had only known each other for six months. But I loved her dearly, and I could see in her eyes she felt the same. 'Don't worry,' she said, 'I will be counting the days. Just come back safely.' I thought afterwards how lucky I was – and still am to this day.

At that time, I had no idea what lay ahead. Both May and I knew that, after giving up my job at Birchall's, this was now my career path and my main source of income. May realised this and gave me her blessing as the four of us once again said goodbye at Liverpool Lime Street Station on 29 January 1963. I was thinking of the future, having saved up quite a lot of money from the first Hamburg trip and I would save even more this time, as it would be twice as long.

I also knew, of course, that Miss Doyle was the girl for me. Being away from her was not easy, but the music got me through those two months and as a pop/rock group, we felt we could now go on to better things. In those days, people still wrote letters, especially to their loved ones, when apart – a bit like soldiers, I suppose. I wrote a lot of letters. Miss Doyle would write even more addressed to the Star-Club, where I would eagerly await them. Speaking on the telephone was sometimes a problem (not many people had private telephones in those days), so we arranged for me to call at a certain time in the evening on a certain day. It wasn't always successful.

Then came an exciting period for the band. Returning to Liverpool the second time, at the beginning of March 1963, things had really started to take off. Record companies in London had realised there were other groups in Liverpool apart from the Beatles. However, success was not handed to us on a plate. For instance, during our two-month contract at the Star-Club we played a total of 128 sessions – long, hard nights. There were plans for a live recording with various artists, but Chris made a very strong case for us to record our own album. Our recording time was very limited and only relatively primitive equipment was available.

We recorded 19 tracks, on which all the band members shared vocal duties: 'Sweets For My Sweet' (Tony), 'Ain't That Just Like Me' (Chris), 'Listen To Me' (Tony and me), 'I Can Tell' (Chris), 'Sick And Tired' (Chris), 'Mashed Potatoes' (Tony), 'I Sure Know A Lot About Love' (Tony, Chris and me), 'Rosalie' (John), 'Learning The Game' (Tony and me), 'Hey Joe!' (me), 'Always It's You' (Chris, Tony and me), 'Hully Gully' (Tony), 'What'd I Say' (Chris), 'Beautiful Dreamer' (me), 'Sweet Nothin's' (Tony), 'Shakin' All Over' (Tony), 'Sweet Little Sixteen' (me), 'Don't You Know' (me) and 'Maybellene' (Chris).

We deliberately chose classic rock and pop songs by many of the artists who had most influenced us: Chuck Berry, Fats Domino, Ray Charles and Buddy Holly. We proved we were a tight, professional, talented band playing music in the raw, and it sounded great.

Thirteen of these cuts appeared on the LP *The Searchers At The Star-Club, Hamburg*, released in the UK on the Philips label in October 1963. The single of 'Sweet Nothin's' with 'What'd I Say' on the B-side, was released by Philips in the UK in September 1963 and achieved No. 48 in the charts. The other tracks were released as singles, EPs and LPs over the following two years on the Philips and Star-Club labels in Germany, Holland and Japan, and by Mercury in the US and Canada.

In 1964, Mercury released an LP called *The Searchers Meet The Rattles*, mixing some of our live Star-Club recordings with tracks by a popular German band. The LP also bizarrely includes 'It's All Been A Dream', the B-side of our recording of 'Sweets For My Sweet' for Pye. That LP reached No. 63 in the US album charts and stayed in the charts for seven weeks.

We didn't get paid for the recordings. The record company and the Star-Club's owner, Manfred Weissleder, got the money.

In 2002, all 19 live tracks were released on the CD *The Searchers At The Star-Club* by the German label, Bear Family Records.

I had very mixed feelings when we signed a third contract to go back to Hamburg. Could I take May with me next time? But I thought that she would have to give up her job and her independence. Could I really take that lovely girl to the seedy atmosphere of Hamburg? The answer was 'No', but then fate stepped in again.

Our manager, Les Ackerley, had hawked around the acetate we had recorded in January before we left for Hamburg. Pye Records, through their producer, Tony Hatch, were very interested. He came to see us in action at the Iron Door and was even more impressed. Les bought us out of the Star-Club contract. Our lives were about to change for ever.

Les Ackerley played a major role in the group's development during our pre-Hamburg, pre-recording period in Liverpool. On our return from Hamburg, the Iron Door was packed for our first gig back and we got a great welcome with a very large banner that said *'Home of the Searchers'*.

CHAPTER 7

Sweet Success and the British Invasion

Tony Hatch selected 'Sweets For My Sweet' as the ideal track for our first single.

Just like today, bands in the '60s needed a first hit single to give them chart success, plus national and international publicity. As a young Liverpool band, we found ourselves in that position early in 1963. At the request of our manager, Les Ackerley, we had recorded a demo tape of several songs at a session at the Iron Door club.

The first track was a little-known song, 'Sweets For My Sweet', which Chris Curtis had found on a Drifters LP in Hamburg a few months earlier. Written by the established American team of Doc Pomus & Mort Shuman, it had been a minor hit for the Drifters in the US. They wrote many songs which became big hits, such as 'Save The Last Dance For Me' and 'Teenager In Love'. We listened to 'Sweets For My Sweet' and felt it was pretty ordinary, so we put our own, strong Mersey beat stamp on it. The song really suited Tony's voice and our demo tape was made into an acetate, then circulated to several record companies in London.

Decca were not interested – but then they had already turned down the Beatles! Pye Records producer Tony Hatch was sufficiently impressed by what he heard to make the journey to Liverpool, to see us in action at the Iron Door. We were quickly offered a recording contract by Pye.

In April 1963, the local newspaper in Bootle ran a story with the headline 'A Day to Remember for this Local Rock Group'. Underneath a publicity photo of the band, the article reported that we had, on the previous Friday 'cut our first disc to hop onto the Mersey beat bandwagon' after signing for Pye Records. It also said 'the blazing lights, the breathtaking whirl into stardom, have at last caught up with the Searchers'.

The article went on to say that 'their brand of music is unforgettably stamped onto the memory by the skilled guitar-work of Mick Prendergast, the leader, who lives at 98 St John's Road; by the throbbing music of rhythm guitarist John McNally, who lives at 29 St John's Road; and by the beat of drummer Chris Curtis, who lives at 30 Florida Street. Bass guitarist is Tony Jackson, of 23 Ritson Street, Liverpool.' The writer concluded: 'Some say the Searchers will be a challenge to the Beatles – that is as may be...if local reaction can tell a tale, the Searchers will be up there with the best of them, shouldering their way to international fame.'

Tony Hatch selected 'Sweets For My Sweet' as the ideal track for our first single and we re-recorded it at Pye's studios at Marble Arch, London. It took three takes to record in one 45-minute session. Tony made a tiny error on his lead vocal, but it was not important and went unnoticed. Producer Hatch was in the studio with us with his engineer, Ray Prickett, and we all enjoyed working with them. We didn't know it then, but these guys would shape our lives and careers over the following years. We frankly didn't have an immediate feeling the track would be a hit. Its chart progress was slow at first, but I remember getting a telegram from Pye saying it had entered the charts at No. 44. It was an incredible feeling for us to get to No. 1 with our first single. 'Sweets For My Sweet' will always hold a very special place in my memory and for all fans of the original Searchers.

In those days, it was important to get plays on Radio Luxembourg. I remember hearing 'Sweets For My Sweet' played many times by deejay Jack Jackson while I was still living at home with my parents. Some very favourable comments from

John Lennon about the record on a radio programme certainly helped to promote it. Our appearance on the *Thank Your Lucky Stars* TV show also helped. The record catapulted up the charts to reach No. 1 on the *NME* chart on 2 August 1963, taking the top spot from Frank Ifield's 'I'm Confessin''.

This was at the time of another big step into the limelight when well-known London agent Tito Burns became our manager. Les Ackerley knew he would lose us and a deal was worked out between him and Tito, who did a great job making us world-famous. Our first LP, *Meet The Searchers*, released in August 1963, reached No. 2 in the charts.

People looking back, when talking of the past, sometimes remember only the bad times, and we had a few of those. Nobody is perfect and certainly not in the entertainment/recording business. When you are looking after four people with big egos and different personalities, it would test anyone's resolve. By this time Chris had become the dominant influence within the band.

We arranged a meeting with Tito, Tony Hatch and Louis Benjamin, Chairman of Pye, because our second Pye single, 'Sugar And Spice', had made No. 2 in the UK music charts – and No. 1 in one or two other charts. Chris and I felt 'Needles And Pins' had to be the next single. I suggested to Tito and Tony that we needed to move from our previous 'Sweets For My Sweet'/'Sugar And Spice' style to a more serious, true-to-life storyline for the next single – it *had* to be 'Needles And Pins'.

Before its release, that song was not the most popular choice with all concerned. Louis Benjamin took the business view of 'if it ain't broke, don't fix it'. He wanted us to record a similar type of song to the first two singles. Tony Hatch, to his credit, was on our side and agreed with us that we should go with 'Needles'. Tito was undecided, probably because he knew that Louis Benjamin liked to get his own way. After all, Louis was Pye Records. If I remember correctly, Tony and John were undecided about 'Needles And Pins', but Chris and I were adamant that it had to be our next single. Modesty aside, how right we were, as it turned out to be the biggest selling record ever for the band.

Then came 1964, easily our best year for record releases – five Top 10 records and on TV every other week – but marred by one big upset, more of which in a later chapter. Yes, as Louis Walsh would say today: 'Mike you look like a pop star, you sing like a pop star, you once were a pop star!' But, although we found fame, we did not find fortune, and certainly not the kind of fortune associated with today's pop stars.

From 1963 to 1966 we were a household name, and our fans had our pictures pinned to their bedroom walls. Life was good and I wasn't complaining. We were each paid a weekly wage of £200, a lot of money in those days. But, unlike a solo artist, the fees we earned were split five ways between us and Tito. I wasn't concerned about income tax in those days, but I should have been more aware of it, as I am today After all, we were in the large income bracket, and, for every pound we made, the Government allowed us to keep half. Needless to say, we all had the tax bills to pay later on.

In November 1963, our second LP, *Sugar And Spice*, got to No. 5. Later that year, after we had scored with two major hit singles, Tito told us if we were to make it big in the recording business, we needed three consecutive big hits. He was so right.

I was so confident that 'Needles And Pins' would be a big

hit, I asked Miss Doyle to marry me. I knew life was going to get hectic and the band would have to be away from home a lot, as a US tour was coming up. She was unsure at first, saying she would prefer to wait at least until the summer. I know now that she wanted a big-occasion wedding, like every girl does. When I explained about being away on world tours, in recording studios and spending a lot of time in London, she finally agreed. I didn't want to lose that lovely girl, or even take a chance on losing her.

We had the quietest wedding ever – I didn't even tell the band, or Tito. But that is what I have always done: once I make my mind up, I do it. And so May and I were married on 2 December 1963 at St John's Catholic Church, Kirkdale, and we have lived happily ever after, or since. Following the success of our first two records, we bought our first house for £2,250 on the Wirral, a supposed upmarket place near Liverpool. I wrote out a cheque, paid the guy, and we moved in – no estate agents or solicitors. After just seven weeks of married life, I had to leave the homestead once again.

Although Miss Doyle was about to be made lonely again, it wasn't as if it was going to be two months at the Star Club or anything like that. We were only gone for about ten days, as I recall, during which time Miss Doyle and her sister, Veronica, who was staying with her, spent all my money furnishing our new home. I am joking of course, but I still tease her about it!

Above: Me, aged one, 1942.

Right: Still cute at six
years old in 1947.

On holiday in Ireland, 1950:
O'Connell Street, Dublin.
Dad, Mam, Aunt Cathleen,
me and Cousin Brian.

Plate 1

St Winefride's Football Team, Champions 1953/54.
Headmaster Mr Toolin is on the left, coach Mr Rooney on the right.
I'm on the back row, fourth from the left.

Bootle SchoolBoys 1955/56. I'm on the back row, second from the left.

Plate 2

Front and back of my Cup Runners-Up medal from the match at Anfield.

My sister Maureen marries Michael Gilligan, a lovely man, 1957.
That's me in the suit, on the far left.

Plate 3

My first real guitar!

Big Ron and I
meet again,
Edinburgh, 2012.

Plate 4

The first Searchers line-up.
Left to right: Joe Kennedy (out of shot), Joe West, John McNally and me.

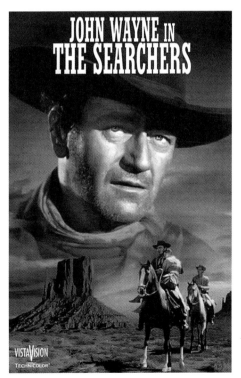

Above: The infamous Watkins
Dominator amplifier, or
rather one just like it!

Left: The inspiration for our name.

Plate 5

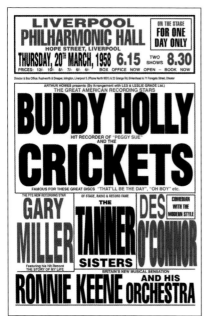

Buddy Holly and the Crickets were a huge influence.

Having a pint with my mates. My good friend Pete Dolan is far left.

Plate 6

Starting again!
① At first, the group consists of
   Tony Jackson, me and John
   McNally.
② I meet Chris Crummey (later
   Curtis) and we are now four.
③ Then Bob Wooler suggests
   we get a lead vocalist and
   we are joined by Johnny
   Sandon.

Plate 7

The Cross Keys pub in Liverpool where I first met Tony Jackson.

Johnny Sandon and I share the vocals at the Odd Spot, 1961.

Plate 8

Picture taken at our last appearance at the Iron Door, 1963.

The imposing entrance to 'The Home of the Searchers'.

Plate 9

Miss Doyle, circa 1961.

My one-year passport photo
circa 1962.

The train that took us part of the way to Hamburg.
Liverpool Street Station, London, 1962.

Plate 10

With the great Fats Domino at the Star-Club in 1962.

Meeting up with rock'n'roll legend Jerry Lee Lewis
many years after our Star-Club encounter.

Plate 11

Plate 12

Above: Our last appearance at the Cavern, 26 July 1963.

Left: Newly married!

Far left: Rehearsing at Pye.

Plate 13

Performing 'Sweets For My Sweet' on *Thank Your Lucky Stars*.
Looks like a *Doctor Who* set!

Thank Your Lucky Stars Mersey beat special featuring the Beatles, the
Searchers, Billy J. Kramer & The Dakotas and Cilla Black.

Plate 14

Welcome to America, 1964.

We make the *Ed Sullivan Show*!

Plate 15

Happy times and white shirts.

Keith Fordyce interviews us on *Ready Steady Go!*

Plate 16

CHAPTER 8

Welcome to America – The Glory Years 1963-65

We had incredible success in those golden years from 1963 to 1966, with fifteen UK chart singles.

How can I forget 1964, our first big year, with lots of hit singles, EPs and LPs, TV shows, concerts and world tours?

In January, Tito Burns took us to the USA, which he wanted to break, having failed with Cliff and the Shadows. When we arrived at the hotel in New York, it was surrounded by screaming girls. Immediately after the Beatles' tour, British bands going to the US got a similar welcome – screaming girls and police cordons. We had breakfasts of pancakes and syrup on the same plate as bacon and fried eggs – it was all very strange to us, but it tasted wonderful. We also had something called 'pizza'.

Tito knew we had to get on the *Ed Sullivan Show* to get the vital break, and made it the main objective. To get real recognition you had to be on that show. To begin with, there was a problem with the producers, who, although they liked the group and the song 'Needles And Pins', wanted something more than another group singing and playing guitars After a lot of negotiation, Tito finally won the day and we duly appeared.

The sound was not great, but the audiences in the studio and at home loved us. I couldn't believe it – we were actually on the *Ed Sullivan Show*, just like Elvis and Buddy Holly had been! Years earlier, I remember going home from work just before I left

Birchall's and seeing one of my rock'n'roll heroes, Buddy Holly, on the *Ed Sullivan Show*. And now, here we were. I thought about seeing Buddy at the Phil in Liverpool on that night in 1958. Now, fate had brought us to one of the jewels in the showbiz crown. God bless America, 'home of the brave, land of the free'. New York was brilliant and a great place to be. We enjoyed riding round in those famous yellow taxis.

We didn't stay long on that first trip to America, as Tito Burns had told us before we went that the visit would be mostly for promotional purposes. 'Love Potion No. 9', a track from our first LP, was a major hit for us later in the US. After the *Ed Sullivan Show*, we did a few other TV and radio shows, plus five or six gigs in and around New York State, before flying home. I couldn't wait to get back to my new wife after our success.

At the end of the US trip, Tito was over the moon. We had achieved exactly what we had wanted to do, and, thinking back, especially as it had an American connection, my choice of name for the group was paying off, thanks to those other Searchers, John Wayne and Jeffrey Hunter. Tito soon had us headlining major tours over the following months and into the next year – 1964-65. We toured with many top stars including Roy Orbison, Bobby Vee, Dusty Springfield and Bob Luman, plus many of our other contemporaries from the UK – the Zombies, Brian Poole & The Tremeloes and Freddie & The Dreamers to name a few. We also did several world tours in that period with people like Del Shannon, Joe South, Tommy Roe and Roy Orbison. If I've missed anyone out, please accept my apologies. One of the last big tours we did in the UK was with Dionne Warwick and the Isley Brothers – a strange combination for the Searchers, you might say, but we left everything to Tito. Life was so hectic, you didn't get time to think about where the money was going.

Mersey beat was to be heard pounding out from just about every street corner in early-'60s Liverpool, but it wasn't every day you found it literally in the middle of the road. Neighbours in Deacon Street, Everton couldn't believe their eyes when they were treated to an impromptu concert by us, right on their own

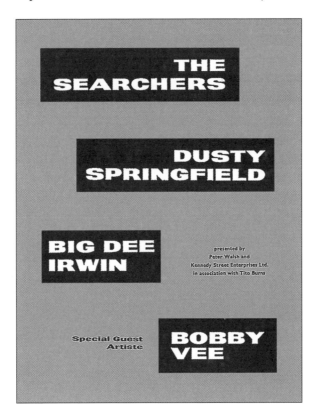

THE SEARCHERS

DUSTY SPRINGFIELD

BIG DEE IRWIN

presented by
Peter Walsh and
Kennedy Street Enterprises Ltd.
In association with Tito Burns

Special Guest Artiste

BOBBY VEE

doorstep. We were mobbed by excited fans when we went outdoors to perform 'Needles And Pins' in front of the television cameras for the BBC's *Top of the Pops*. I remember seeing a photograph of this event somewhere.

When we toured the UK with Roy Orbison in 1964, Tony Jackson and I took Roy to a football match. Everton happened to be playing Chelsea at Stamford Bridge that Saturday and our gig that night was near London. Tour manager Fred Perry came with us, mostly to keep an eye on Roy. Poor Roy could not get the hang of it and didn't really understand our national game.

We had incredible success in those golden years from 1963 to 1966, with fifteen UK chart singles (including three No. 1s), seven hit EPs including two No. 1s, and four Top 20 LPs (including one No. 1). For our third single, Pye had wanted us to record another old Drifters song, 'I Count The Tears', but we had been impressed by Jackie DeShannon's recording of 'Needles And Pins' and, as already mentioned, our arguments in favour of that song won the day.

Released in January 1964, 'Needles' reached No. 1 within a few weeks. Then we had our third No. 1 from our first four singles for Pye, when 'Don't Throw Your Love Away' got to the top of the charts in April. Our third album, *It's The Searchers*, came out in May 1964 and included our last two No. 1 singles, plus our version of Don Gibson's 'Sea Of Heartbreak'. The album reached No. 4. Our first three albums, released within twelve months, were all major chart successes – which was not bad going. Disappointingly, our next single, 'Some Day We're Gonna Love Again', only made No. 11. With hindsight, I have to agree that was not a great song, but it was all we had at the time. We had left it to Chris to find songs for us – to pick a winner, as they say.

We certainly picked a winner for our next release. Our recording career had stalled somewhat, and the music writers on *NME*, *Disc* and other publications made an issue of it and claimed our popularity was on the wane. This to an extent was true, but they soon changed their tune after our success with 'When You Walk In The Room'.

Jackie DeShannon recalls writing the song's main riff on the guitar, but says Glen Campbell played the distinctive 12-string line on her recording of it. Glen did a lot of session work early in his career, including many tracks with the Beach Boys. We listened to the DeShannon version of the song with great interest. Without being critical, I thought it was pretty light.

As I recall, our mood at the recording session at Pye's Marble Arch studios was buoyant and happy. Chris and I were the main contributors on the recording. We decided to double-track my vocal and also double-track my 12-string Rick, adding Chris's harmony vocal. We all went home very contented that night. (On the subject of double-tracking, singers with really strong voices don't need their vocals to be double-tracked. Frank Ifield, for example, had a great voice which didn't need double-tracking, and there are many others like him. But double-tracking has been around for a long time now and lots of artistes and groups use it.)

Tony Hatch was a happy man that night and guaranteed us

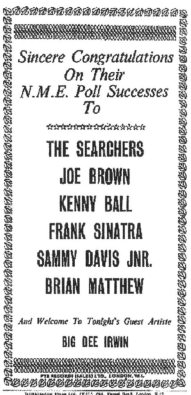

that 'When You Walk In The Room' would be an instant hit. How right he was! People tell me 'Needles And Pins' and 'When You Walk In The Room' sound similar. As the latter did not make No. 1 in the charts, 'Needles' has to come out on top. Today, the Searchers song I most enjoy performing is undoubtedly 'When You Walk In The Room', but for listening it has to be 'Goodbye My Love', which got to No. 4 in 1965 – an atmospheric sound, with lots of echo.

On another note, we had a bit part in the Michael Winner film, *Saturday Night Out*, performing the title song (the B-side of 'Needles And Pins'). By this time Chris had bought himself a flat in London. He loved the social life: his many friends included Alma Cogan, Dusty Springfield and her manager, Vicki Wickham. Chris had expensive tastes and was a frequent visitor to Harrods. I remember he took me to Kutchinsky's, a jewellers in Chelsea, to help me buy a Piaget watch for May. It felt like the big time.

In the summer, after the runaway success of our three No. 1 records and one No. 2, we were booked for the *New Musical Express*'s annual Poll Winners concert at the Wembley Empire Pool stadium. We had been voted runner-up to the Beatles in the vocal category. At that time, it was the ultimate pop show, broadcast live on television. But, like all outside live performances at that time, the sound suffered a bit. You can see some of the show on YouTube. Have a look and you'll see and hear what I mean. Everyone who was anyone in the pop world at that time was there, so it was certainly a feather in our caps. I still have the silver cup that was presented to us.

Our follow-up EPs were also keeping up the high standard: *Sweets For My Sweet* made No. 5 in the EP chart, *Hungry For Love* got to No. 4, and *The Searchers Play The System* (from the Oliver Reed/Julie Foster film) reached No. 11.

As a result of our first US tour and our appearance on the *Ed Sullivan Show*, 'Needles And Pins' reached No. 13 in the US charts. 'Don't Throw Your Love Away' got to No. 16. Our first US LP, *Meet The Searchers*, reached No. 22. Even two albums of our old Star-Club recordings, *Hear! Hear!* and *This Is Us* reached No. 120 and No. 97 respectively in the US charts.

In December 1964, our recording of the American anti-nuclear folk song 'What Have They Done To The Rain' was released, reaching No. 13 in the UK and No. 29 in the US.

So, 1964 was a very eventful year for the band, especially when we lost Tony Jackson – but why?

CHAPTER 9

Ego and Bad Vibrations – Losing Tony

In the early years, we had played music for kicks and beer money.

One of the most talked-about and repeated questions by fans and the general public over the years has been: 'Why did Tony leave the band?' Why does anyone leave a band? You could say it is inevitable that all musical groups, especially pop groups, split up sooner or later. History tells us the person most likely to leave is the vocalist or the 'main man'.

Take one of my inspirations, Buddy Holly. As we know, Buddy starting his recording career as a member of the Crickets. Even though the other members of the group all played their part, Buddy was the voice and the inspiration. When he left the band, the fans (including myself) and the record-buying public were disappointed, and couldn't understand the reasons for his decision.

Before we get to the reasons why group members leave, let's just look at some of the groups who became household names and then split up: the Jackson Five, the Supremes, the Osmonds, the Shadows and the Four Seasons. These are just some of the biggest names; there are hundreds of others we will never get to hear about.

One of the main reasons that people leave is ego. Let's be honest and say 99% of 'pop stars' (depending on their status) have large egos – some larger than others. But we all have one –

yes, me as well. There are certain times when 'Mr Ego' will surface, but most people will keep him quiet until he is fed by others in the same line of business. My 'Mr Ego' has been fed many times over the years. Who would have – or could have – thought that, as early as July 1964, fate would strike amid the great times and the group I had brought together would lose its bass player, Tony Jackson?

Looking back, at the time it came as no surprise to me, as relations in the band had reached a point where it could be seen what was about to happen. John, Chris and I were still compatible – just – but Tony was growing away from us. Chris and Tony were never the best of friends, and Tony, being the oldest member of the group, always felt he knew best when decisions had to be made about which songs to record, or where the group should be going. I could see he was not happy and wanted more from the world of show business. Tony was divorced from his wife, Margaret by this time, and it could be seen that, once he was introduced to the world of wine, women and money, his marriage would suffer.

He was my close mate in the early years and we did most things together. We just had our music and Everton FC. We would meet in the Why Not pub in Liverpool on Saturday lunchtimes and go off to Goodison Park to see our heroes, Roy Vernon and Alex Young, in action. But one thing I learned as I got older is that everything changes. And so it was with Tony and me. We drifted apart, especially after I met May.

In the early years, we had played music for kicks and beer money. We had been happy to play in Liverpool's 'sweat cellars' – the Casbah, the Lowlands, the Cavern, the Iron Door, and many other dives. But then came success and we took ourselves seriously – the fantasy became a reality and we were household names. Our personalities changed – and Tony's changed most of all.

Tony was born on 16 July 1938 in the Dingle area of Liverpool – his contemporaries Billy Fury and Ringo Starr were also born and brought up there. By his early twenties, he had acquired the ominous nickname Black Jake, and had the Elvis (he preferred Clint Reno) 'attitude', which I saw in action at the Cross Keys.

When I first met him. Tony made himself a Fender-style bass guitar and an amp to go with it – he was an electrician by trade and very good with his hands. He got Adrian Barber from the Big Three to make a huge cabinet for his amp – we used to call it 'the coffin' – and he taught himself to play with some help from me, and became a good bass player. He later bought a Hofner violin bass.

Tony sang the lead vocal on our first recording, 'Sweets For My Sweet', and I joined him for the vocals on 'Sugar And Spice'. His driving bass was prominent on both recordings. Tony also sang lead on our biggest success stateside, 'Love Potion No. 9'. On our first album, *Meet The Searchers*, Tony featured as lead singer on most of the tracks. At his best as a vocalist, he could give Little Richard a run for his money.

Tony didn't sing on any of the tracks on our third LP, *It's The Searchers*. Chris would tell him his vocals were not needed and he was to play bass his (i.e. Chris's) way. In his 1998 interview with Spencer Leigh for *Record Collector* magazine, Chris gave his opinion on the vocals issue over 'Needles And Pins': 'Tony Jackson was the lead singer for "Sweets For My Sweet", and his was the best voice we could have for that song. Unfortunately, it wasn't the best voice for "Needles And Pins"; he tried it, but he was singing "I saw her today" totally without meaning, just like he was singing the words off a page. It was much better with Mike Pender.'

From the moment it was decided that 'Needles' would be our first single with me as the lead vocalist, not Tony, the trouble really started, although I never realised it at the time. Tony became increasingly moody and very argumentative. It came as no surprise when Tito arranged a meeting between Tony and Chris to calm things down and to try to bring the whole group back together again.

'Some Day We're Gonna Love Again' was the third single in a row to feature my lead vocals, rather than Tony's. Then along came Frank. Chris had struck up a friendship with a young guy we called Frankie – Frank McNeice – who as 'Frank Allen' was the bass player with Cliff Bennett & The Rebel Rousers. We had first met up with them at the Star-Club in Hamburg. Chris and Frank became good friends in Germany and also socialised in London when Chris moved there. Frank, Cliff Bennett and the other members of that group were all from the London area.

Internal tensions within the band worsened when certain people neglected to tell Tony about recording sessions and policy discussions. Totally alienated, he walked out in July 1964, after nearly a year with the band, and shortly afterwards Frank Allen became our new bass player.

Tony did not go quietly. It was headline news and a great shock to our fans when he left the band. He reputedly spent £3,000 of his own money to put his new band together and to have cosmetic surgery on his nose, to make it smaller and have the bump taken out. The surgery cost £250. There is a first-hand description of the auditions for his new band – who were to be called the Vibrations – in Paul Francis's excellent autobiography, *Drumming Up Vibrations*.

An up-and-coming drummer whose previous bands had played on the same bill as the Rolling Stones, Paul was already a professional musician at the tender age of sixteen. He read in a newspaper that Tito Burns, who, of course, managed us, would also be representing Tony. The article also said Tony was putting his own band together. Paul wrote to Tito to offer his services and was promptly invited to attend auditions at the Roaring Twenties club in London's famous Carnaby Street.

It was rather disconcerting for the young man to find that 400 other musicians were also being auditioned! It was a bit like *The X Factor*, with Tony sitting at a table with two other men. He needed a guitarist and a keyboard player, in addition to a drummer. Ironically, Paul was asked to play along with a track by the Liverpool group the Undertakers, 'Hell's Bells'. The Undertakers, like us, had been regular performers at the Iron Door. At the end of the auditions, Tony chose Paul and two other young guys, Martin Raymond (keyboards) and Ian Buisel (lead/rhythm guitar).

From that point, things happened very quickly: meetings with Tito Burns and recording sessions at Pye with Tony Hatch, using the studios that we knew so well. Their first single, the Mary Wells number 'Bye Bye Baby', produced by Tony Hatch, was released in September 1964. In the national press, Tony was quoted as saying he had left the Searchers over a 'policy dispute': 'I found the soft, sweet approach of the Searchers too watery – I prefer the gutsy, strong beat we followed in the early days back home in Liverpool,' he told the *Sunday Mirror*.

An appearance on top TV music show *Ready Steady Go!* was quickly followed by a 29-day national tour with the Hollies, Freddie & The Dreamers, Marianne Faithfull and the Four Pennies. On *Ready Steady Go!* presenter Cathy McGowan asked Tony why he'd had a nose job. 'Because it was terrible, like yours,' replied Tony. He also unhelpfully added that he thought our recording of 'What Have They Done To The Rain' was 'terrible, just about the worst thing they've ever recorded'.

Apparently, the audience reaction to the first gigs by Tony and his new bandmates was excellent, with hordes of screaming girls pursuing them. Unfortunately for him and his young band, this promising start did not continue for long. 'Bye Bye Baby', the first single by Tony Jackson & The Vibrations (Tony didn't want to use his name, but Tito Burns insisted on it) reached No. 25 in one chart and No. 28 in another, in spite of considerable publicity and promotion. The song was a radical departure from what Searchers fans might have expected. Their second single, 'You Beat Me To The Punch', another Mary Wells cover, failed to chart.

'Love Potion No. 9' was chosen as the next single, although of course Tony had sung the lead vocal on our version, which had recently reached No. 3 in the US chart. Tito Burns was noted in the press as saying the 'famous feud' between Tony and his former group was now over. 'They shook hands in this office,' said Tito. 'It was silly for them to continue this battle.' And so, with everyone's blessing, Tony and his band released 'Love Potion No. 9' in February 1965. It reached No. 37 in the UK and No. 12 in Sweden. It was an obvious attempt to capitalise on our success with the same song in the US charts. They even performed at the Cavern and at the Star-Club in Hamburg, which must have brought back happy memories for Tony.

Inevitably, our paths were to cross several times. Both bands appeared on the same edition of the TV show *Thank Your Lucky Stars*. We were also on the same bill for an 11-date UK tour in March 1965, with Dusty Springfield, Bobby Vee and the Zombies. I was always pleased to see Tony and we were still friendly, but the atmosphere was somewhat strained with Chris and John.

The strain was also starting to tell on Tony. Being on the bill with us, he felt he had more to prove. They played good sets, but he was drinking more and more, which could be a problem at times. Perhaps Tony didn't want to be up front as the vocalist. Perhaps he felt more at ease playing bass as part of the band. After that tour, I heard reports that he had been involved in fights before, during and after gigs.

If Tony's unsuccessful last single for Pye in July 1965, Goffin & King's 'Stage Door', had been recorded by us, it would almost certainly have been a big hit. His first single for CBS, 'You're My Number One', released in January 1966, sounded like 'the Searchers meets the Beatles'. By this time, Tony had now changed the band's name to the Tony Jackson Group. His next effort, 'Never Leave Your Baby's Side', predated the Byrds' early sound. His last single, 'Anything Else You Want', likewise sank with without trace in December 1966, and CBS did not renew his contract. By the summer of 1966, UK work for Tony and his band was drying up. Following unsuccessful tours of Germany, Spain and Portugal, he and his band fell apart around February-March 1967. A final EP was released in Portugal by the Estudio label in 1967.

When we were still in New York after our 1964 *Ed Sullivan Show* appearance, Tito Burns had spoken to us about other avenues that might be open to us. I noticed Tony's ego surface immediately as Tito mentioned the movies and acting parts for those who were successful in the pop world. He told us that Brian Epstein had done a deal for the Beatles and that we, as a group, could have the same opportunity, depending on how long we could be successful. It's easy to get carried away when people tell you how good you are, or how good you look. It's great for your ego, but it can also be your downfall. This was the start of Tony's frustration and his slow alienation from Chris, John and myself.

Tony had very much enjoyed our bit part in the *Saturday Night Out* film, performing the title track. He was smitten, being the oldest and having the biggest ego, to the extent of seeing himself in the role of Ben Casey, an American television series about a hospital with actor Vince Edwards in the lead role. Tony had been likened to that character many times since the show had been on British TV.

The seed had been sown and Tony's ambition now became to make movies. Tito went on to say that he could see me in a bit part in a Western movie, as many pop stars were used as props to promote Western films, which were still in fashion at that time, but I have to admit this was rather tongue-in-cheek and Tito must have had too many Martinis. Still, the mention of something like that does stir the imagination. It took me back to my childhood, dreaming of being up there in the saddle with my Western cowboy heroes – the Durango Kid, Hopalong Cassidy, and of course John Wayne.

Tony was the hard man in the band, as well as being the hard drinker. It has been rumoured that he and I had a fight before a show in Cardiff. It was even mentioned by the *Daily Mail* in their obituary for Tony. The truth is, it was only a 'handbags' situation, as they say in today's football terminology.

When I first met him at the Cross Keys, he was a warm, friendly character and we became friends very easily. I would stay at his house, where his wife Margaret would cook us a meal. She was always happy with the situation that Tony and I would be together a lot, especially with 'going to the match' as we called it. In those early days, before I met up again with Chris, I looked up to Tony, probably because he was older than me. Funny thing was, I can't remember age being mentioned until much later.

Tony, John and I never played at the Cross Keys as a trio,

and I can remember only two gigs where we did. Tony also said, in a later interview, that he and Chris Curtis were asking other people to go to the Star-Club, Hamburg with them as replacements for John and myself. This was a fabrication. John and I would not leave our jobs. Speaking for myself, I loved my job and got on very well with my workmates, and was allowed to take a month's leave to fulfil the Star-Club gig. John then had to leave his job, which he did – but not until I asked him to do just that. Tony invented the story about replacements, probably because his music career fell apart in 1967. It would be 25 years before he returned to performing onstage.

CHAPTER 10

Frankie Joins the Band

I've met up with Frankie a couple of times since the split and we've always shaken hands, which is more than I can say about John.

So Tony left, and Frankie, as I sometimes called him, joined us. Chris had first met Frank and introduced him to John and me in Hamburg. I can't remember if Chris knew him before Hamburg, but you could say that John and I didn't have a say in Frank joining us. I felt it was decided by Chris and, to a certain extent, Tito Burns. I do remember at the time thinking, *Frank seems a nice lad – a good bass player, looks OK, don't know if he can sing, he will do for the time being*, but my impression was that Chris was besotted with Frankie and he was going to have him in the band whether John or I liked it or not. Frankie always came across as an honourable and honest young man. We became good friends and I realised shortly after he joined us how good it was for the band that he had joined. We had some good years after Chris left.

I can remember staying at Frank's house a couple of times during those early years. His mum and dad were lovely people and Frank had lots of friends – or 'mates', as we called them in Liverpool. The few times I stayed at Frank's and met all his friends reminds me of the film *American Graffiti* – Ron Howard, Harrison Ford, Richard Dreyfuss, and the guy I remember most from that film, John Milner. He had the hot rod race with Harrison Ford at the end, and was killed. It is one of my all-time favourite films, along with *Shane* and, of course, *The Searchers*.

You may well ask why I am going on about the times with Frankie. I believe that, when writing memoirs, you have to be honest, and not just write about the bad times. I've met up with Frankie a couple of times since the split and we've always shaken hands – which is more than I can say about John.

When we attended Chris Curtis's funeral, John arrived at the same time as May and me. It was one of those awkward moments which I'm sure we've all experienced. I didn't want to ignore him, so I offered my hand, but John declined, saying, 'I don't think so, Mike,' and walked on. I thought, as I entered the church, *Eat your heart out, John!* When the time came for reading the eulogy, I mentioned that John and Frankie were also in the church, but that was all. I must add that Frankie is the complete opposite to John: after the service, he gave May a hug, we shook hands, and, although there was not much conversation, it was an honourable meeting.

I have many fond memories of my time with Frankie in the band, like the time when May and I, and our three children, had moved into a new house (one of the many moves). It was the time when people had a craze for woodchip wallpaper. This house was open plan, with lots of arched entrances instead of normal doors So we decided on the woodchip. We were doing three nights at a Liverpool venue and Frankie came round for a couple of days to help with the wallpapering – happy days. We called the house 'Les Arches'. If Frankie ever gets to read this, he'll laugh.

Before ending this short chapter on Frankie, there is one generous gesture I must include – one I will never forget – when he sent a letter of condolence to my dear wife, May, after our youngest son, Nathan, was killed in a tragic road accident some years ago. I know his letter helped May in her hour of need, just to know that friends from the past were thinking of her. If and when I next meet Frankie, I will give him a hug in memory of Nathan.

OUR DEAREST NATHAN
1970 – 2009

Nathe's life was cut short under tragic circumstances, which has come as such a shock to us all.

Born in April 1970, at Christiana Hartley's Hospital, Southport, Nathe began life in Aughton Green with his mum, dad and siblings, Michael and Stephanie. Following the family's move to Blundellsands, he began his schooling at Ursuline Convent School, and at age seven, he sat and passed the entrance exam to attend St Mary's Boys School. Although he was not particularly studious during his school years, we always felt he had a good brain and an enquiring mind. He obviously came to regret the missed opportunities he'd had at St Mary's, and sadly, it was not until later in life that Nathe developed a thirst for knowledge and a desire to better himself. He went on to complete, under his own steam, several higher education courses, including a Computer Programming degree and courses in First Aid, Health & Safety and Law. Following various office jobs, and doing some Road Crew work with his dad, Nathe eventually began a career in Telecommunications at Lake Technologies in St Helens, where he quickly became a much loved and trusted member of the team.

His best friend in the world was his beloved mum, who was his confidante. He struggled, at times, with his demons, but his mum was always there for him and he found great comfort in sharing his problems with her.

One of Nathe's passions in life was his music and he was an avid fan of the rock band "Marillion". He followed them relentlessly and saw them perform live many times, all over Europe. He even struck up quite personal friendships with some members of the group and their families. In the opinion of many, he had the potential to become a musician himself, and although he would never admit it, he had a real flair for the guitar. Those who knew Nathe well, however, would agree that he was a very modest person and never had the confidence to just pick up the guitar and play for people. But, the lucky few who were close to him would see him in relaxed mode, at various family celebrations, where he would feel comfortable enough to "have a go" and he would astound us all with what seemed to be a natural ability to "freestyle" on either an acoustic or electric guitar.

His other passion was his motorbike. He had always wanted one, and hard as his mum tried to dissuade him from getting one, she realised that she could not fall out with him over it and it was ultimately his decision. He went ahead and got it, and for the couple of years that he had it, he only ever rode it when the weather was good; not because he felt it would be more hazardous to drive in poor conditions, but simply because he didn't want to get his precious bike wet in the rain. He usually drove to work in his car, but sometimes, on the quite rare occasions when the weather was fine, he would don his leathers and helmet and enjoy an exhilarating journey to work on his bike. And, it was on such an occasion, that Nathe took the bike option, and on the warm, sunny evening of Tuesday 2 June, he left work on his bike for the last time. Nathe was always sensible and a very careful rider, and yet, through no wrongdoing on his part, he paid the ultimate price.

He did not want much out of life. He was not "showy" or materialistic. All he wanted was to meet a nice girl who would love him and care for him and one of his biggest regrets was that he never got the chance to become a dad. The next best thing for Nathe, was being uncle to Alexander, and one of his proudest moments was standing as Godfather at Alexander's christening, a responsibility he took very seriously. He adored him and we are so glad that they shared so many happy times together.

Nathe was quite a complex person, but he was the most honest, decent guy that you could ever wish to meet. He was sometimes very serious but more often very funny in his observations of life. He touched the lives of everyone who met him and had a deeply caring side to his nature.

We take great comfort in the fact that only the weekend before he passed away, we were all together to watch the FA Cup final, and although Everton didn't win.....we enjoyed the whole weekend together as a family.

We can't believe he is gone, but we're truly grateful for the many, many happy memories we have of him. He will be forever in our hearts until we see him again.

CHAPTER 11

My Love Affair with Rickenbackers and Other Guitars

It wasn't long before the group's reputation grew, and we became one of the top five bands in Liverpool.

From a very young age, I was, and to a certain extent still am, a guitar freak. I can remember seeing, at the early age of ten, the electric guitar left in my grandmother's parlour every Sunday, after it had been played the previous night at the local pub in or around Milford Street. It was not far from where John McNally, Big Ron Woodbridge and I would give one of our first performances some years later at the Convivial.

Grandmother's guitar was my first introduction to the guitar. I would hold it and wonder how on earth people could play such a thing. It wasn't until my last years at St Winefride's Secondary Modern School that I picked up another one, this time in John Bargen's front parlour. John was a classmate and also the school's head boy. Along with my other mates, Pete Dolan, Pete Davies and Brian Woolvine, we would all turn up at Banjo's (John's nickname) house, not far from the school, where we would all have a go at playing his guitar, but all we could ever do was to pretend to play it.

In my last year at school, I traded – or 'swapped' – as we

used to say, my collection of American comics (*Tales from the Crypt* among others) for an old, battered acoustic guitar. This was more or less how I met Big Ron, who also collected American comics. Collecting comics was a big thing for young boys at that time. The collecting bug is still with me today and helped me make inroads into another exciting time – of which more later.

That battered acoustic guitar served me well until I persuaded my dad to put a deposit down on a brand new electric/acoustic guitar. It was a sunburst colour, with 'f' sound holes. I thought it was a brilliant guitar! I remember it was Christmas 1955, a few months before my fourteenth birthday. There was the usual snow everywhere and obviously it was very cold outside, but it was lovely and warm inside Rushworth's, one of the biggest music stores in Liverpool at that time. I can't remember the make of the guitar (there's a picture of it in the book), or how much my father paid, but it was a 6-string. 12-string Rickenbackers were then a thing of the future.

I was so proud of that guitar, but I cannot remember what happened to it. I probably traded it in for the Hofner Club 60 a few years later when I could afford to buy it myself, as I was about to start my floor-laying job. Through that job I met another good friend Dougie Tartt – he also bought a Club 60, and, as mine was the blonde version, Dougie went for the sunburst finish.

The Club 60 was a brilliant guitar, but it didn't have the greatest of actions by today's standards. It had a great body, with lots of white piping and tortoiseshell inlay. This was the guitar that would take me through some of our early Searchers gigs when, as already mentioned, John McNally and I were the only two Liverpool group members using them.

Later, when we started playing instrumentals like '3.30 Blues', 'Walk Don't Run' and one or two Shadows hits, I realised I needed a guitar with a tremolo facility, as most instrumentals featured that method. Although I could achieve the same effect by bending the strings, I felt I needed the real thing, just like Hank Marvin. I dreamt of having a Fender Stratocaster, but that's all it was: a dream. The nearest thing to a Strat that you could find in Liverpool at that time – early 1960 – was a

Futurama. It was similar to a Strat, but only a poor imitation. Whatever my next guitar was going to be, it would have to be small-bodied, with a tremolo arm and three pickups, and most of all affordable. Enter the Burns Tri-Sonic cherry red with tremolo arm. My job at the time must have paid well, as I didn't need to trade in my Hofner Club 60 to buy the Burns. So now I had two guitars – wow!

The next twelve months saw the band play all the major venues in Liverpool and surrounding areas such as the Iron Door, the Cavern, the Odd Spot, the Civil Service Club, Lowlands, the Casbah, Wavertree Town Hall, Orrell Park Ballroom, Litherland Town Hall and St John's Hall, Bootle, among many others. It wasn't long before our reputation grew and we became one of the top five bands in Liverpool. The next big step was our trip to Hamburg for our performances at the Star-Club. The Burns Tri-Sonic was still with me and was the lead guitar sound on the Star-Club recordings, as well as on our first two big hits, 'Sweets For My Sweet' and 'Sugar And Spice'.

By the time we recorded the hit that made us a household name, 'Needles And Pins', I had changed to a top-of-the-range Gibson. That was a fabulous guitar, so I said goodbye to my faithful Burns Tri-Sonic. Why, you might ask. I often ask myself the same question. There was absolutely no reason to part-exchange it for the Gibson Stereo. I well remember our manager, Tito Burns, telephoning Ivor Mairants (a famous guitarist from the '50s) at his music shop in Piccadilly Circus, to ask Ivor to make sure he did me a good deal. Even so, I should have kept that guitar.

In his excellent book, *Rickenbacker Electric 12-String*, Tony Bacon quotes Tony Hatch as saying the Searchers' first hits in 1963 were recorded using a four-track Ampex tape recorder. 'Sweets For My Sweet' and 'Sugar And Spice' were recorded 'live' direct to the four-track machine and then mixed to a two-track. By late 1963, Pye had acquired a second four-track and the two machines were placed side-by-side in the control room of Studio 1. At that time, the two four-track machines couldn't be electronically synchronised, although Tony's engineer, Ray

Prickett, could often get them running in sync for up to a minute. Part of a vocal could be lifted from the second machine and put on the first one.

Tony adds that, from 'Needles And Pins' onwards, 'we had the flexibility of being able to record instrument tracks on the first four-track and then mix and copy them to the second machine, adding instrument overdubs (such as the second guitar) and/or vocals at the time or later. I'm not saying we did this all the time – it all depended on the song and how we wanted to handle it.'

I have read the story about our recording of 'Needles And Pins' and sound engineer Ray Prickett's request for myself and John to play octaves to create a chiming jangle. It's a nice idea, but like the Wreckers and the Confederates (two fictitious pre-Searchers groups I invented to spice up the sleeve notes for our first LP, *Meet The Searchers*), it's a myth. Listen to the record: there are no octaves, just my Gibson Stereo with John's Hofner Club 60 behind – both 6-string guitars. We doubled my Gibson, just to enhance the A-chord riff. Our first hearing of 'Needles' was not from the original Jackie DeShannon version, but from seeing Cliff Bennett & The Rebel Rousers (with Frank Allen on bass) perform it in Hamburg. They did it much slower than us, and my pronunciation of the words was totally different to Cliff Bennett's when we eventually recorded it. But you take a song and make it your own. It was our second UK No. 1 single.

When people ask me about 'pinza' or 'pinsa', I explain that it was just what happened on the session. I apologised to Tony Hatch, but he said it sounded OK, so it was left in. I always sang it onstage, when we all had our own songs. There was no issue then about who was the band's lead singer!

The Gibson ES-345 took me and the band through a couple more hit records, 'Don't Throw Your Love Away' and 'Some Day We're Gonna Love Again'. Chris by now was enjoying life so much that his talent for finding 'okay songs' and turning them into hit records was diminishing and he would soon burn himself out. But not before we would once again find ourselves near the top of the charts with our next offering: a song that would not only revive our career, but would also change our direction slightly.

A few weeks previously, while recording *Thank Your Lucky Stars* in Birmingham, I happened to be watching the TV in our dressing room when the Beatles came on to perform their latest single, 'A Hard Day's Night'. The guitar riff George Harrison played in that song, although nothing special, did have a unique sound a bit like the Greek bouzouki instrument.

Rickenbacker, the California-based company, had given one of its earliest 12-string guitars to George during the Beatles' first US tour in early 1964. They were the first guitar-maker to bring the electric 12-string successfully to market and, of course, went on to define the instrument. I had seen John Lennon's 6-string Rickenbacker before, but this Rickenbacker guitar was different. Straight away, I knew it was a 12-string electric Rick. Time for a new guitar.

'Some Day We're Gonna Love Again' was an okay song, but that's all it was. The next single needed to be a resounding success – and it was. 'When You Walk In The Room', written by Jackie DeShannon, was – and still is – one of the best songs we ever recorded. After hearing her version, we all felt, especially Chris and me, that we could do it better and make it our own.

A few months before we actually recorded the song, while we were rehearsing and finding the right keys for the vocals and instruments, I played the guitar riff on a 6-string and it sounded like something Duane Eddy would play. The riff for this song needed to be a different sound. It was, and would become one of the most instantly recognised guitar riffs from the '60s, even providing the inspiration for Tony Hatch's famous *Crossroads* theme.

Crane's music shop in Liverpool was pretty upmarket in those days, and I knew they had Rickenbacker 12s in stock. To my amazement, they did me a straight swap for my Gibson ES-345, which at the time I thought was a great deal. Crane's obviously knew their guitars and probably got the better of it, but I wanted that Rick!

I have to admit that, although I really wanted the 360/12 model I'd seen George Harrison play on television, when they showed me the Rose Morris 360/12, I changed my mind, as I much preferred the 'f' sound hole to the 'slash' type on George's guitar. Looking back, I know that I should have kept the Gibson. There was no need to part with such a lovely instrument. I often wonder where my ex guitars are now.

In *Rickenbacker Electric 12-String*, Tony Bacon claims that British beat group guitarists lined up during 1964 and 1965 to join the electric 12-string club, and some chose Rose Morris's newly available Model 1993. He goes on to say 'the Searchers stand out now as an important group in the unfolding story'.

I am just one of several '60s lead guitarists who fell in love with electric 12-string Rickenbackers and their jangling sound – George Harrison, Pete Townshend, Brian Jones and Roger McGuinn of the Byrds come to mind for a start. Notable later converts include Tom Petty, Peter Buck of REM, Bruce Springsteen and Paul Weller. The Rickenbacker Rose Morris 360/12 (Model 1993) was, without doubt, my second love. Hand-crafted in California, I was very lucky to get one, as demand exceeded supply at the time. Rickenbackers have been made at that factory for more than 70 years.

When my Rick was stolen in late 1969 from the Lafayette nightclub in Wolverhampton, it was, of course, a huge disappointment. But these things happen and would happen again in later years. That night in Wolverhampton, I vented my anger and frustration on our road manager, a young musician called Chris Cotterell, who came from Kingston upon Thames. Of course, I apologised to him later and we stayed good friends. To be honest, I could not really blame him 100%, because there was so much gear to look after – too much for one person.

After my Rick was stolen, I temporarily used a Danelectro Belzouki 12-string (memories of 'When You Walk In The Room'), the two-pickup model. I didn't really like it that much and it was never played on any recordings, but it saw me through at the time.

In 1969-70, things were not so good gig-wise and money was tight – so tight, in fact, that I was unable to buy another Rickenbacker. In any other band with our reputation, another Rick would have been provided instantly. But in the situation in which we found ourselves, there was little money in our capital account and we were just about earning enough to pay the wages. Things picked up for us a bit in the early '70s, and in 1974, while on a tour of the USA, I bought my next guitar. Yes, it was another Rick, which I bought from the world-famous Manny's Music shop in New York. This time I went for the smaller-bodied 456 6/12 converter in maple glow. That guitar took me and the band through the next ten years, from RCA Records to the Sire sessions and albums.

As a matter of interest, little has changed in the production of Rickenbacker guitars and basses. Using modern tools and equipment, Rickenbacker selectively captures technology to ensure improved quality is the only reason for not performing the operation in a traditional fashion. The most skilful and demanding work is still done today entirely by hand. The 'fireglo' finish was part of the popular attraction. The red sunburst from the native maple wood grain in the centre of the guitar body moved to a darker shade around the edges. Rickenbackers are not cheap – they are superb, very valuable instruments with a unique, clear sound. I have been known to travel on planes with my Rick on the seat next to me! I used my Rick 360/12 for all recording and performances from 'When You Walk In The Room' until it was stolen. The Model 1993 is a legend nowadays and not easy to find. Alas, many of the instruments did not make it past the '60s: necks were broken easily, due to the heavy loading of the twelve strings, compared to six.

After I bought my Rickenbacker 456 converter, I used it regularly onstage up until 1982-83. I was not the only member of the band to have a Rickenbacker. MPS guitarist Chris Black also owned a 1968 Rick. It was one of only two such models in the UK – the other one being mine! Much later, Frank Allen had a 4001 jetglo (black) bass. Anyone who would like to know more about those iconic guitars should read Tony Bacon's book, *Rickenbacker Electric 12-String: The Story of the Guitars, the Music and the Great Players.*

As mentioned earlier, the 12-string Rickenbacker kind of changed our direction slightly, when, after the success of 'When

You Walk In The Room', Chris's dominance in the band and especially in the recording studio showed through once again. He suggested that, for our next single, we should record a folk-type song we first started doing in the band's early years at the Star-Club. This in fact was a protest/anti-war song' associated mainly with Joan Baez, whose version we took it from. It was actually written by a Californian lady named Malvina Reynolds, who did record the song but never got the recognition for it! I've never heard her version.

'What Have They Done To The Rain' was a major departure for the band. The guitars are there: my Rick 12 and John's Club 60 (now sprayed black), but they are low in the mix – a Tony Hatch idea – which highlights the harmonies. It is, perhaps, one of the first British folk rock records, pre-dating artistes like Donovan, an electrified Bob Dylan and the Byrds in the US, who some say adopted our Rickenbacker-led sound and vocal harmony.

I used two guitars for our three live recordings in Sweden in February and December 1964 and May 1967, now available on CD as *The Swedish Radio Sessions*. My Gibson ES-345 was on all the songs except the last two on the second recording, 'When You Walk In The Room' and 'What'd I Say'. I played John's Burns greenburst Double-Six 12-string on those two songs.

We had recently been given a set of English-made Burns electric guitars. I used the Double-Six on some recordings, as well as for TV shows and concerts. On one TV appearance to perform our December 1964 single, 'What Have They Done To The Rain', John and I each played a Double-Six. My guitar was finished in white and John's in green.

In the late seventies, just before Seymour Stein signed us to Sire Records, we were all given new guitars by Aria, a relatively new company trying to get their instruments onto the UK market. They were Japanese, with a factory on the outskirts of London not far from where Frank Allen lived. Frankie had met Aria's chairman, who just happened to be a Searchers fan. We were all duly invited to visit the factory, where we were given new guitars. John and I chose a 12-string and a 6-string, and

Frankie obviously went for an Aria bass. I was a bit cheeky and also asked for a 12-string acoustic!

The 12-string electric Aria was quite impressive, with a great action – very important on a 12-string – and not too big a body. Its only failing, as I recall telling John, was that its neck width/fingerboard was too wide and not as comfortable to play as the Rickenbacker 12-string. But, because we were honourable people and Aria had been so kind, we decided to give our new instruments a go. I have to say they were excellent, and it also looked good for us to have nice, new, shiny guitars, all the same make.

I still have the Aria 6-string and the acoustic 12-string, but the electric 12-string was one of the ones that got stolen. They gave me a replacement, but not the same model. It was a brand new model, more stylish and much lighter than the stolen one. It was also easier and more comfortable to play, as the neck width was narrower. The main difference between the two guitars from the audience's point of view was the colour. Both guitars were Aria Pro-11s. The stolen one, the Aria Pro-11 Aquasound, was a very dark sunburst colour. The replacement, the Aria Pro-11 Revsound, was a stunning blue colour – only slightly different, but a much better guitar.

This guitar, which I still have today, was the subject of every guitarist's nightmare. On a five-week MPS tour to Australia in February-March 2006, the neck of the guitar fractured during the outward flight. This was at a time when airport security was still on red alert after the 9/11 Al Qaeda attacks. Qantas Airlines insisted, like other major airlines, that our guitars had to go in the hold with all the other baggage, as our instruments were in hard cases. We didn't give it much thought at the time, as that was normal practice.

On arrival in Perth, we were met by promoter Danny Ryan and a nice limo to take us to the hotel. Most times when I arrive after a long-haul flight, especially to the USA or Australia, I always check on the condition of my guitar. Yes, you've guessed it, I didn't do it this time and, as we had a day off before the tour started, I didn't check it until the following day. When I opened the guitar case, you can imagine the scene: the Aria 12-string was fractured at the neck end, just before the nut which clips the strings before they splay out to each separate tuning key.

I gave Qantas Airlines a new title that day. I can't repeat my exact words here, but they went along the lines of 'Go away, you fatherless Qantas'. I didn't have a spare guitar with me – there's nobody I know from the '60s who does take a spare guitar with them. So there I was, just about to start a major tour of Australia with Mike Pender's Searchers and no 12-string guitar!

As it was still early in the day and 24 hours before the first concert, there was some time to try to find a replacement if I could. We tried the two music shops in Perth. They could sell me a Rickenbacker for the equivalent of £2,500, but they wouldn't let me hire it. As I had two Rickenbackers at home, I didn't want another one. So I bought a 12-string Yamaha electric guitar, small-bodied and with a close action, for about the equivalent of £500. We got through the tour with flying colours, and I still have that little Yamaha guitar. (Incidentally, Frank and John were also in Australia at the same time with their Searchers. I was told later that some of their shows were cancelled. I hope it wasn't because I was there!)

On our return, May and I moved into the country house where we still live today and I had the blue Aria 12-string repaired. They did a great job on it, and, looking at the guitar today, you can't see where the neck was fractured. That was more or less the end of my guitar acquisitions – but not quite.

After my agent, Tony Sherwood, told me that Derek Franks was putting on a new show called *ReelinandaRockin* with lead vocalists from several major '60s groups, I decided it was time for a new Rickenbacker. So I went out and bought a 660 12-string in jetglo. I was going to get the Rick 660 12-string that Tom Petty plays, until I realised the guitar still retained the old-style trapeze tailpiece – not a good idea in my opinion, as the normal and octave string for each key are both in the one hole at the tailpiece end. I thought about the tuning, as both strings would be touching – I'd already experienced this unusual set-up with my Rose Morris Rick. So I went for the 660, which has the separate tailpiece and a separate 'bed' for each string. It is the same model used by REM guitarist Peter Buck. I use this Rick for all the major gigs and tours like the *Solid Silver '60s Show*. It plays very well, and, I'm told, sounds great too.

Since buying my first Rick 360/12 in 1964, I have experimented a little and now play 12-string guitars – including Arias and others – with the octave string 'in front of' the normal 3rd, 4th, 5th and 6th string. As all guitarists know, the first two strings on any guitar are the E and the B respectively. The two E and two B strings on all 12-string guitars are always in unison with each other, the reason being that, if you tried to octivate them, as with the 3rd, 4th, 5th and 6th string, the tension would twist the guitar neck and would break the string. So, as we all know, you can only have octave tuning on the G, D, A and E strings and if you (as I do) have the octave string before the normal! In my opinion this produces a more jangly sound, but you may have to change the nut to do it.

There is one other guitar I haven't mentioned: the Fender Stratocaster. I bought it in Kansas City on an American tour with John and Frank in the early '70s. It's a 1963 model, and, from what I've been told, quite rare and collectable. It even has the original bridge cover, which, apparently, is usually missing.

So there we have it: my guitars and the life they have given me.

CHAPTER 12

Recording for Radio

Our continuing frustration with the Beeb's recording restrictions led to a big bust-up in the studio and we were never invited to do another session again.

We recorded a lot of sessions in London for various BBC radio programmes between April 1963 and May 1967. We also did a series for Radio Luxembourg sponsored by Pye which went out live. And we had many loyal fans in Scandinavia, so we also recorded several sessions for Swedish Radio.

Our sessions for the BBC's Light Programme started soon after our first single, 'Sweets For My Sweet', came out. Sessions we recorded for the BBC's top radio programme for pop music, *Saturday Club*, were also used for other programmes such as *Top of the Pops* (not to be confused with the TV show), *Top Gear* and *Saturday Swings*. Radio 1 and Radio 2 were to start in 1967. Brian Matthew presented *Saturday Club* and the late-night weekday show, *Top Gear*.

The sessions were recorded at the BBC studios in Maida Vale, the Playhouse Theatre, or the Paris Theatre. It was a lot of pressure for us, as it was for several other leading bands including the Beatles, the Kinks and the Hollies, as the BBC sessions were squeezed in between very busy tour schedules. We would have done a gig the previous night and then would have to be at the BBC studios early the following morning. We were always under pressure in the studios too. There was no time for warming up or sound checks, and no chance of any overdubs. We were always pushed for time. Some of our performances were not as good as we would have liked, given more time and more technical support. There is just one example on the CD released in 2004 – a slightly dodgy vocal opening to 'Magic Potion' recorded in April 1965.

The sessions often included short interviews with all members of the band, although Chris handled most of them until he left in 1966. He also introduced many of our songs. Brian Matthew always tried to make us feel at home and at ease, as did his producer, Bernie Andrews. On the Searchers' *BBC Sessions* CD, you can hear my rather stumbling attempt to explain why Chris had left the band. It was a very difficult question to answer. The first track on the CD is 'When You Walk In The Room' from 1964, because no tapes exist of our earlier sessions for the BBC. The tapes of our sessions for Radio Luxembourg have also never been traced.

In Britain, as in Sweden, what we performed at these sessions was usually decided by our latest release, whether it was a single, an EP or an LP. Our new singles were plugged as often as possible on the Light Programme, as were key tracks from our EPs and LPs. B-sides were also performed, such as 'This Feeling Inside' (the flip side of 'What Have They Done To The Rain'), 'I'm Never Coming Back' (from 'When I Get Home') and 'Too Many Miles' (from 'Take Me For What I'm Worth'). We recorded no fewer than six tracks from our 1965 LP, *Sounds Like Searchers*, for the Beeb, plus four off our next album, *Take Me For What I'm Worth*.

We also cut several songs for the BBC that we did not record for Pye: Chuck Berry's 'Sweet Little Sixteen', a favourite from our early days (and nights) at the Iron Door/Cavern/Star-Club. Bob Dylan's 'Blowin' In The Wind' was recorded during a radio date in May 1966. Cover versions of big hits by other groups included Carl Perkins' 'Glad All Over' and the Ronettes' 'Be My Baby'. Our medley of 'See See Rider' and 'Jenny Takes A Ride' was borrowed from the popular versions by Mitch Ryder & The Detroit Wheels.

In February 1967, we recorded our next Pye single,

'Popcorn, Double Feature' and a cover of Ike & Tina Turner's 'Goodbye, So Long'. The following month, we taped 'I'll Be Loving You', a poor song written by Chris, which is something of a rarity, according to the sleeve notes of the BBC CD.

The last surviving set of our BBC sessions, recorded in May 1967, includes the obscure 'I Don't Believe', originally released in the UK in late 1965 by a US band called the Guilloteens. We liked the song, but weren't convinced enough to record it, so it was a bit of a filler for the BBC. Regrettably, our continuing frustration with the Beeb's recording restrictions led to a big bust-up in the studio and we were never invited to do another session again.

British pop music had been very popular in Sweden since the beginning of the '60s, with the Beatles touring there in the autumn of 1963. Many British groups were to follow them over the next few years. We were also very popular there and we made many visits to that country for tours, recordings and live performances for Swedish Radio.

The Swedish Broadcasting Corporation, or Swedish Radio for short, recorded three of our live sets in Stockholm between February 1964 and May 1967. The three separate sessions are featured on a Sanctuary/Castle CD released in 2001.

Tony's great vocals stand out on the first session, recorded in the Karlaplan studio in Stockholm on 18 February 1964, as we rock our way through songs from our early days in those sweaty cellars: 'Money', 'Some Other Guy', 'What'd I Say' and 'Ain't That Just Me', as well as 'Sweets For My Sweet' and 'Needles And Pins'. John took the lead vocal on Fats Domino's 'Let The Four Winds Blow'. We all enjoyed playing those old songs again, – especially me playing all the old guitar riffs for those songs from our early days, which also featured on our first two LPs. Chris talked to the audience and joked with them, giving the recording a feel of what it was like to be at one of our concerts in the '60s. He even thanked them in Swedish for their applause!

Ten songs were broadcast on 2 March on Swedish Radio Channel 2 in a 30-minute show called *Pop Guests in Stockholm – The Searchers, a Group from Liverpool*. Back home, 'Needles

And Pins' was about to hit the top spot in the charts.

On the second session, recorded on 4 December 1964, Chris introduces new boy Frankie before launching into a thunderous performance of his party piece, 'What'd I Say'. Our session was broadcast on two channels on 4 and 29 January 1965. Two recent hit singles, 'When You Walk In The Room' and 'What Have They Done To The Rain', are also included, as well as some classics often also played by the Beatles in their Cavern days: 'Red Sails In The Sunset', 'Memphis, Tennessee' and 'Hi-Heel Sneakers'. I again used my Gibson ES-345 for most of the songs, switching to John's Burns greenburst Double-Six 12-string for the last two, 'When You Walk In The Room' and 'What'd I Say'. Frankie played a Gibson EBO bass, which had a more mellow sound to the Hofner violin bass that Tony used. John played his sunburst Fender Telecaster.

Frankie did frontman duties for our third and final session on 31 May 1967, which featured two of our latest singles, 'Have You Ever Loved Somebody' and 'Western Union'. I played my Rickenbacker 12-string for the whole session. Reviewers in Sweden commented on the change to our sound brought about by our new drummer, John Blunt, whose heavier, all-action style was very different to Chris's. As with our two previous Swedish Radio shows, we closed our set with a rocking finale: a version of Mitch Ryder's 'See See Rider–Jenny Takes A Ride' medley.

Three months before our last session, the Byrds had recorded a session for Swedish Radio on 28 February, complete with Roger McGuinn and his Rickenbacker 12-string. Like us, they were very picky about their harmonies.

We enjoyed a great deal of chart success in Sweden between 1963 and 1966. 'Sweets For My Sweet' reached No. 2 on 17 September 1963. 'Needles And Pins' remained in the charts for 32 weeks, getting to No. 5 on 22 February 1964. Top honours went to 'Don't Throw Your Love Away', which quickly reached No. 1 on 9 May 1964 and remained in the charts for nine weeks. 'What Have They Done To The Rain' reached No. 7 in January 1965, and 'Bumble Bee' got to No. 6 in June of that year. Three hits reached their Top 10 in 1966: 'Take Me For What I'm

Worth', 'Everybody Come Clap Your Hands' (a track from the *Sounds Like Searchers* LP not released in the UK as a single) and 'Take It Or Leave It'.

Our Swedish Radio recordings and our other performances in Sweden between 1964 and 1967 have been meticulously researched and chronicled by great Searchers fans Björn Eriksson and Peter McCormack. This research includes copies of original documents from the Swedish Radio archives in Stockholm, such as the set lists and the 'band protocol sheets' for each of the three recording sessions. Accounts of our open-air concerts at the Folkets Parks in the summer of 1964 and in 1967 are included in their research. I remember it often being very cold at those shows.

They have also documented the history of Rickenbacker 12-string guitars and my use of those lovely instruments. When I visited Stockholm some years ago, I autographed a Rickenbacker Model 1993, which is now exhibited in the Rickbeats Models Library in that city.

For our many fans in Europe, we also recorded several of our early hits in French and German. These recordings were for record releases, not for radio broadcast.

CHAPTER 13

Losing Our Golden Touch

John was not happy. By this time, his close relationship with Chris had ended, and 'hell hath no fury', as they say.

Our last two EPs, *Four By Four* and *Take Me For What I'm Worth*, both failed to trouble the charts in 1966. In his book, *Liverpool: Wondrous Place*, Liverpool author and rock music writer Paul Du Noyer summed up – in rather harsh terms – what happened to us, and to other Merseyside bands, in and around 1966: 'The Mersey beat acts were mostly working-class lads, whose values were those of traditional entertainers. They never had the scholarly obsession with obscure blues that Jagger, Richards and the others had. They liked the bright, accessible pop of Tamla-Motown and the Brill Building. They had no interest in the emerging counter-culture; their roots were in semi-pro show business. When pop became rock, and rock went weird around 1966, the Liverpool groups were left behind; and with the rise of deejay-dominated discos, the beat groups weren't even needed for dancing to. They faced oblivion or exile on the chicken-in-a-basket circuit. Cream and the rest became rock gods. The Swinging Blue Jeans became a good night out in Widnes. Liverpool lost its supremacy in pop music, but suddenly became famous for pop art.'

For us, 1965 was a bumper year, not helped by several newspapers referring to a reported management takeover bid for the band, and Dusty Springfield, by Brian Epstein. I was quoted as saying, 'We don't know what's happening', which was the truth. Chris said he didn't think it would be a good idea to have Dusty and Cilla under the same management.

When You Walk In The Room, was the title of our fifth EP, which entered the EP chart on 27 March 1965 and rose to No. 12. Our fourth album, *Sounds Like Searchers*, included some lead vocals by Frank Allen, such as on 'Everybody Come Clap Your Hands'. It got to No. 8 in the charts in the spring of 1965. Building on our transatlantic success with the singles 'Love Potion No. 9' and 'Bumble Bee', an EP with the latter title entered the chart on 8 May 1965 and buzzed straight to No. 1. And the hits kept coming, with 'Goodbye My Love' (UK No. 4, US No. 52), followed by our one and only self-penned A-side, 'He's Got No Love' (UK No. 12), released in July 1965. The last of our EPs to make the chart, *Searchers '65*, on 25 September, achieved two re-entries and peaked at No. 15.

In his second book, Frankie claims that 'He's Got No Love' was the start of our downward spiral record-wise. But I suspect that, like John McNally, he resented the fact that Chris and I had written and produced the song with Tony Hatch's blessing. This was made more apparent when we later performed it on TV. The scowls on one or two faces said everything!

'When I Get Home' is a song we had found in America. Again, I have to disagree with Frankie and say that it was a good pop song. Had it been recorded in our early career, it would have been a certain hit. It was only our dwindling popularity among fans that kept it from chart success. Our next single, P.F. Sloan's 'Take Me For What I'm Worth', was much stronger and made the Top 20. Before our Australian tour with the Rolling Stones in early 1966, Messrs Jagger and Richards had given us 'Take It Or Leave It' for our next single, which gave off warning signs by only reaching No. 31.

On this tour with the Rolling Stones, I also came up with the idea of 'He's Got No Love', but I didn't have a clue about the title or the storyline. I played the slide guitar figure and the chord sequence to Chris. He put down the lyrics and we both came up with the group's first self-penned Top 20 hit. John was not happy, and when Tony Hatch gave his approval to release the song as our next single, Frank did not have a say in it either. By this time, his close relationship with Chris had ended and 'hell hath no fury', as they say.

John, and to a certain extent Frankie, were not in favour of this song being our next single. There are many reasons for this, not only writing royalties, but also because Chris and I would take the plaudits for an original, almost-Top 10 record. It reached No. 12 and spent ten weeks in the UK charts. As it turned out, 'He's Got No Love' was to be the last big recording by the group. Those that followed were of little or no consequence. I've been asked many times why Chris and I didn't follow on from the success with that song and keep writing more hits. Part of the answer lies in my inability to write lyrics.

Our fifth album, *Take Me For What I'm Worth*, released in December 1965, was a strong mix of pop, folk and rock. Tracks included Jackie DeShannon's 'Each Time' and 'Four Strong Winds', later recorded by Neil Young. The Hollies generously gave us what proved to be our last UK Top 50 single, 'Have You Ever Loved Somebody'. Featuring our new drummer, John Blunt, it was released in September 1966, and reached the dizzy heights of No. 48 in the UK and No. 94 in the US.

Incredibly, our former drummer, Chris, produced a rival version of the same song with Paul & Barry Ryan which also scraped into the Top 50. Chris Curtis was certainly aware of the rise of the new 'heavy' rock music, and after leaving us in 1966 he helped to establish Roundabout, the band that was to become Deep Purple.

In 1967, we released our three final singles for Pye: the almost-psychedelic 'Popcorn, Double Feature', a cover of the Five Americans' 'Western Union', and lastly 'Secondhand Dealer', written by Frankie and myself.

When Pye did not renew our contract at the end of 1967, we moved on to Liberty. That label showed little interest in us and four singles came and went without attracting much attention: 'Umbrella Man', 'Kinky Kathy Abernathy', 'Somebody Shot The Lollypop Man' (released under the pseudonym 'Pasha') and 'Shoot 'Em Up Babe', which was only released in Germany. A cover of Stephen Stills' great protest song for Buffalo Springfield, 'For What It's Worth', remained unreleased until it appeared in 2003 on the *40th Anniversary Collection* CD.

When the *Anniversary* CD was in the making, I was not consulted at all – probably because I was on the other side of the world touring with *ReelinandaRockin*, and it wasn't until I arrived home and found a copy of the CD in my mailbox that I knew it had been released. I was happy enough with the cover, but, sad to say, whoever designed it got it wrong with the Rickenbacker guitar. Although similar in looks and design, it is the 'George Harrison' 360 12-string model that is pictured on the sleeve, and not my 360/12 Rose Morris, as used on the 'When You Walk In The Room' recording session. For guitar freaks and purists, the defining feature is the hideous slash on the 'Harrison 360' compared to the sexy f-hole on the Rose Morris, which, as mentioned in a previous chapter, was the reason I preferred it.

CHAPTER 14

Chris Rolled Over by Stones

Chris showed great self-confidence and he could handle a crowd better than any of us.

So, what happened to Chris? We were on a world tour in early 1966 and, in Australia with the Rolling Stones, we as a band were rushing towards our 'sell by' date. We would soon be past it as far as hit records went, mainly because we did not write our own material. We suffered through lack of original ideas and original songs. I thought about this long and hard, and realised we couldn't go on depending on Chris to find another big song. He had come up with the goods so many times, and we took for granted his knack of finding hit songs that had fallen by the wayside that needed just a few changes to make them smash hits.

Chris knew this, of course, but was now becoming frustrated, not only with our recording strength, but also with our performances onstage and our popularity with audiences. The Aussie audiences loved the Stones on that tour and they got all the headlines in the newspapers. In this business, you have to realise that when you've been the group or artiste that makes the No. 1 slot overnight – you can't always be No. 1. With Mick Jagger making the front pages and getting most of the television coverage, Chris could not handle it. It began to show, as he started taking antidepressants. On another tour, again in Australia, with Del Shannon and I think Roy Orbison, as I recall it was getting near showtime and Chris could not be found anywhere. When he eventually turned up, I was angry and lost my cool. We ended up throwing all his pills down the toilet.

Chris was the only member of the original band not to be born in Liverpool, but on the other side of Lancashire (a 'Blitz baby', like myself) in Oldham. He moved to Liverpool at the age of four, and I first met him when we were both pupils at St Winefride's Primary School in Bootle, but then we went our separate ways. Chris passed the 11-plus exam and went on to St Mary's College – definitely the brainy one in the band and the self-appointed leader. He left school at sixteen and went to work as a clerk at Swift's furniture shop in Stanley Road, where he stayed until joining us. Although he claimed in the sleeve notes on the band's first LP that he had been in a rhythm & blues group before joining the Searchers, I suspect it was another Confederates/Wreckers spice-up.

As already mentioned, I bumped into him by accident one Saturday morning. He was on his way back from Frank Hessy's music shop, having made a payment for his drum kit. He told me he'd had it for a few weeks and was teaching himself to play. Before long, we'd all got ourselves down to Chris's house and started rehearsing like mad. He turned out to be a pretty good singer and his record collection was fantastic. He'd be playing us records we didn't know by artistes we'd never heard of.

In his 1998 interview with Spencer Leigh, he said I asked him to join the band for a gig that night at the Wilson Hall in Garston. It was actually several days later, after our first rehearsal sessions. Chris said that first gig was 'a bit like busking for me – they were doing songs like "Oh Lonesome Me",' but at the time he showed great self-confidence and could handle a crowd better than any of us. This was true from the very early days at infamous venues like the Wilson Hall and Hambleton Hall in Huyton, which were notorious for fights. Chris was the one who did most of the chat between numbers – something that seemed to come very naturally to him.

He was self-taught and not the greatest of drummers, but he had a great voice and provided the soft, high harmonies that became essential to our sound. You could say he was a natural-born leader. I have a good early example of that leadership quality: a couple of letters that he wrote to the Star-Club management on behalf of the band in 1962, to try to renegotiate our contract (see pages 54 and 55).

He had a very distinctive look, with long hair, black leather trousers and jacket. He stood out in a crowd. He changed his surname to 'Curtis' one day in the Cavern, when Tony Jackson left out his unusual surname when introducing the band to some journalists. Chris looked round and saw the name 'Lee Curtis' on a poster on the wall and adopted his new surname on the spot.

He would always wear his leathers for our early sessions at the Cavern or the Iron Door. His style of drumming, often standing up, was also unique. There was an almost manic quality about some of his performances – look at YouTube to see him repeat his show-stopping party piece from our early days, Ray Charles's 'What'd I Say', at the *New Musical Express* Poll Winners concert in 1964 at the Wembley Empire Pool.

As I said before, he had a very large collection of records, including rock'n'roll, folk, and a lot of US soul by artistes like Etta James, Dionne Warwick, Kitty Lester and Nina Simone. Bill Harry, founder and editor of the *Mersey Beat* newspaper, interviewed Chris in 1964 for an article called 'Chris – And His Mammoth Record Collection'. Chris said he had 'boxes and boxes of records in the house, and I've lost count of the number. There must be hundreds and hundreds. I'm particularly interested in collecting records that haven't made it in the States – and soul records are my favourite.'

Chris carried lots of records around with him in a large case which also held a portable record player, and he was constantly listening to them. He explained that the Searchers chose most of their own records from lesser-known American recordings. 'In fact, every one of our A-sides, with the exception of "Sugar And Spice", was chosen in this way. We also use a lot of these numbers on our LPs,' he said. He also told Bill Harry that his favourite artistes were Bessie Banks, Dee Dee Warwick, Lou Johnson, Jackie DeShannon and Aretha Franklin.

In his book, *Bigger Than the Beatles*, published in 2009, Bill Harry discounts the theory that Liverpool groups were different from groups in other parts of the country because 'Cunard Yanks' brought them records that couldn't be obtained elsewhere in Britain. ('Cunard Yanks' were Liverpudlians who worked on ocean liners and brought presents back for their families, including American records.) Bill describes it as a nice theory, but 'something of an exaggeration'. He is right about that, although it is true that we all, in one way or another, got American records from relatives and friends. However, most of the American songs played by Mersey beat groups in their early days were available in Britain through the normal channels.

Chris was a talented writer and was interested in record production right from the start of our contract with Pye. He chose the American songs for the band for our Iron Door demo tapes and the live session at the Star-Club recorded by Philips.

He had taught himself to play the piano as a child. He wrote the B-side of our first single, 'It's All Been A Dream', using that piano. He was also a perfectionist in many ways. He was furious when he found out, for example, that Tony Hatch had kept from us the fact that he'd written 'Sugar And Spice' under the pseudonym of 'Fred Nightingale'. Chris had disliked the song intensely and did not want us to record it. He explained in an interview that it had the same or similar chords to 'Sweets For My Sweet'.

In his April 2003 interview with Spencer Leigh, Chris claimed Tony Hatch had 'tricked me into recording that rubbish'. As I recall it, nobody was 'tricked' into anything. At the time, the four of us didn't have a clue how the recording industry worked – especially the writing/publishing side. Looking back, we did not have a great deal to offer in the way of songs, and after the success of 'Sweets' any good song, even if similar in style, would probably have been a success. None of us really liked 'Sugar And Spice' on first hearing. It was a tape recording played on piano (which should have given us a clue as to who wrote it – but what did it matter anyway?). It may as well be Tony Hatch as anyone else, as he was now our mentor. Chris said Tony Hatch told him he had heard 'Fred Nightingale' singing the song in a pub. Nevertheless, 'Sugar And Spice' still made it to No. 2 in the charts.

Chris was a very strong character who did not like to be crossed. His working relationship with Tony Jackson was rocky from the start. Tony was to say, many years later, that Chris's addition to the band was 'a gimmick – a drummer who had long hair and leather pants'. A lot of nasty tricks were played on Tony after Chris had met Frank Allen at the Star-Club, and had decided to get his close friend into the band at Tony's expense. That was not Chris's finest hour by any means, but in some ways Tony had pressed the self-destruct button. Tony was never going to be a team player.

Chris had the ability to write good songs, such as 'I Pretend I'm With You' and 'No One Else Could Love Me', which were relegated to B-sides but were good enough to have been A-sides, but lost his golden touch temporarily with our version of Bobby Darin's 'When I Get Home'. In an interview with Brian Matthew in October 1965 during our BBC sessions, Chris was confident about its success and talked about how he had found the song. I actually liked the song – we had found it on a jukebox while touring the US. Chris had also spoken at an earlier BBC session about 'Goodbye My Love'. Both brief but intriguing interviews are on the *BBC Sessions* CD and on the new *Hearts In Their Eyes* box set.

'When I Get Home', released in October 1965, only reached No. 35 – our worst chart position to date. We hit back at the end of the year with 'Take Me For What I'm Worth', described later by Chris as 'a profound statement, it could have been a gay anthem'. Our accompanying LP was the first of our five with Pye not to make the charts, although it had strong tracks like 'Each Time'.

By this time, Chris was living in London in his own apartment. He preferred to be on his own, away from the Pont Street apartment that Tito Burns had rented for us the previous year. As Tony Jackson was no longer with us, Tito decided we now didn't need our Pont Street abode. So, with Chris now part of the London social scene, John and I would commute between London and our homes in Liverpool.

Chris became an important part of the social scene among music artistes in London, and his circle of friends included Dusty Springfield and her manager, Vicki Wickham (who had also produced the television show *Ready Steady Go!*), Brian Epstein, Lionel Bart, Alma Cogan and Madeleine Bell.

One of Chris's last decisions with us before going his own way was to choose 'Take It Or Leave It' as our next single. Both Chris and I were in Tito Burns' office when Mick Jagger and Keith Richards arrived with the acetate of the song as a demo. We thought it would be good for us to record, and there were no objections from Mick or Keith. The song would later also appear on the Stones' *Aftermath* LP.

We made great efforts to try to dissuade Chris from leaving the band after we returned from our traumatic tour of Australia in March 1966. I tried, but by then his ego was in control. When we returned from Australia, Tito told us that Chris wanted to get into recording and production. We had a chat and Chris told me he thought he had done it all with the band. He hated touring and now wanted to do something else. A lot of people in the music business in London had made various business proposals to him. Losing Chris was a major blow from which we never properly recovered.

Chris recorded just one solo single, the Joe South song, 'Aggravation', which failed in the UK but made the Top 10 in Sweden. He really gave it the hard rock treatment, with both Jimmy Page and John Paul Jones playing on the session. The B-side was 'Have I Done Something Wrong'. Both tracks are included in the *Hearts In Their Eyes* box set.

However, he got into big trouble with Tito Burns and us when he produced 'Have You Ever Loved Somebody' (written by the Hollies) for Paul & Barry Ryan, in direct competition with our recording of the song. Chris claimed Graham Nash had given him the song. Our single just crept into the Top 50.

He produced a single for Alma Cogan, 'Snakes And Snails', which also featured a star-studded line-up of backing singers including Dusty Springfield, Doris Troy and himself. Jimmy Page and John Paul Jones played on this session too.

In 1967, Chris formed a group called Roundabout with Jon Lord and Ritchie Blackmore, later transformed into Deep Purple. 'Deep Purple' by Nino Tempo & April Stevens was one of Chris's favourite records.

After quitting the project with Roundabout, he gradually disappeared from the music business in London as his financial resources ran out. He returned to his family in Merseyside in 1969 and went to work for the Inland Revenue at their offices in Bootle. He retired after 19 years due to ill-health reportedly caused by sick building syndrome.

In the mid-1970s, Chris was invited to join a Merseyside group called Western Union, but his style did not go well with the synthesised instruments. He was still writing and producing demos of his songs but became almost a recluse, refusing to give interviews until he gave two to Mersey beat author and BBC Radio Merseyside presenter Spencer Leigh in 1998 and 2003.

The 1998 interview – his first for 30 years – was broadcast on BBC Radio Merseyside and also published in *Record Collector* magazine. Chris described how he took over some of the vocals when Johnny Sandon left the band, and got inspiration from listening to records by the Clovers and the Coasters: 'White boys singing black man's soul – and it worked.' He also told a story about nearly being banned from the Cavern by owner Ray McFall for criticising the state of the toilets.

His liking for wearing leather jackets and leather trousers for gigs at the Iron Door or the Cavern made him even sweatier than the rest of us, which didn't go down well with his mother. She also, apparently, was not happy about him being in a beat group. Even when we were famous, she still would have preferred Chris to work in a bank

He admitted to his interviewer that he had wanted to control the band's musical direction and would often throw a tantrum if any of us crossed him, although he would apologise the next day and give us each a present. He said that, in effect, he was the leader of the band: 'The moment I had them thinking on my wavelength, I knew we couldn't go wrong.' He took most of the credit for choosing our singles and claimed he was right 'ten times out of ten'.

Chris told the story about how pleased P.J. Proby was that we had recorded his song, 'Ain't Gonna Kiss Ya'. We were probably the first UK act to record one of his compositions. Chris also admitted that 'He's Got No Love' was based on guitar licks similar to the Rolling Stones' 'The Last Time'. It was wrong of Chris not to mention me, as it was I who had the idea for the song. But, by the time he did that interview, he would have been sick that I had formed Mike Pender's Searchers.

The interview did not go down well with John McNally, who described it as 'so distorted'. 'Anything good that the Searchers ever did is down to him and he washes his hands of everything else,' he added. Frank Allen thought it was very funny – and typically Chris.

Chris's second interview went out on BBC Radio Merseyside on 13 April 2003. Three 'new' Searchers albums had just been released: *The Iron Door Sessions*, *The Searchers At The Star-Club* and *The Swedish Radio Sessions*.

Chris described the recording of 'No One Else Could Love Me' with a basic drum track, to which he had added castanets and Spanish bells, with Tony Hatch playing the piano. After his tirade about 'Sugar And Spice' and what he saw as Tony Hatch's deception, he talked about the importance of the Iron Door club to the band: 'We used to do doubles at the Iron Door and the Orrell Park Ballroom. It was difficult to get down the stairs with my drums at the OPB, and then down another flight to the Iron Door. The stage was only a foot high and it was a strange place. The room had a divider in it and Roger McGough used to stand between the doors.'

He said the Star-Club management had realised the band could play for long sets: 'I would sing "What'd I Say" and the audience would go absolutely nuts.'

He recalled how he had his long hair cut when we had our first hits: 'I thought, *If you want to be as successful as Cliff, it will have to go*.'

He talked about finding old records in Liverpool shops like NEMS and the Rotunda: 'I loved obscure B-sides and loved finding really wonky songs.' He had found 'Love Potion No. 9' in a backstreet second-hand record shop in Hamburg. 'For some unknown reason, I reckoned it would be a good single for the States, as they like dopey stuff like that.'

Spencer Leigh asked him if he any problems in persuading the band to do the songs he chose. 'No, they knew I had picked the hits, so I must know something. They went along with it.'

He described his close working friendship with Dusty Springfield, who had lived in Liverpool for a time, including some work on production for *Ready Steady Go!* for herself and Otis Redding.

Talking about our Swedish Radio sessions, he praised my performance on the 'See See Rider' track. Chris said he had preferred performing live and had hated miming: 'I always lost track. I could do it, but it was only all right.'

He concluded the interview by describing George Harrison as 'one of the nicest, quietest people I have ever known'.

CHAPTER 15

Clocking On with the Family

By then, I had developed a keen interest in antiques, especially old clocks and duelling pistols.

Music and popularity always goes in cycles – every pop star or group have their time at the top. I was fortunate to have been able to be a family man and develop other interests, some with financial prospects. But there were troubles ahead and not much harmony in the Searchers as a group.

As early as 1968, the Searchers had run their course as a hit recording group. By the end of the 1960s, gigs were becoming thin on the ground and, of course, our popularity had dwindled as the hit records dried up. We had had four very good years from 1963 to 1966, but from then on we were just thankful to be earning a living. My old mate Tony Jackson had gone, to be followed by Chris Curtis. Frank Allen had replaced Tony on bass, and John Blunt had replaced Chris on drums, only to be himself later replaced by Billy Adamson.

Neither Tony nor Chris achieved much success in their solo careers. Over the following twelve years, several record companies tried the 'Lazarus effect' on us, but failed to resurrect the group into recording stars once more. Up until 1980, we struggled as a group and had to take a lot of work in countries such as Germany, Sweden and Denmark, which meant I was away from May and the children for long periods. It was always a month for Germany and five weeks for places like Australia. The work was just not there in the UK.

Although there were many disappointments musically and professionally, May and I had many happy times with our young family. For me, music has not always been the most important thing in life – I am a very strong family man. May chose the name Michael (no surprises there) for our first child, born in September 1965. I remember we were so proud of him, as all parents are of their first-born. May bought the most expensive pram she could find and took Michael everywhere to show him off.

1966 was a very happy year, with Everton winning the FA Cup and we were all at Wembley (except little Michael) to see the match. I remember Everton did not get the headlines they deserved, coming back from two goals down at half-time to win 3-2. Perhaps the reason was that England won the World Cup later that year.

Two years later, our second bundle of joy arrived. May had decided well in advance to call the baby Stephanie. I remember saying before the birth, 'He's not going to like that name when he grows up!' But it turned out to be a Stephanie.

We were by this time living at Five Gables, a huge Victorian mansion just outside Liverpool, at Aughton Green. We spent many happy years there and, as my interest in antiques grew, we furnished the place with many wonderful things. Stephanie and Michael would play with the suit of armour in the large hallway. Michael would hide his Corgi toys under one of the moving parts of the 'tin man', as the children called him.

There was a full-sized snooker room in the house, which was one of the features that attracted me on first viewing the property. We had lots of parties and family gatherings, with visits from footballers from both Everton FC and Liverpool FC. When we weren't playing snooker, I would run my Hornby Dublo train layout on the snooker table. Life was still very enjoyable, although the gigs continued to take me away from May and the children whenever the USA, Australia or Europe called. I realised that everything in life comes with a price.

Then came the 1970s, which were really hard years for the group. When rock bands like Deep Purple and Led Zeppelin came along we, as a pop outfit, were left behind and gigs in the UK dried up. This meant long months away on the German circuit, doing two shows a night – echoes of Hamburg's Star-Club. But, as they say, that is the nature of the business. It is ironic when I remember it was Chris Curtis who helped to form the band that later became Deep Purple.

By then, I had developed a keen interest in antiques, especially old clocks and duelling pistols. I would take large reference books about antiques on the road with me. It was a good way of killing time, or rather passing time.

A clock is a fascinating piece of machinery, but it's also a nice item of furniture. I invested much of my earnings from the '60s in cased duelling pistols, buying quality rather than quantity. This also applied to clocks. Some of the sets of duellers in their original cases which I bought in the late '60s and early '70s are today worth many thousands of pounds. Any flintlock set in mint condition (as mine were), and in their original case with all the accessories, will today fetch upwards of £20,000. I had many of those sets and would buy them for between £600 and £2,000. Many had never been used, or even fired.

My habit of taking those books on the road with me paid off one day in 1972, when May and I were driving in Lancashire with Michael, Stephanie and baby Nathan. We used to take them out a lot, especially if I had been away for several weeks. We'd decided we would drive across on the A59 towards Harrogate and stop on the way for lunch, but we didn't get anywhere near Harrogate that day! On a whim, I decided to call at a transport café I knew of called the Five Barred Gate, where I had previously bought some antiques from the guy who ran the place. The children would have preferred to go to a Little Chef, but stopping that day for bacon sandwiches changed our lives a little, especially mine.

The café owner, who shall remain nameless, took me upstairs to his antiques 'den' to look at a pair of duelling pistols. They were in excellent condition and in their original case, but something else caught my eye. Under an old table, covered in clutter and dust, was a large ebony table clock. To the untrained eye, there seemed nothing special about it, but my reading of 'boring' reference books, as the guys in the group called them, would now come to fruition.

I lifted the large clock onto a table. As there was no maker's name on the dial, I turned it round to find on the back plate, the magical words – *Eduardus East, Londini*. To most people this would appear to be a foreign name, but my researches into English horology told me that this was how English clockmakers in the seventeenth century signed their clocks. Of course, it could have been a fake, but my gut feeling was that it was genuine. It was not a pretty clock and May was not impressed by it. The rather eccentric guy knew that the clock had some value and asked £425 for it – he wouldn't take a cheque. This was not a great deal of money for what I considered to be a rare and very collectible item. Not wanting to take any chance on losing what I new to be a bargain, I took May and the children home and went straight back with the cash.

My research over the next few weeks showed that Edward East had been clockmaker to Charles I and Charles II, and that he signed his name in Latin! I called Richard Swainson who was producing a new album with us, as the band were still with RCA at the time, and asked if May and I could stay at his London apartment for the night, before going to Sotheby's the next day to have the clock valued.

Their expert, a Mr Vaughan, was very impressed with the clock and could not believe the circumstances in which I had found it. It was put up for auction at Sotheby's with a reserve price of £10,000, which I thought was a bit steep. Although it didn't sell at the auction, a private collector very soon afterwards offered £12,000 for it! I agreed to sell it as a private sale, which meant I had no commission to pay. That was a lot of money back in 1972 – more than a year's wages working with the band.

It was after that stroke of fortune that we decided to open an antiques shop in nearby Southport, next door to our good friend David Glover, who was an experienced antique dealer. This was a great adventure for May and myself, and we had some fun over the next couple of years. I would find many antiques while on the road, gigging. These were mainly longcased clocks and the

Americans loved them. We met many interesting people in the antiques business. I have formed many friendships and made successful investments in the collecting world.

As the '70s progressed, I was slowly growing away from the music business. I wanted to enjoy my family life with May and my three children. I didn't want to be schlepping up and down the UK's motorways for the rest of my life doing gigs I didn't really want to do for a third share of something that was never going to get me to where I wanted to be in life. I was now really into the world of art and antiques, and by this time (mid-'70s!) found I could make more money from antiques than from 'Searching' with the band.

There were, however, various attempts to get back into the recording studios. We had tried our luck with RCA, complete with a new drummer, Billy Adamson. We re-recorded our hits for the *Second Take* album in 1972, but more interestingly came up with some fine singles. 'Desdemona' got to No. 94 in the US in September 1971 and also charted in Germany. 'Vahevala' had a great Caribbean beat to it, with almost obligatory steel drums.

Richard Swainson, A&R man at RCA, had suggested that we record a song called 'Solitaire', written by Neil Sedaka. It was not our usual type of number, like country rock or good three-part harmony material.

The string-and-percussion backing track was recorded and I did the vocal – it was a solo performer's song really. After everyone was happy with the recording, a release date was planned by RCA – the good news. The B-side was a cover of the Bee Gees' 'Spicks And Specks'. Then all our hard work was wasted when RCA dropped their support for it, allowing CBS to jump in with the Andy Williams version, which became a worldwide smash. The Carpenters did very well with that song too, but our version was out before either of them. We were incredibly unlucky to miss out with our version of 'Solitaire', as it showed signs of being a hit.

It was at this time that leaving the band was put to me as an option by Richard. So that came to be the story of my foreseeable future After the disappointment with 'Solitaire',

Richard asked me if I would be interested in making a solo album. RCA were testing out several lead singers from various '60s groups and had just released an album by Allan Clarke of the Hollies. The label was keen to sign me as a solo singer, though this did not mean I had to leave the band. Although we never discussed it, and they certainly never pursued it, John and Frankie must have known the situation. I had to make a decision. As it was not my intention to look for a recording deal for myself at that time, I didn't pursue the idea. I was not ready yet for a solo career.

In his second book, Frank claims that I recorded a song – or songs – behind their back This was while we were with RCA and Richard Swainson. Firstly, this was done in my own time and was something that many members of groups find themselves doing – like in 1965, when Chris recorded stuff in his own time. It had nothing to do with me at that time and it didn't interfere with the band's plans or itinerary. Even Frank would ask his good friend Norman Newell to record him, I seem to remember.

So, when Richard Swainson phoned and asked if I would put some tracks down, I said I would, as long as it didn't interfere with the band's itinerary. I did not need John or Frank's approval and we didn't have any written contract. But, because I was not ready to make the change and leave, there was no point in mentioning it to the others. I am, and have always been, my own man. I have made quick decisions in my life – most of them for the good, thank God.

It had been rumoured in showbiz gossip as early as 1964 that I was leaving the group. It was even announced on the national television news! I had been interviewed by a young lady from a music magazine and had been totally misquoted. I was as gobsmacked as everyone else when I saw the news bulletin.

May called me the next day while I was on tour, to say that a lot of reporters from London were outside her mum's house, wanting May to comment on the news report. I told her to put on her best frock and tell them not to believe everything they had seen on television, and say I had been misquoted in a magazine article by a young journalist looking for some glory. May was on the front page of the next day's *Daily Mirror* – something I had never managed myself, though I did get a mention and a small photo.

During our time with RCA under the direction of Richard Swainson, a promotional concert was organised for us to perform with the Everly Brothers. It was around this time that I got hold of a song by Phil Everly (an Albert Hammond composition) which I thought would make a great single. Richard agreed with me about the song, but John was not impressed, and Frankie just sat on the fence, so to speak. Before we knew it, another group had recorded it and it reached No. 2 in the charts. That group was the Hollies and the song was 'The Air That I Breathe'. That made *two* songs John and I had disagreed about.

After leaving RCA with a few more failed singles under our belt, we went back on the road, including a month in Germany, working for the promoter Rainer Hass – a great guy. He had a lovely mum who always wanted to come to our shows in Germany to hear me sing 'Running Scared'.

So that was it for the next few years. I enjoyed performing when the gigs came in, but it was the cabaret bookings that gave us a living. Music was still an important part of my life, but it wasn't the most important. By the time I had established Mike Pender's Searchers in 1986 there were many other irons in the fire. I could now afford to choose when I wanted to perform, so that left time for other interests – some business, some leisure, but all enjoyable.

May and I would often go to auctions at country houses, mostly for works of art. Those trips were not always successful. At one such auction, an early eighteenth-century seascape painting was up for sale – a fabulous picture. We were late arriving (no satnav in those days), and as we entered the marquee where the contents of the country house had been moved to, I could see the painting on an easel next to the auctioneer's rostrum. He was in full flow and I naturally thought he was taking bids on the painting, so I jumped straight into the bidding, which was quite low. After a few more bids, it dawned on me that the bidding was for something completely different. I almost found myself the owner of a Victorian dining table!

After antique pistols, clocks were always my forte and I have bought and sold many valuable collectors' clocks over the years with the help of my good friend Ron Musker, who, although a Red (Liverpool supporter), is one of my closest and valued friends – and I don't have many. After selling the *Eduardus East* clock to a collector, I had the chance to buy another collector's clock, coming from the workshop of England's greatest clockmaker. According to Mr Vaughan, the expert at Sotheby's, it could be worth more than the *Eduardus East*. This clock is what most people would call a grandfather clock, but to the collector it is a longcase clock. We have now had it for about forty years and I know its value!

CHAPTER 16

John and I –
A Difficult Relationship

I found myself wanting to move on several times during the '70s and early '80s.

Looking back, the 'disagreements' we had in the band seem a bit petty. John and I were never close friends, only guitar friends, as it was the guitar that brought us together in the first place. In all the years of working together in the Searchers, we could count on one hand the number of times we socialised. In truth, we saw so much of each other on the road while working, that we both needed a break from each other when not gigging. However, as the years went by, especially going into the '80s and the Sire period, it eventually became a pleasure to be away from him. I have no doubt the feeling was reciprocated.

I sometimes felt John had a chip on his shoulder and resented much of my input into the band. This was most apparent when Tony Hatch decided that 'He's Got No Love' would be released as a single. From then on, John and I would either compete or disagree, whichever way you look at it. On another occasion, when we were signed to RCA, John resented my choice of a single, 'I Really Don't Have The Time'; he preferred 'Sing Singer Sing'. It would be interesting to know what Searchers fans thought.

The late 1960s were a lean period for the band. To be honest, we were not making enough money for the amount of work we were doing. I put it to John that, as we were a limited company, we should put things like telephone bills, fuel and all personal travel bills through the company bank account.

Regarding travelling together to gigs, John and I needed each other, as he would drive if he picked me up, and vice versa. We never invested in a reliable vehicle and consequently had many problems, mostly breakdowns. Whichever one of us drove to the gig, the other would drive home and keep the car until the next time.

On another charge – me not being ready when he called to pick me up – this is news to me, but doesn't surprise me one bit, as it confirms what I've said about competing. But that remark has to go down as really scraping the barrel. Even bitchy.

Frank Allen refers to a Nottingham gig that he claims caused a lot of trouble within the band. I think this story refers to a gig that either I didn't have in my diary, or a gig that came in late and I had already made other arrangements. I seem to remember a birthday party organised with many people coming to the house (John was not invited) and finding out about the gig only a few days before we were due to appear.

By 1984, there were major rumblings within the band – John and I were now further apart than ever. The closest we'd ever got to each other was in the early days, at the Star-Club in Hamburg. In truth, this was mostly because we both missed our home life and being with our girlfriends, both of whom were later to become our respective wives.

While at the Star-Club, Tony and Chris would always be going out to do their own thing, and they both soon made friends with the locals. Tony and I had been very close, almost like brothers, ever since I had first met him, but after meeting Miss Doyle at the Cavern, most of my time when we weren't gigging was naturally spent with my future wife. So, with Chris and Tony otherwise engaged in Hamburg, John and I would keep each other company. We would pass many hours playing our guitars or playing each other on the football machine in the bar next to the Star-Club. We also spent a lot of time writing letters to our girlfriends, or looking for a telephone kiosk to phone home.

During our years at the top, between 1963 and 1966, when Tito Burns was running the show, John and I were pretty close because we had to be, always travelling home together by train or plane. From the early years of success until I decided to form Mike Pender's Searchers, John and I also lived fairly close to each other. Our children went to the same schools. When hard times came, and gigs became thin, we bought a car between us We were no longer pop stars; we had become survivors, along with most other pop groups from the '60s. Only the creative groups survived and were able to sustain themselves with royalties from writing their own material. I found myself wanting to move on several times during the '70s and early '80s. Certainly, by that point, John must have known the split was inevitable. Even he has to admit it was the best thing for both of us. I know it certainly was for me.

I must also comment on what Frank Allen calls, in his second book, 'small acts of betrayal'. I recall that, during our time with RCA Records, our producer and recording manager, Richard Swainson had more than once spoken of a separate deal for me, but still within our Searchers contract. This would have been similar to the deal that Coral Records had to release singles by both Buddy Holly and the Crickets at the same time.

Richard and I discussed the idea many times. If you listen to my solo recording of 'Solitaire' – because that's what it is, a solo recording – you can see where Richard was going. After that record, Richard told me about RCA's plans to record a solo album with Allan Clarke of the Hollies, and a proposal to do the same with me. This was no secret, and John and Frank were well aware of the situation.

When Richard called me at home during a lean time, to ask if I would put vocals onto some tracks for some of his songwriter friends, I said, 'No problem.' That's all they were, demos – which I still have – and I could have done my own deal with RCA, but that would have meant leaving the band. I often wonder why I didn't take that course.

In his second book, Frank also accuses me of arrogance and of having a 'monstrous ego and self-obsession' over interviews, especially one before the band performed on a live BBC TV programme in June 1977 to celebrate the 25th anniversary of HM the Queen's accession to the throne. I was looking forward to this performance – I think they wanted us to do 'Needles And Pins'. As I left home that morning to drive to London, I told May and the children to watch the show and I would give them a wave. I fully expected to be the one interviewed by the presenter, Bob Wellings.

During the rehearsals for the show, Bob said he would speak to John immediately before we performed the song. I promptly asked him whose idea it was to interview John. 'That is what we were told by your agent,' said Mr Wellings. I told him nothing like that had been mentioned to me and there were now two choices – either do the interview with me, or not at all. I can only guess that John had informed our agent that he would do the talking. I note from Frank's book that he thought my interview was 'bland'. He may have thought so, but my kids thought it was great!

CHAPTER 17

The Sire Sessions

Sire Records had given us the chance, although in some ways their efforts were half-hearted and uncertain.

After the years of fighting for success, and among ourselves, could we be great again? Was the infighting and unhappiness going to be worth it? How long would it last? Comments like 'The band's rebirth shows they haven't lost their touch' spurred us on. Were we really were past our 'sell by' date?

After RCA's offer of a possible solo contract and my rejection of it, the Sire deal in late 1978 was a breath of fresh air for the band. The chairman of Sire Records, Seymour Stein, said to me – and I quote, 'Mike, your voice still sounds great. You guys are gonna be big again.' There was no upfront money from Sire, mainly because we still couldn't write strong enough material, but I realised we were now going to make records for a new generation. We were almost twenty years on, but yes, it could happen again.

Rockfield Studios are in South Wales, just outside the lovely old town of Monmouth. Rockfield claim to be the world's first residential recording studios and the Searchers are by no means the only famous band to have recorded there since the facility opened in 1965. Artistes as diverse as Del Shannon, the Undertones, Coldplay, Queen and Echo & The Bunnymen have all recorded there. Nowadays, you don't even have to be in a band to stay at Rockfield: the complex offers bed & breakfast and self-catering accommodation for visiting this attractive corner of the

Welsh countryside.

Dave Edmunds helped to put the studio and its associated Rockfield record label on the music map when he recorded 'I Hear You Knocking' there: it spent six consecutive weeks at the top of the singles chart in 1970. Perhaps the studio's grandest moment* came in 1975, when Queen recorded 'Bohemian Rhapsody' for their new album, *A Night At The Opera.*

We actually lived on the premises, as it was a self-contained studio with living accommodation and kitchen, etc. Dinner was served to us each evening. These facilities were something totally new for the band – I have to say it was great. Pat Moran – a lovely guy – was our producer and he lived not far from the studios. We all got on very well, considering that Pat was from a much younger generation than us

Although I enjoyed the sessions, I sometimes lost my cool, as I had the biggest workload. Pat loved his work and I felt always had a lot of respect for me as a vocalist. He was always agreeable if I wanted to re-record a vocal, sometimes staying late into the night or into the early hours. I got off home at every opportunity, just for a day or two.

Sire Records had given us the chance, although in some ways their efforts were half-hearted and uncertain. Seymour Stein was obviously a Searchers fan, and, like many before him, still thought we were worth another shot. He initially came to see for himself if we still had enough quality, six months before offering us the contract. He liked what he saw and heard, but we never saw him again after that first introduction. He left all communications to Sire employee Paul McNally (no relation to John).

The two McNallys got on too well together for my liking, and I could see problems ahead. Just like the other McNally, Paul and I would clash, as would John, Frank and myself, during our time with Sire. This was nothing new, as we had three band members all of whom had separate identities and were slowly drifting apart.

It was only Pat Moran at Rockfield Studios who kept me interested in the whole thing. He would keep me going when I got tired, and I would keep him interested when I wanted to change

On tour with Dionne Warwick.

The 200th edition of *Thank Your Lucky Stars* featured an all-star cast including the Seekers, Mike Sarne, Jim Dale, Helen Shapiro and us.

Plate 17

Rehearsing for *Ready Steady Go!*

The inscription on our *NME* Runners-Up trophy.

Plate 18

Signs of discontent.

Tony with his new band, the Vibrations.

Plate 19

Frank Allen joins the band, 1964. This rare pic of us with our manager, Tito Burns, was taken shortly after.

Burt Bacharach with Dusty and some pop group at the back.

Plate 20

1966 world tour, Australia.
Our distinctive sound was now firmly established on three continents,
with the Rickenbacker 12-string a notable feature.

Stolen in late 1969 from the Lafayette nightclub, Wolverhampton, this
Rick 360/12 would today be worth many thousands of pounds, not only
for its market value, but also for its unique historical and inspirational
value in the world of popular music. I wonder where it is today.

Plate 21

Live performance at Radio Luxembourg.

Frankie and I
arriving at
Manila Airport in
the Philippines,
1966.

Plate 22

Televised press conference at Manila Airport,
with Julie Rogers providing the glamour.

We played four sell-out shows at the huge
Araneta Coliseum in Quezon City, Philippines.

Plate 23

Two photos taken in the three years young John Blunt was in the band (1966-69).

Plate 24

Charles II period table clock as I found it in 1972.

Signed 'Eduardus East, Londini', clockmaker to Charles II circa 1665.

Plate 25

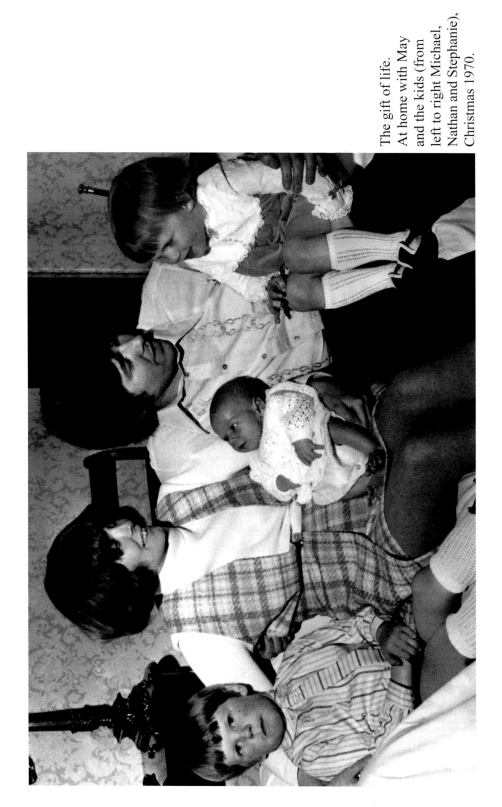

The gift of life.
At home with May and the kids (from left to right Michael, Nathan and Stephanie), Christmas 1970.

Plate 26

Our new Aria guitars.

The Sire years:
Frank, Billy
Adamson, John
and me.

Plate 27

Playing a Rainer Hass gig in Germany, 1975.

Jack Charlton invites us to a training session with Middlesbrough FC, 1976.
A very young Graeme Souness is at the very back!

Plate 28

May and I with a familiar face at the *Royal Variety Show*, 1981.

Whole Lotta Shakin' (hands, that is).
HM the Queen and more familiar faces, *Royal Variety Show*, 1981.

Plate 29

Deep in thought at Rockfield Studios, 1980.

Edinburgh, Scotland... and we are smiling!

Plate 30

This rare photo with my old mate Tony Jackson
was taken at the auditions for Mike Pender's Searchers in 1986.
Left to right: Chris Black, Steve Carlisle, me and Tony.

Bass player Barrie Cowell *(far left)* was chosen instead.

Plate 31

End of another show.
Left to right: Barrie, Mike Jr, me and Keith Roberts, 2014.

Joe Brown, but
not the Bruvvers!

Plate 32

something. For some reason, Paul McNally saw fit to bring in another recording expert, or producer if you like. This came as a complete surprise, and for me took the edge off working with Pat Moran.

Ed Stasium was a new breed of producer. He was a nice enough guy, but I felt we didn't need him. He and Paul McNally would try and make the Searchers into something we were not. This was never more evident than after one publicity gig in London, when Paul McNally mentioned to John and myself that we should replace our drummer, Billy Adamson, permanently.

Although we never found out who initially wanted a replacement drummer for the Rockfield sessions, we went along with it – or, should I say, were compelled to do so. In all honesty, I saw nothing wrong with Billy's drumming. So, when Sire put it to John and me about losing Billy, our reaction was 'We don't really want to go down that road', but John and I did talk about it on the train going back to Liverpool.

The first thing I thought of on our journey home was: would Sire give us the real deal if we replaced Billy? After all, we had been down that road before with other record labels, but this was different. This could work. John and I were both reluctant about the idea on the journey home, saying we would put Frank in the picture the next day.

When we told him, Frank, to his credit, didn't even want to talk about it – probably because he was closer to Billy than John and me. Both Frank and Billy lived in the London area and would socialise occasionally, but I suspect Frank also didn't want the hassle and the very likely unfair dismissal claims we would have, if we sacked Billy. As it happened, we didn't grant Paul McNally his wish and Billy stayed with us.

I felt I had worked very hard on the Sire sessions, even at one stage wrecking my voice, although other song parts could be put down while I was resting. As most of the work was down to me as the vocalist, Pat Moran suggested I took a break and go home while he and John did some guitar fills and other bits. When you are the main vocalist, you expect to be worked the hardest – as always happens when doing a couple of albums. Also, we had not written any of the material, so I had to learn all the words as we were recording, when I would ordinarily have had time before the session started to get the words into my brain.

Although I was only a couple of years off my 40th birthday, I didn't feel any concern about my age – John, Frank and I still considered ourselves to be quite young. At times, I felt shattered, especially as we still had to gig occasionally while we were still recording. If Sire had done the proper thing and given us an advance, I for one would have been much happier, instead of feeling insecure and asking myself if it was all worth it. John and Frank didn't seem to mind too much about receiving a pittance, but I always thought we were being used, as opposed to being invested in. But I played along and 'worked my balls off ', as they say.

A few years later, in 1985, when I decided enough was enough, I would remember times like Rockfield Studios trying to make things happen again for the band, giving everything and not getting much back. I knew then that it was time to move on. I had a family to look after and they were worth more to me than anything. I sometimes took my two sons, Michael and Nathan, to the studios, as both of them were into music, groups, guitars and drum kits. As I've already mentioned, during our six weeks at Rockfield we needed to do gigs to survive. However, the sessions were going so well, I was pretty convinced we were on the way to renewed success.

During our talks with Sire before starting the recording sessions, the powers that be at the record company suggested we look at ourselves in a new light, so to speak. It was suggested that, instead of me playing lead guitar and singing the lead vocal, as in years gone by, I should concentrate on the vocals and leave the lead guitar to John. This was a good idea, as Sire still wanted to retain the 12-string guitar, but mainly for filling the sound out doing live performances. The vocals would have more guts in them now, compared to the old Pye/RCA days.

After spending a fortune on recording and promotion, Sire decided to drop us in favour of the Pretenders, who were starting to have major success with hit singles like 'Brass In Pocket'. To this day, I still feel our first Sire single, 'Hearts In Her Eyes', would have been a chart success if someone like Tito Burns had been at the helm.

We also had to grasp the situation regarding certain matters within the band. But, in truth, we had come too far down the road, and seen the inside of too many recording studios – me especially – and I wanted out. If the Sire interlude had worked, then it could have been my springboard. Too many people had brought up the subject of me recording in my own right. Our Sire producer, Pat Moran, had joked about it, and many others including RCA's Richard Swainson, Jeff Lynne, Leo Sayer and Bill Kenwright had raised the issue. But the day was coming – John and Frank must have known it would happen eventually.

1979's *The Searchers* album, the initial product of those sessions at Rockfield, was widely acclaimed by the far-from-gullible British rock music press. It was considered to be as contemporary as any album released that year. Four tracks were selected by several reviewers for special praise: 'Hearts In Her Eyes', 'Coming From The Heart' written by Bob Dylan, Tom Petty's 'Lost In Your Eyes', and 'It's Too Late'.

Produced by Pat Moran, it was recorded and mixed at Rockfield Studios between April and July 1979. The credits stated that Ed Stasium remixed 'It's Too Late', Bob Jackson played keyboards on 'Lost In Your Eyes' and 'Coming From The Heart', and I was credited with '12-string electric guitar, lead vocals and harmonies'. The sleeve notes stated that the album was 'probably the first so-called "comeback" album to thoroughly justify the coming back', and that our trademark harmonies 'highlighted by Mike Pender's emotion-charged lead vocals, have simply matured over the years'. As a band, we thought our instrumental work was melodic, tight and precise. The album was also very well-received by self-confessed admirers of our '60s sound, such as Tom Petty & The Heartbreakers.

'Hearts In Her Eyes' was released as a single, got some great reviews and built up some airplay. However, for reasons best known to themselves, Sire recalled the album, reissuing it immediately with a different sleeve and a slightly revised track listing. The US release included the Bob Dylan song, but not John Hiatt's 'Back To The War', and vice versa for the UK release. The result was a loss of impetus at the vital time. An ecstatic review in *Rolling Stone* magazine helped it get to No. 191 in the US *Billboard* chart. The US release is available now on CD.

Rock music correspondent Peter Trollope also gave our new album a good review in the *Liverpool Echo* on 31 October 1979. Describing us as 'a group that refused to die', he added that we were 'as fresh today as they were in their glorious Mersey beat heyday', with an album 'crammed full of contemporary songs'. He reported that plans were under way for us to promote our new single, 'Hearts In Her Eyes', and the album, with a UK tour. He quoted John as saying we were as excited now as we were back in the '60s, and how things seemed to have gone full circle. John also said we were hoping the album would do well in America and that we would be able to go over there. We were still getting fan mail from the US almost every week. We might have been out of the limelight in this country for some time, but we were back now, and that's the way we liked it.

Trollope continued: 'Mike and John are the guitarists from the original line-up – it is their playing that gives the group its unique sound'. He also reported that we were due to play three consecutive nights in November at Blighty's club in Farnworth, a venue which regularly attracted crowds from Merseyside. (Later on, it was also the venue for my first gig as Mike Pender's Searchers.)

The reviewer in the *Evening Times* of 19 October 1979 said *The Searchers* was an album we could be proud of – there were some good songs on it and one or two excellent ones. 'If they are going to get back into the singles charts, then "It's Too Late" could be the song to do it', he wrote. He quoted Frank as saying that Sire had given us eight weeks to finish the album, whereas our previous LP, ten years before, had been completed in ten days. John said that the band had continued for so long after many of our contemporaries had fallen by the wayside because 'we play for the audience, not for our own ego'. Billy said, 'The new album has given us a new lease of life. We chose the songs we wanted to do, and we couldn't do any better than that.'

Melody Maker gave us a two-page write-up on 17 November 1979 to tie in with the release of *The Searchers*. Headed 'Someday We're Gonna Rock Again', Allan Jones said that, having inspired folk rock and power pop, we were back with 'an album which wouldn't shame Rockpile'. His view of our new album was very favourable, like so many others both here and abroad. He described it as 'an honourable return that reminds us of former triumphs without being nostalgic... the performances were crisp, surprisingly fresh... the songs have been chosen carefully, with taste and some discernment'. The tracks he picked out for special praise were 'Hearts In Her Eyes', 'Feeling Fine', and particularly 'No Dancing'.

He had previously been our guest at our gig at the Rhydyfelin Non-Political Club in Pontypridd on a very wet Tuesday night. Unfortunately, when he arrived, the committee members on the door had difficulty in believing he was actually with us and I had to push through the crowded tables to rescue him. The place was packed and noisy – we were squeezed into a small dressing room. He described the air in the hall as being 'thick with cigarette smoke, aftershave and perfume'. We told him we'd played worse places and we'd had to survive. Frank was quoted as saying that we didn't really mind playing these places: 'I mean, we're really not bothered, we've never been over-endowed with integrity.'

Allan also reported the story that Seymour Stein had heard the Ramones' cover version of 'Needles And Pins' and had decided to find out what the Searchers were doing now, which led to our contract with Sire and the sessions at Rockfield. The article also referred to our influence in the '60s on Californian bands like Buffalo Springfield, Love and the Byrds, who in turn had influenced the phenomenal later success of the Eagles. Five years after his glamorous night out with us in South Wales, Allan Jones was appointed editor of *Melody Maker*. In 1997, he became editor of *Uncut* magazine, a position he still holds at the time of writing.

Time Out magazine described 'Hearts In Her Eyes' as 'a new Searchers classic', even though the Radio 1 playlist panel had ignored it. Their journalist went to our gig at a social club in Bristol: 'The extraordinary thing about Mike Pender's voice is that it is so good when he's doing "Take Me For What I'm Worth" yet again, in a social club north of Bristol, to a beery audience hidden beyond the lights by 20 yards of empty dance floor. When in front of an audience who might be impressed by it, he sings "Running Scared". No one takes on one of Roy Orbison's bizarre, operatic crescendos lightly, perhaps not even the "Big O" these days. Mike sets up the drama against a simple throb from Frank and drummer Billy, and before you've had time to choose between prawn cocktail and soup of the day, he's cranked into a tonsil-splitting swoop that threatens to splinter the cashier's spectacles. On quieter numbers, he can pitch and crack the lyrics as if he's just discovered them, but with a control bred by the years. John and Frank weigh in with harmonies, ooh-aahs and responses that sound like a studio-polished backing tape.'

The highly respected rock music writer, Robin Denselow, welcomed our first album since 1974 in the *Guardian*. He commented: 'If every deejay in Britain was doing his job properly, the opening track and single, "Hearts In Her Eyes" would be a smash hit.' He quoted me as saying: 'When we first made it years ago, we didn't accept or enjoy it, but to make it twice would be wonderful.' Denselow concluded our new album was 'in part at least, very good indeed'.

He also reviewed our gig at the Venue in London for the *Guardian*, commenting that 'there could be no more opportune time for one of the classic '60s bands to be snatched back from the scampi-in-a-basket circuit, hopefully to be repromoted to the mass audience they deserve'. He praised our new songs and described our sound as 'crisp and neat', although we looked to him more like 'nervous, enthusiastic and optimistic newcomers than returned veterans'. He said John and I 'sounded genuinely enthusiastic' as we played our old hits. We were even attracting attention from the punk rock generation – former Sex Pistols Paul Cook and Steve Jones were in the audience at one of our London gigs, with other new wave personalities.

Smash Hits said our single release from the album, 'It's

Too Late', 'knocks spots off most current releases. Pop with a rich, glowing capital "P" teems with ability and experience to produce a sure-fire gem. Don't miss it.'

Record Mirror prophesied that 'the future of the Searchers looks to be on firm foundations with classic pop of the standard of "Hearts In Her Eyes" and "It's Too Late".' Their reviewer said we had always turned out exemplary songs, and that the band's 'rebirth shows they haven't lost their touch'.

Although our album failed to chart in the UK, Seymour Stein was sufficiently encouraged to give the go-ahead for a second LP. *Play For Today*, was recorded at Rockfield between August and October 1980. Released in 1980, it was retitled *Love's Melodies* for the US market, because the track 'Love's Melody' had been released as a single. Produced by Pat Moran and Ed Stasium, it included John Fogerty's 'Almost Saturday Night', plus songs written by John David, Alex Chilton and Randy Bishop – and two ('Little Bit Of Heaven' and 'Another Night') credited to McNally, Pender & Allen! Mick Weaver played keyboards on some of the tracks. Two tracks, 'Everything But A Heartbeat' and 'Almost Saturday Night', deserved to be singles. It was a great selection of songs, but the album failed to chart in either the UK or US.

One reviewer described both our Sire albums as 'a formidable slab of new wave power pop, with classic Brit beat overtones.' Sire did make efforts to break the band again, but, like all record companies, they had other bands and artistes to promote at the same time as ourselves.

Our old label, Pye, had sold our back catalogue to Castle, along with those of various other '60s artistes who had also lost some of their popularity. In late 1982, however, we found ourselves back in the old Pye studios in London. Pye did not exist any more and the studios were owned by PRT (Precision Records & Tapes).

Their A&R man, Matt Haywood, had faith in the band and came up with a song published by Bruce Welch of the Shadows, 'I Don't Want To Be The One'. It had been written by Steve Thompson, a prolific songwriter. Matt, who worked closely with Pete Waterman, thought we were still capable of coming up with a hit. We met with Matt and Pete to discuss the promotion of the record. They were very enthusiastic and talked about a possible album and how we were going to be big again. Pete even had me believing the record could make the charts. Before we recorded the song, Matt and I had met up with producer Peter Collins, who would record us at the old Pye studios. We would have a new single on PRT, a new label, and a chance to get back in the charts.

In the recording world, it doesn't matter how good a song or record is – what really matters is promotion. 'I Don't Want To Be The One' was good enough to be a hit, but the promotion was not there. Matt Haywood worked his socks off. We appeared on the *Leo Sayer* TV show, on which I sang live to a recorded backing track. Leo complimented me on my vocal. Matt also did a deal with Woolworths to sell the single, but all to no avail.

Pete Waterman lost interest after that one single – another disappointment. 'I Don't Want To Be The One' was a very good effort, but PRT and Pete were more interested in much younger up-and-coming bands. A projected album was never completed and everything just fizzled out.

After failing with 'Hearts In Her Eyes' and then with 'I Don't Want To Be The One', I became convinced we were never going to make it back to the charts, and that I would soon have to make a big decision. I stayed friends with Matt Haywood and we joined up again later, when we recorded a song ironically titled 'It's Over'. I still play 'I Don't Want To Be The One'. That record, you could say, was the last group effort at attempting a chart comeback.

Over the next few years, things got gradually worse within the band, especially between John and myself. Soon my decision to leave and the band's worst nightmare would finally happen. When the Sire affair eventually fizzled out, it was the beginning of the end for me. Sire Records and Seymour Stein had put their faith in the band, but the lack of any kind of backup (i.e. manager, publicity agent) and fading compatibility within the band, all our hard work had come to nothing.

I had given my all in the Rockfield studios – much more than at any previous time – because of the interest shown in us by so many other artistes and songwriters such as Tom Petty, Will Birch and John Wicks. I really felt this was it, things were going to happen. The end product was there. It was up to Sire now and they must know what to do. But Sire didn't do it, and the anti-'60s 'you belong in the past' brigade – including BBC radio deejays and producers – all got their way. 'No plays today – it's too late,' as Paul Jones once said when reviewing our earlier RCA single.

I'm listening to 'Switchboard Susan' as I write these words. We had done the business in the studio – the tracks were all ready and waiting. It *had* to be a success, but as we all know, it wasn't. And so I was left with only one conclusion: we really were past our 'sell by' date. Our contract with PRT had also ended in tears, as they say. I knew then that I would have to make some very important decisions in my life.

CHAPTER 18

By Royal Command

One of the most annoying things for any performer when appearing on television is the fact that some presenters and cameramen don't do their homework.

Royal Performance
in the presence of
Her Majesty The Queen

at 8pm
on the evening of
Monday 23rd November 1981
at the
Theatre Royal, Drury Lane

It was a big night for us, but the camera was not on me for the performance. After some tentative approaches, we had been booked for the *Royal Variety Show*. Tim Rice (now Sir Tim) has always been a big fan of the group as it was in the '60s. Back in 1981, he got my telephone number from Bill Kenwright who, at that time, was starting to build up his theatre empire. Bill and I go back a long way, to when we first met at the *Top of the Pops* studio in Manchester.

We were both mad fans of Everton Football Club, and Bill at that time was a regular on the TV soap, *Coronation Street*. He would arrange for Everton tickets to be left for his brother Tom and myself. We became good friends. He would organise charity football matches and would always be the centre forward, copying his Everton idol, Dave Hickson. I was his partner striker and laid on many a goal for him.

But to get back to that telephone call, Tim Rice had told me he was planning to have a '60s music segment for the *Royal Command Performance*. Although that idea had been approved in principle, he told me that some of the artistes who had been invited had not been confirmed. Tim was very honest and said he was trying to get us on the show. It was for this reason I didn't jump in and say, 'Yes, we can do it.' I told him that, unless it was a definite contract, we could not say 'Yes', as I knew we were contracted for a tour of Finland and Norway at that time.

Tim wanted us so badly, he put it to me that, if he could get a definite contract from the producers of the *Royal Variety Show*, would I give him a 'Yes'? I remember thinking that, as the show was on a Monday night, there would not be a problem with our Scandinavian promoter, as he would not have a gig for that night – 23 November 1981. I put this point to Tim and asked him to get back to me within the week.

Our promoter in Finland gave us his blessing and we flew back to the UK, going straight to the Theatre Royal on Drury Lane for rehearsals. Tim was there to greet us, and he told me it was Louis Benjamin who had swung it for us, insisting we should be on the show. Louis Benjamin had signed us to Pye Records in 1963. He was instrumental in the band's early success, albeit he wasn't keen on 'Needles And Pins'. He and Tim Rice had convinced Bernard Delfont, the president of the *Royal Variety Show*, to have us on the bill. The other acts with us in the '25 Years of British Pop' segment of the show included Acker Bilk, Marty Wilde, Lonnie Donegan, Donovan, Lulu, the Shadows with Cliff Richard, and Alvin Stardust.

One of the most annoying things for any performer when appearing on television is the fact that some presenters and cameramen don't do their homework, especially when a group of musicians is appearing. And it is *really* annoying when it happens in front of Her Majesty the Queen! You can check it out for yourself if you watch the Searchers on the *Royal Command Performance* on Monday, 23 November 1981 on YouTube. The first shot of the film shows Frank miming to my vocal!

It's easy to see what happened. That nice cameraman I've smiled at has got it all wrong. As Frank is positioned in the middle of the band, the cameraman thought he was singing. When he finally realised his mistake, he immediately swung over to me – but it was too late. John's Aria guitar looked good, though. Ironically, Frank wasn't even on the original record. This type of thing happened a few times over the years and it looks bad, mainly because either the other guys in the band don't know the words when the camera goes on them, or they are not in sync with the music.

CHAPTER 19

The Last US Tour

This was to be my last trip to America with John and Frank.

In 1983, we all decided to try America one more time. To his credit, it was John who suggested the idea. Our second Sire album, *Play For Today*, had received good reviews when it was released in the US a couple of years before as *Love's Melodies*. Even *Rolling Stone* magazine said that it was 'good, even great'. Sire also gave it a different picture cover, which I wasn't pleased with.

As there was no demand for the band from the US, we had to organise our own flights to America, and transport to and from the gigs. Looking back, I have to say the trip was something of a disaster. The few gigs we did get were low-key. The worst part of the whole tour for me was the driving. We each took turns while the others slept – and America is a huge country.

Ray Reneri was our contact from our previous US tours, but he found it very difficult to get us decent gigs. A handwritten handbill for our show in Baltimore described me as 'ex-Moody Blue, Jack Bender' – something of a confusion between Mike Pinder and Mike Pender.

The best gigs we did in the few weeks we were over there were two shows in New York. Ray just happened to know the owner of one of the biggest discos in New York. That guy was also a fan of the band, and, like Ray, was still a strong '60s music fan. We played his club, which was packed out, as most discos in New York were at that time. We tried to inject some 'heavier'

FROM LIVERPOOL, ENGLAND.
THE "LOVE POTION #9" "NEEDLES AND PINS"
SEARCHERS
ALL ORIGINAL MEMBERS!
FEATURING EX-MOODY BLUE
JACK BENDER
ALSO APPEARING: THE RE-SEARCHERS!
TUES. NOV. 8th
SHOW STARTS AT 10 P.M.
AT: THE MARBLE BAR
306 W. FRANKLIN ST.
CALL 727-5336 FOR MORE INFO!

songs into the show and we still looked pretty good for our age.

A good many of the younger generation gave us the 'wow' factor, but to be honest, the show was still steeped in the '60s. We had some really good songs in the set. 'Fooled Around And Fell In Love' (a minor hit for Elvin Bishop) and other non-Searchers songs helped give the band a new dimension, but, at the end of every show, the overriding factor and mainstay of the band, as it were, was the 'Needles And Pins' riff and my 12-string introduction to 'When You Walk In The Room'.

We had some rave reviews for our gig at a relatively small, trendy club in New York called The Other End. The headline in one newspaper read 'One of the greatest shows, ever'. It was the last night of our tour, our first for ten years. The club was packed to the rafters. One guy was rumoured to have travelled from Australia especially for this gig. Joey Ramone was also in the audience that night and met us after the show. Ritchie Blackmore, Chris Spedding and David Essex had attended our other New

York shows.

Our new songs from the Sire *Searchers* album drew the kind of applause normally reserved for our established hits. The reviews in the New York media singled out 'Hearts In Her Eyes', 'Love's Melody', 'It's Too Late', and a ten-minute electric version of 'Switchboard Susan' which brought the house down. Frank got a lot of laughs when he introduced me as 'the Boy George of Liverpool, not quite so butch, though'. He also described the 'riotous' nature of the tour: 'Overdosing on 7-Up and stepping on the cracks in the pavement.' One reviewer said either John or I could give Roger McGuinn of the Byrds a few lessons on the 12-string guitar', even going as far as saying we were 'the greatest band of his generation'. I should add that he was on his second bottle of Jack Daniels at the time.

This was to be my last trip to America with John and Frank, as the next time I set foot on those distant shores was three years later with my own band. But, before that, I had to plan for the future.

CHAPTER 20

It's Over –
Splitting from John and Frank

I suppose I was a fool, really, to think the band would keep me informed.

There is no doubt that, in the recording and entertainment world, the ideal situation is to have success with your own music and lyrics. This ensures that, if you are successful and sell lots of records, you not only have your recording royalties for the sales of CDs, records and tapes – which all artistes have, regardless of who wrote the lyrics – but you also have writing royalties that bring you in much more income than recording royalties.

There is no better example of this than Elton John. You don't *have* to perform every night, week in, week out – although that's OK when you're young. This income ceases when your records stop selling, as happens to almost everyone. I still get royalty cheques, but only because Universal still release compilations of the Searchers' back catalogue, which they now own.

I realised many years ago that not being able to read or write music was a handicap in the pop music business. Writing lyrics also did not come naturally to me, and I could not read or write music. I knew, all those years ago, that life in general would get difficult for us as the Searchers once the bubble had burst and the band would become a 'Whatever happened to...?' act. So, I needed to channel my other attributes into reality.

Whatever you do in life, if you are successful, it's because you love what you do. I love performing, I love singing and playing my 12-string Rick. But I couldn't do it night after night. I'm lucky in that, although I don't have the writing royalties, I do have other interests and investments that ensure my family and I have a full and enjoyable life, and at the same time help our children and grandchild. We all want to make a better life for ourselves, especially if we have a happy and loving home life. I have all these things and count myself blessed, even though May and I have had the heartbreaking experience of the tragic loss of our youngest son, Nathan. But God, in his wisdom, has given us our lovely grandson, Alexander.

I suppose I was a fool, really, to think John and Frank would keep me informed as to when we would play our last gig together. I was being as honourable as I could, by seeing out all remaining contracts, as we had agreed, to give them time to find a replacement. I realised then, of course, that I should have just left when I had made my decision months before. Perhaps they thought I would change my mind. How wrong they were! The desire to leave always came from other people and not from myself.

People often ask me the question: Why did you leave the band? I would like to set the record straight about the final parting of the ways, and about the last gig I played with the band, which is very different to the account by Frank in his second book. Frank's account is second-hand. He did not travel to Liverpool with John and me after that last gig, on 23 December 1985 at the Albany, Deptford, on the outskirts of London.

It was, predictably, a sombre affair in many ways. Before the show, the atmosphere in the dressing room, or what passed for a dressing room, was depressing, with stilted conversation and a sense of 'Let's get it over with'. I had initially told John and Frank I would honour all contracts up to 26 January 1986 – the date of the last booking in the diary.

We all had agreed on this, as I felt it would give me time to sort out our financial affairs within the partnership. But then they suddenly informed me they had a replacement, Spencer James,

```
                          Engagements Diary.

OCTOBER      31st)
NOVEMBER      1st) Willows Variety Centre, Salford, Lancashire.
              2nd)

              3rd  Yatton, Bristol.

              6th)
              to ) London area, (exact dates not known at present).
              8th)

              9th)
              to ) Chessford Grange Hotel, Kenilworth.
             11th)

             15th)
              &  ) Iceland
             16th)

             22nd) Milton Keynes Rugby Football Club.

             23rd) Marine Centre, Esplanade, Great Yarmouth.

             29th) Maesteg Town Hall, Wales.

             30th) Kings Country Club, Eastbourne.
DECEMBER      6th) Forest Glen Pavillion, Telford.

              7th) Brittania Hotel, Piccadilly, Manchester. (possibly private function)

             11th)
              to ) Scotland (various venues).
             17th)

             18th) Telford (private function?).
JANUARY       3rd)
 (1986)       &  ) Newmarket Cabaret Club.
              4th)

             23rd)
              to ) Merseyview, Frodsham.
             25th)

             26th) Hexagon, Reading.
```

and had rehearsed with him. They now wanted the split brought forward – and then came another surprise which made me quite angry. As we had a gentlemen's agreement that I would stay until they found a vocalist, I purposely didn't make any press announcements about leaving the band, preferring to wait until the final gig, whenever that was going to be.

I found out at a gig in Leeds – one of the last we did together – that they had chosen a replacement and had been rehearsing behind my back, knowing I had given my word to honour all gigs into the following year. However, I was not unduly worried, as I was in no hurry to find and rehearse my new band, and was planning to take some time off, anyway.

Before 1985, there were occasions when I had thought about forming another band. The signs were there as early as 1964-65, although I was misquoted. The young female journalist was guilty of wishful thinking when she asked if I would be making a solo album. I replied then that I had no wish to do anything on my own and that the band still had more success to come. Tito Burns also brought up the subject of a possible solo album at least twice, before he gave up on us.

When the band signed to RCA in the early 1970s, the opportunity was there for me to record a solo album. I asked Richard Swainson if RCA would still keep the band if I did the solo album. He said no, as RCA had already gone over budget. I could have gone my own way then, but decided to turn down the offer. The time wasn't right, and besides I didn't have the capital, seeing as RCA were not giving moneys upfront with this venture. As I said earlier, I remember thinking the desire to leave always came from other people and not from myself, so I declined. I wasn't ready, but if I'm honest, I knew it would come.

While the Searchers were signed to RCA, there was no record success. RCA wanted to let the band go, but keep me signed to the company. John did not like the idea, but doing that would have given us another avenue, and, with a little luck, the chance to make the charts again. This made sense, and, had Tito Burns still been the band's manager, he would have been in favour.

In early 1985, I realised our recording career was over. As a group, once rated second only to you-know-who, we would not have chart success again as a foursome. The most we could hope for was that, somewhere in the distant future, a compilation of our hit recordings would appeal to the record-buying public – and that did actually happen some 25 years later, when the *Very Best Of The Searchers* compilation reached No. 12 in the UK album charts.

But back to 1985: after the failed US trip two years earlier, I realised that, from then on, it would be performances only. I decided it was time for me to make more of an impression onstage and not to leave all the talking to Frank. Singing and playing guitar were easy-peasy, but talking to an audience and getting them to listen was something else. Actually, you can do too much talking, as Frank often did, to the annoyance of many people. Times were when Frank would be rabbiting away and a voice from the audience would shout, 'Get on with it!' or 'More music!' Frank was a good raconteur, but at times he overdid it.

In those 18 months leading up to the summer of 1985, I spoke with a few people within the business, most of whom were '60s-music-orientated and very good friends of mine. As you know, Bill Kenwright was someone I'd known from the very early days. He was one of the people I told I would be splitting to form a new band. Bill had tried to sign the Searchers years earlier, when nothing much was happening record-wise. I remember him driving to a gig down south somewhere for a meeting with us. John and Frank were reluctant to go ahead with the deal.

When people often ask me the question, 'Why did you leave the band?', I usually say, 'Why not?' One of the main reasons for my leaving was that I needed control of my own destiny. I could see no future for myself and my family in staying with the band. In 1985, we, as the Searchers, were and always would be living off past glories. That's all right, because that's what we all do in the record business with a few exceptions.

In 1985 we were not doing well as a business. We were three partners with three employees: a drummer, an agent and a road manager. In 1974-75, we, the Searchers, earned £31,662 for the year. After expenses of £19,087, that left just £12,575 between the three of us – less than £90 per week. At the same time, I was making more money from investing in antiques and works of art. Ten years later, in 1984-85, although earnings were now much better, they were only really in line with inflation. I needed to be in a position where I would have capital to invest for the future.

Turnover in my first two years after leaving the band was very good: £358,480. After deducting expenses of £192,101, my capital account looked good. I was now able to invest in works of art and property, and at the same time provide for my family. I had taken a calculated risk and was now where I wanted to be.

That was 1986-87, and all these years later it still feels good. From the time I said I was leaving, August 1985, up until my final departure at the Albany, Deptford that December, John and Frank contrived to keep me away from the spotlight, which gave me more of an impetus to get away.

As a gesture of goodwill, I left them my well-worn stage suit, not thinking for a minute they would actually use it. But, apparently, the new lad squeezed himself into it.

CHAPTER 21

A New Beginning – Finding Myself

1985 was a long time coming. But it was the year that I found myself, 28 years after that fateful afternoon at the Regent Cinema in Crosby.

A new dawn was beginning for me, and it felt good to make the break. To have confidence is always the key when starting a new venture, but I was quietly confident about what I had to do. However, before I did anything, I took a couple of months' holiday.

When forming Mike Pender's Searchers, it never occurred to me, or even entered my mind, to bring Tony Jackson or Chris Curtis back into the fold, as it were. My agent and manager at the time, Robert Pratt, would always bring up the idea of having 'three original Searchers' and I would be right back where I had started. I told him: 'No way!'

I had met Chris Black a couple of times over the years when his group, Sons and Lovers, appeared on the bill as our support act. They were a very popular harmony group and made many live appearances on television shows during the '60s. I remember thinking that, when the time came for me to split, he would be good for my new band, especially as I was looking forward to performing songs with strings and piano backing, both of which Chris could provide. Another plus was that he also played a Rickenbacker 12-string – the exact same model as mine:

the 456 6/12 converter. He was also very good vocally and sang perfect harmony (no one's that good)!

Before I'd had a chance to rehearse some of the many drummers we had in mind, Chris called me to say he knew just the guy we needed and he would be perfect – and he was. Steve Carlisle was one of the best singing drummers around at that time and would have been able to give Don Henley a good run for his money!

Robert Pratt would come down from Scotland and stay over for a couple of nights to give me his opinions and ideas for my new venture. He was instrumental, in those early days, helping me when I was putting the band together. Although we didn't see eye to eye on a lot of things, I needed his experience and backing if I was to make an impact.

Although I was still living in Liverpool, in the Blundellsands area, most of the remaining months of 1985 were spent travelling to and from Nottingham. I decided to make Nottingham my base, as it seemed much easier for me to go over there and rehearse the band, as Chris Black and Steve Carlisle were living there. More importantly, Chris's friend, Sons and Lovers' bass player Eddie Cooke, had very kindly offered us his outlying farm for the rehearsals and for temporary accommodation for me. Eddie has a remarkable voice, and also wrote most of the group's original material.

I had Chris Black and Steve Carlisle who were perfect, but the recruitment of a bass player became a bone of contention between Robert and myself. Eddie Cooke temporarily stood in while we all went through the repertoire of songs old and new. Robert then came up with the idea of contacting Tony Jackson, who we knew was managing a golf club in Windsor. I could see where this idea was going and how Robert's mind was working, but from the outset I knew that it would be a mistake to go back over old ground. With this in mind, I told Robert that no way was I about to rehash the Searchers. But Robert was one step ahead of me. He had already contacted Tony on my behalf!

Out of courtesy, and the fact that Tony and I had been good friends all those years ago, I agreed to go through the motions, as it were. I picked him up from Nottingham railway station the following day. By now, most of the applicants for the bass player vacancy had been vetted. I had settled for Barrie Cowell, a young man from Skelmersdale, a place not far from my home. Baz, as we later called him, was put on hold, as Robert had also arranged a photo session with Tony Jackson as part of my new band.

We did the shoot and then ran through a couple of songs with Tony. It was good to see him again, but he was clearly struggling with both playing and singing. However, I was not really concerned, as I knew that it would not happen. That night, after Tony had gone home to Windsor, I told Robert there was no going back to the old days. Forget about Tony Jackson and Chris Curtis, the original Searchers are history. I telephoned Tony the next morning and told him that it wouldn't work. I also thanked him for coming to the rehearsal. That was the last time that I would speak to him until our memorable meeting six years later, when I invited him up onstage at the Birmingham Town Hall. You can see this performance on YouTube.

After I had totally dismissed the idea of Tony and Chris Curtis in those early stages, Robert came round to my way of thinking. He finally realised that it had to be 'Mike Pender with a Searchers connection'. But Robert and I were on shaky ground from the beginning, as I always felt that he wanted to control my future. It was a little bit like Tito Burns in the days when I was a 'shrinking violet' – not any more! By this time, I had reinvented myself, or, as this book will tell you, I had found myself. So it came as no great surprise when, on a tour of Northern Ireland in 1986, Robert and I had the mother and father of all arguments and our short working relationship came to an end.

I wasn't the first artiste to fall out with their manager or agent, and I won't be the last. It happens all the time in this business. But I have to give Robert his due: apart from our few differences regarding the way I should go forward, he did an excellent job in the short time we were together. This was especially evident from our nationwide tour with Ben E. King, when he made sure Mike Pender's Searchers got top billing.

Robert organised many TV promotions for us. and also the recording of 'It's Over'. He was my mentor, and his drive and confidence in me went a long way towards establishing my new career in those early days.

After 'It's Over' failed miserably, I think Robert became disillusioned with the whole scenario. We were having constant problems with agents, promoters and venues, who were advertising us incorrectly as 'The Searchers' instead of 'Mike Pender's Searchers'. John and Frank's solicitors were harassing us and threatening legal action. This was something that Robert had not bargained for – perhaps he thought John and Frank would just disappear. And so our relationship came to an abrupt end, and he informed me that Tony Sherwood would be handling all my future business.

Tony first came into the business as a deejay, working in London, Nottingham, Derby and Manchester. He also sang with the resident band from time to time at various ballroom venues, such as the Plaza in Manchester. It was there that he first met people like Wayne Fontana, Peter Noone and Dave Berry, forming friendships that are still strong today. Herman's Hermits were his regular group. You could see them at a lunchtime session for the princely sum of sixpence. Tony, of course, did start very young. It was also at the Plaza where he met his wife, Barbara. After a number of years as a deejay, he talked his way into an agency in Nottingham called Banner Productions. Amongst others, they looked after a local group called Sons and Lovers who had a young guitarist called Chris Black in their original line-up!

I have to thank Robert Pratt for introducing me to Mr Tony Sherwood. It was the start of a very long, happy and successful partnership. Once Tony had taken over the agency, and after we later sorted out the problems with the 'other side', things went really well for me and for MPS (apart from a few unscrupulous promoters and others who shall remain nameless). I am so glad that Tony stayed in my corner for so many years – he was the best and most trusted agent that I could have found.

My life had definitely changed for the better and I now

started to earn my just rewards. After 25 years of being part of a world-famous musical quartet I had initially brought together, it was now time for me to go my own way. I had enjoyed some of those years, but not most of them, and had realised that nothing lasts for ever – especially in the music business.

History will always identify the four members of the group I founded – John, Chris, Tony and me – as the Searchers, the originals. Just like John, Paul, George and Ringo, we conquered America and became a household name on both sides of the Atlantic.

CHAPTER 22

See You in Court!

The two people who, at one time, loved me like a brother and to whom I had devoted my all, during more than twenty years, were now trying to have me incarcerated.

As the years roll by, more and more people are amazed that the rift was so prolonged, the end so sudden, the line so thin, and that the bitterness lingers on. Confusion led to court action: their Searchers *vs.* my Searchers.

As I've already mentioned, one of the reasons why Robert Pratt became increasingly disillusioned with Mike Pender's Searchers and myself was the amount of harassment from John and Frank's solicitors over the name of the band and incorrect billing. I suspect he was concerned that the whole scenario would eventually lead to the law courts – which of course it did – and wanted out. This is what prompted Robert to ask Tony Sherwood if he would be interested in taking on MPS in an agency and management deal. I don't know if there was a fee involved and I never asked Tony about it.

I could not have wished for a more honest, dedicated and caring person than Tony to take me on. At the beginning of 1987, my new career took off with a bang. Tony couldn't keep up with the demand for Mike Pender's Searchers and had to take on another agent to help with the bookings. The new guy was Tony's old friend and colleague, Mick Fulwood.

We would get people calling the office to book 'The Searchers'. Tony or Mick would tell them they could book *Mike*

Pender's Searchers, to which the callers would often reply that 'Mike *is* the Searchers' (not my words!), so why couldn't they book me as that? Tony and Mick would point out that, if they booked me, they would have to sign a contract stating 'It is essential this artiste is billed as follows: "Mike Pender's Searchers".' It was made clear to people they had to abide by the contract and only bill us as 'Mike Pender's Searchers'.

This alone should have made promoters and agents aware of the situation, but somehow it did not. Many people were still unaware that there were now two groups with the word 'Searchers' in their name. We would actually get people telephoning and arguing about why they couldn't call my group 'The Searchers'.

John and Frankie were now desperate and, in truth, were trying to stop me working – even to the extent of taking legal action to try to have me sent to prison for 'contempt of court', as they put it. This was because, although some of the contracts stipulated 'Only to be billed as "Mike Pender's Searchers",' they unfortunately omitted to state that 'each word must be given equal prominence as to size, colour and type of lettering'. This indeed was desperation to the point of being crass. It was clear that John and Frank didn't like the competition. Let's face it, who in their right mind does not understand the wording 'Mike Pender's Searchers', regardless of the colour or size of lettering?

There is a well-known phrase, which, although a cliché and often used in the wrong context, most certainly applies here: there is a very thin line between love and hate. The two people who, at one time, loved me like a brother and to whom I had devoted my all for over twenty years, when record companies only signed us because I was still the voice of the band, were now trying to have me incarcerated because they couldn't stand to see me have success in my own right. The truth was – and is – that there is still room for both groups. We are both tributes to the once-famous four.

And so it was brought to our attention that I had signed a couple of contracts that were incorrectly worded. The contracts should have specified that all promotional material must have

'Mike Pender's Searchers' in the same typeface and colour. Oops. In MPS' early days, there were so many gigs coming in that Tony would bring a whole load of papers to a show for me to sign, rather than posting them to me. Many of our gigs were in the Nottingham area, which was also convenient for Tony.

When I think back now, it is easy to blame Tony for the three or four contracts that never mentioned colour or size of wording, but, as the trial judge said, and I quote, 'A very large number of [contracts]... have been disclosed, and so far as the contracts disclosed are concerned, it is accepted that they do all carry the relevant wording.'

Mr Justice Whitford said committal to prison or granting leave to issue writs of sequestration 'would be wholly inappropriate'. He also dismissed the possibility of a fine for several reasons, including 'the very full apologies which have been offered'. He concluded that 'the only order which it is appropriate to make upon the motion, is that the defendant should pay the plaintiffs' costs on an indemnity basis'.

This was not a judgement in favour of John and Frank, only an obligatory motion from the judge. That morning in court, with my lawyer, Philip Conway, I had tried to convince John and Frank that only the solicitors and barristers would be the winners, but they refused to compromise. I was proved right when Mr Justice Whitford in reality threw out their case.

A complete transcript of the official tape recording of the judgment appears in *Appendix V.*

CHAPTER 23

Stopping the *QE2*, Touring Oz and the Poison Pen

We celebrated the 30th anniversary of the Searchers' first big hits and my 30 years in the music business in some style in 1993.

So, I was back on the road at home and abroad, and busier than ever before, but having more time for my family and friends. Among Mike Pender's Searchers' first gigs we had some really high-profile ones and met some exciting people. I remember talking to Sir Alex Ferguson when he was manager at Aberdeen and some years away from his glory days at Manchester United and his knighthood. Aberdeen had just won a big European game and we were invited to perform at the Aberdeen Hilton. Later that night, I found out Sir Alex was a big Searchers fan and that his favourite film was... *The Searchers*. He added that he was also a big John Wayne fan.

During the conversation, Sir Alex told me that, when the topic of who was going to be the entertainment came up, he had asked for the Searchers and had thought no more about it. He had then been informed there were now two 'Searchers' groups, each with an original member. Now, we all know that Sir Alex has a broad Scots accent, but I managed to understand him enough to hear him say something like, 'We must have the guy who sang "Needles And Pinsa"!'

Another early MPS gig that comes to mind was the *Irish Open* golf tournament held in Dublin and hosted by the Sangsters, who were top in the horse racing business at the time. I don't know if that still applies. Anyway, it was a great gig and Terry Wogan was master of ceremonies. Who else in Dublin? The singer and film actor Howard Keel was one of the celebrities in the audience that night.

In 1989, we recorded eleven of my favourite Searchers songs for a cassette tape imaginatively titled *Mike Pender's Searchers*. It was recorded at Dave Williams' Music Works in Nottingham. I used 6- and 12-string guitars, and Chris Black played acoustic guitar as well as keyboards. Barrie Cowell and Steve Carlisle joined in with the vocals as usual. The cassettes were available to MPS fan club members and were sold after our gigs. We needed to do that to satisfy the demand for merchandise from our fans after concerts. I also needed to let people know what I sounded like, although they could obviously still buy the original Searchers' recordings. Twenty years later, when I was sitting in on Mike d'Abo's radio programme on BBC Radio Gloucester, Mike commented that the MPS version of 'Goodbye My Love' sounded better than the original which I sang with Chris Curtis in 1965.

Our fan club secretary, Gill Westwood, also arranged for T-shirts to be printed to promote the band. Gill had just taken over from Margaret Brown, who had been with us since 1986, from the very beginning. She had also initiated the *Pinsa* newsletter.

In 1990, we recorded three new songs I had co-written with Barrie, 'Blue Mondays', 'Broken Hearts' and 'Red Ferrari', as well as a new and very different arrangement of 'Needles And Pins'. They were released in Germany in 1991 along with ten tracks from our cassette on a Karussell CD called *Sweets For My Sweet*, and have all since been licensed to various other labels.

With several other artistes, I also made a charity record for EMI in 1991 called 'As Time Stood Still', in support of *Gulf Aid*. Among those in the recording studio that day were my old Mersey beat pal Gerry Marsden, Brotherhood of Man, Sonia and Rose-Marie, as well as celebrities like Frank Bruno, Timmy Mallett and Tessa Sanderson. The *Sun* newspaper had set up the project to raise money for the Government-backed charity for

British servicemen and their families. MPS also performed at the London Palladium on 24 February 1991, for the *Sun*'s *Gulf Aid Gala Show* featuring a host of well-known artistes including Dame Vera Lynn, Gerry Marsden, Brotherhood of Man and Mike Yarwood. Later that year, Martin Hartwell of Aria Guitars, presented Barrie, Chris and myself with lovely new guitars.

In the summer of 1992, MPS had a great time doing a *'60s Revival* summer season at Tivoli World in Spain with lots of old friends including Brian Poole & The Tremeloes, Dave Berry & The Cruisers, the Troggs and Cliff Bennett & The Rebel Rousers.

Two of the highlights of 1992 were reunions with my old bandmate Tony Jackson at Birmingham Town Hall on 2 May, and then for a *Mersey Beat 30th Anniversary Show* on 1 November at Guildford Civic Hall with other old friends the Merseybeats and Mike McCartney. Tony brought his band, the Vibrations, with him for the November gig.

In July 1993, we had a great tour of the USA – New York, Indiana, Kentucky and Detroit – with good attendances at all the venues. Gerry & The Pacemakers, Billy J. Kramer, and the Manfreds with Paul Jones shared the bill, and we closed each show. There was also a Beatles tribute band from the USA who were not so good. Our two shows in Louisville, Kentucky were each attended by more than 1,500 people. We did sixteen songs in our set, starting with 'Have You Ever Loved Somebody' and finishing with 'Don't Bring Me Down'.

We celebrated the 30th anniversary of the Searchers' first big hits and my 30 years in the music business in some style in with a gig at the Commodore International, Nottingham in March 1994. It seemed appropriate to choose a venue in Nottingham rather than Liverpool, as Chris Black, Steve Carlisle and Tony Sherwood were closely associated with the city.

We arrived back from a gig in the United Arab Emirates on the morning of the show and were all pretty tired after the flight. May and our daughter Steph had driven over to Nottingham that afternoon, and along with our two sons Mike and Nathe, who were the road-managing for me. We all had a night to remember. Tony was promoting the show and was delighted to tell me it was a sell-out, with many members of our fan club in the audience.

The Piggies kicked off the proceedings with their brilliant impersonations of '60s bands including the Beatles and the Rolling Stones. The popular local group Sons and Lovers followed, giving their first performance since a reunion seven years previously. Chris Black enjoyed the evening as much as anyone, playing keyboards again with his former band. They included some Beach Boys and Drifters material and an excellent Four Seasons medley.

We got a rapturous welcome and it was a highly emotional night for me and the band. Mike and Nathe made sure the sound was good, even great. Chris, Steve and Baz were brilliant that night, even though we were all tired after our excursion overseas. I joked with the audience that my guitar had been damaged on an airport conveyor belt and now only had 10 strings. There were lots of jokes, quips and repartee from Chris and me that night, and, as a special tribute to my wife May, I sang 'Wind Beneath My Wings', knowing she would in the audience with our daughter, Stephanie. I also paid tribute to my two sons, Mike Junior and Nathan.

And there was a big surprise for me at the end: Tony introduced the guest of honour, Kenneth Earle – President of the Agents' Association and head of LSA, the company which organised '60s festivals at Butlins. He presented me with a silver galley tray and a set of brandy glasses, which I promised to put to good use. Beautiful bouquets of flowers were presented to May and to our fan club secretary, Gill Westwood. Copious quantities of champagne were delivered to the stage and a toast was drunk to 'Mike's 30 outstanding years'.

There was still time for us to do 'Needles And Pins' and ELO's 'Don't Bring Me Down', and finish with Bryan Adams' 'Summer Of '69'. The quote of the night came from Tony Sherwood, who, when asked why the show wasn't held in Liverpool, replied, 'There isn't anywhere in Liverpool as good as the Commodore... I'm a Nottingham boy and I'm proud to show Nottingham what I've got.' It was a truly great night, which I will never forget.

In 1994, we were honoured to be the first '60s band to be invited to play on the *QE2*, as part of the world-famous liner's 25th anniversary cruise celebrations. However, our travelling arrangements didn't quite go to plan on what I saw as the gig of a lifetime. Cunard spared no expense in flying us out to join the ship in Barcelona, where we unfortunately arrived late, due to a Spanish air traffic controllers' strike.

We were whisked from the airport to the port, but, horror of horrors, we arrived to see the ship sailing out of the harbour. I was given a radio phone and took a call from Brian Price, the cruise director on the ship. He told me there were two choices: he could have the ship stopped and have us taken out on a pilot boat, or we could meet the ship the next day in Gibraltar.

The pilot boat was clearly the best option. We scrambled onto the small craft with all our luggage and gear, and set out after the huge liner. As we came alongside, a small hatch opened just above the waterline and several crew members appeared to help us get on board. Not a romantic arrival (seeing as May was with me), but certainly an exciting one.

Later that night, seated at the Captain's table, our experience made for some amusing conversation. The Captain told us he always had the last word in these matters, and when he said the *QE2* was to set sail, it set sail. The ship waited for no one. I totally agreed with him. After three days and nights of being wined and dined almost to the point of being pampered, May remarked that it was 'just like a second honeymoon' – which was an ironic comment, given that we never had a first one.

We did two performances for the gala events on the Saturday night. Even after many years of playing in some marvellous settings, I have to admit I was a little nervous before going onstage. The audience for the first show were a bit reserved – remember, we were probably the first '60s group many of them had ever seen. However, everything went well and we thoroughly enjoyed ourselves. It was all over too soon and, after arriving in Southampton the next morning, we were suddenly thrust back into the real world.

In early 1995, we escaped from our winter weather at

home for a six-week tour of Australia in the company of the Manfreds, Gerry & The Pacemakers, Brian Poole & Electrix, Billy J. Kramer and Herman's Hermits. This was a very prestigious tour, and we were delighted to get standing ovations and excellent reviews for our performances. The Aussies wanted an authentic '60s tour and that's what they got. It was a great throwback to the '60s: TV and radio coverage, sell-out shows at national stadia, reviews in the morning papers, fabulous hotels and big money. And it was all thanks to UK promoter Derek Franks.

The egos were out in force on that tour – which was good, as I felt we more than held our own, coming out on top for most of the shows. I felt MPS were now at the zenith of our performances and sounding as good, if not better, than the original Searchers. Steve Carlisle was excellent – he had everything – great drummer, great voice, and great attitude. Steve was a lovely guy, as were Chris Black and Baz Cowell. Just before the start of the tour, Steve got the tragic news from home that his mother had died. When I told him I had been in a similar situation some years before after receiving news of my father's passing, he showed great courage and decided the show had to go on.

Considering Chris, Steve and Baz, were all great musicians in their own right, we all got on very well, and I let them have a free rein – up to a point. I say that, because I was never going to let myself get into the same position I found myself in previously with Curtis, Jackson and McNally. My new bandmates knew they had to toe the line. They knew that, up to a point, I would direct and they would follow. Although I would treat them as equals, they accepted that, in reality, they were my backing band. This approach worked for a long time, and over the years I can only think of a few times when I had to slap someone's wrist to put things right.

The tour, which ran from 7 February to 4 March, was as good as any I had ever been involved in, including the golden years of the '60s. One indication of just how successful that tour became, was when promoter/entrepreneur John Whale informed us that Cliff Richard had been the year before with his *Hit List*

Tour and ours was actually 'putting more bums on seats', as they say. The excellent and efficient organisation of the venues, hotels and flights made one feel like a pop star again. Inevitably, we had some long flights and even longer coach journeys to contend with, but on the plus side we did get some photos of kangaroos and emus. Many of the bigger venues held up to 20,000 people and were all sold out.

We got great reviews in the Sydney newspapers after the show at the Entertainment Centre on 17 February in front of a near-capacity audience. One journalist described us as 'far and away the best group on the bill'. He added that the Searchers' original sound and 'superb harmonies' were still in evidence, 'a sublime mix of Buddy Holly and the Everly Brothers'. Unfortunately, he spoiled things a bit by stating that we 'delivered a great version of the Beatles' "Don't Let Me Down" as an encore'. It was, of course, ELO's 'Don't *Bring* Me Down'.

Many TV appearances and press interviews were involved for all the performers, with all the usual hype, coupled with the still-enormous egos of some artistes. In some ways, that was a good thing because it kept everyone on their toes. But not everyone put 'Mr Ego' back in the cupboard after the performances. With half a dozen million-selling groups and solo artistes on the tour things were always going to get heated, although generally we all got on well – that is until 'The Poison Pen' came on the scene.

After the first week of the tour, when everyone had settled in and got to know each other again, a curious thing started to happen. On arriving at a gig in the late afternoon, some of the acts would find a sheet of writing paper pinned to their dressing room door, or in the room itself. Most of the messages were tongue-in-cheek and not offensive, but as the tour gathered momentum, some of them became unfunny and it became apparent that someone had an axe to grind. The situation soon became the main topic of conversation.

After the Sydney Stadium gig, the Poison Pen really got to work, especially after some unfavourable newspaper reviews the following morning. In my view, the reviewer had gone over the

A S THE near capacity audience left the Entertainment Centre after 3½ hours of pretty much non-stop hits from the Sixties, the patrons were handed a questionnaire which asked: Did you like the show tonight? Which was your favourite act? It then listed the six main acts, seeking a tick of approval and asking at the end "Would you like to see it again next year"?

In the spirit of co-operation the following is my response:

Billy J. Kramer — True Dud. A middle-aged man in white suit who opens his set with *I'm A Believer* (never a hit for old Billy J.), whips through very ordinary versions of his hits *Do You Want to Know A Secret?, Trains and Boats and Planes, Bad to Me* and *Little Children* (which he just couldn't get his voice around) and has to flesh out his performance with nondescript versions of *Runaround Sue* and *Glad All Over*. Should stick to the club circuit and be grateful.

Herman's Hermits — does a band have the right to exist when Peter Noone, forever thought of as the "Herman" in the group, is not on lead vocals and the only original member is the drummer, Barry Whitwam? Let's just call them a down-the-line covers band who, in 25 minutes, offered a set consisting of seven songs including *No Milk Today, Mrs Brown You've Got a Lovely Daughter* and, as a huge singalong finale, *I'm Henry VIII, I Am.* Let them play support for The Beatnix at the local pub.

Manfred Mann — well, actually, most of the original Manfred Mann sans Manfred Lubowitz, who started the outfit. Clearly the most talented bunch of musicians on the night, they were the only band to use a saxophone and harmonica and to even hint at the fact that the concept of "The Best of British" without a few R&B bands was pretty silly. Amazingly Paul Jones and Mike d'Abo, the group's two early lead singers,

POP

BY BRUCE ELDER

The Best of British, Entertainment Centre, February 17

were both in fine voice and the material, which included Bob Dylan's *The Mighty Quinn* and a hugely extended version of Bo Diddley's *Do Wah Diddy Diddy* exposed the thinness of most of the other group's material.

The Searchers — far and away the best pop group on the bill. Mike Pender was the only original member but the group's original sound (a sublime mix of Buddy Holly and the Everly Brothers) was still in evidence as they worked their way through the superb harmonies of *Needles and Pins, Sweets for my Sweet, Don't Throw Your Love Away, Sugar and Spice* and *When You Walk In The Room*.

They delivered a great version of The Beatles *Don't Let Me Down* as an encore.

Gerry and the Pacemakers — True Dud. Should be renamed Gerry Needs A Pacemaker. A very ordinary club/cabaret act, culminating in a truly woeful version of *You'll Never Walk Alone.* Send him back to Liverpool to play in the local pub.

The success of a night like this (and it was truly successful) lies in the audience's commitment and preparedness to participate. There was nothing very special occurring on stage but the songs were all familiar, the impulse to clap and sing along was overwhelming, and everyone seemed to have left their inhibitions at the door.

The frightening thing was that the baby-boom generation were re-enacting what their parents used to do. The only difference was that they weren't standing around a piano singing *Bicycle Built for Two*. Will this generation do the same in 30 years' time? And what will they sing?

170

top in his newspaper column, but the damage was done and a few people were embarrassed. However, it also provided plenty of ammunition for the Poison Pen.

As the tour wound down, so too did the notes left on dressing room doors. We never did find the culprit, although fingers were pointed at Herman's Hermits.

Promoter John Whale was at that time the Roman Abramovich of big-time tours in Ausralia. Although it must have been an expensive tour to put on, he probably came out of it with a large profit. This was MPS' third tour of Australia.

Derek Franks was now planning a tour of South Africa, which we duly played along with the Merseybeats and the Swinging Blue Jeans. In later years, Derek put together the *ReelinandaRockin* and *Oh Boy!* tours. He was a big MPS fan and put a lot of work our way. Derek recommended me to ITV, to appear on the *Brian Conley Show*. Brian himself had the last say on who would appear on his show – and chose Gerry Marsden and yours truly. Later on, he told me he had always been a Searchers fan and one of his all-time favourite songs was 'When You Walk In The Room', which I performed on the show.

In late 1994, Anne Askey took over from Gill Westwood as MPS' fan club secretary, assisted by her husband, Roger. One of their first actions was to publish the first issue of *MPS News*, the official magazine of the MPS fan club. Four issues a year were planned, on a subscription basis. They also produced some great T-shirts to promote MPS. Roger and Anne lived in Halifax and had been avid fans of MPS – and the original Searchers – for many years, going to as many gigs as possible in the North and Midlands. Roger even confessed that I, as a Searcher in the '60s, had been his teenage idol.

We had another memorable reunion with Tony Jackson at Birmingham Town Hall in 1995, where MPS topped a bill which also included the Merseybeats, the Four Pennies, Love Affair, Chip Hawkes, and Twinkle – quite a line-up. Tony joined us for the last few numbers of our set, including 'Sweets For My Sweet', 'Sugar And Spice', 'Farmer John' and 'Needles And Pins'. You can imagine the reaction of the packed audience!

In March 1996, we celebrated the first ten years of MPS. Our celebration gig took place on 26 April at the Victoria Theatre in Halifax, with support from Herman's Hermits. Roger and Anne Askey organised a huge cake in the shape of a 12-string guitar, which was presented to us on stage. It was a real work of art which looked far too good to eat.

We then did a summer season with the great Joe Brown and his Bruvvers at seaside resorts up and down the UK including Bournemouth, Worthing, Skegness, Hastings, Southport, Torquay and Ilfracombe. Joe included Don Gibson's 'Sea Of Heartbreak' in his set, a song I'd recorded with the Searchers as an album track in the '60s.

In October we went off to Dubai to rough it in a five-star hotel with Marmalade, Dave Dee, the Foundations, the Swinging Blue Jeans and Chip Hawkes. Our *Sounds of the Sixties* show played at the Dubai Country Club, a seriously posh venue.

Also that autumn, we released a new 18-track album on cassette and CD. This contained the 15 tracks we had recorded back in 1989 and 1990, plus my versions of 'It's Over' (from the 1986 Sierra single) and 'Falling Apart At The Seams (which I'd recorded with Billy Kinsley's group, Class of '64, back in 1989), and a fantastic new song called 'Two Hearts'. As with our 1989 cassette, the album was simply called *Mike Pender's Searchers* and was sold through the MPS fan club and at gigs.

Not long after it came out, Chris Black emigrated to Brisbane, Australia, to marry a young lady he had met on a previous MPS tour of that country. His last appearance with MPS was a charity gig for Guide Dogs for the Blind at the Llay British Legion Club in Wrexham on Saturday, 5 October. Just before the gig, the agent involved disappeared with half of our fee, but I decided to go ahead anyway as a gesture of goodwill, as the event was for charity.

Chris was giving up his career to care for his wife-to-be, who we heard was suffering from cancer. Everyone sent them their warmest good wishes. In a letter printed in *MPS News*, he expressed his heartfelt thanks to everyone. I can't comment on the outcome, as I don't know the details, but I heard she took him to the cleaners. Poor Chris ended up with no wife and no house. I did warn him to be careful before he decided to leave.

Paul Jackson, an excellent guitarist formerly with Brian Poole & Electrix, joined MPS to take Chris's place. Paul fitted into the band very well and very quickly, his guitar-playing blending in very effectively with mine. I did miss the humorous verbal sparring with Chris onstage, but that had been totally unique. Born in Nottingham in 1962, Paul had played in various bands and had also done some acting work as an extra on some television shows, including *Crossroads* and *Howard's Way*. He later joined Brian Poole & Electrix, which was when I first met him.

On a sadder note, our one-time vocalist with the Searchers in our early, pre-fame days, Johnny Sandon, tragically took his own life on Christmas Day, 1996. He had in recent times been working as a taxi driver in Liverpool and was suffering from depression. John McNally and I, plus many other Mersey beat musicians, attended his funeral. I didn't actually see McNally that day – not that I wanted to – but I heard later that he was there. May and I paid our respects to Johnny's family and of course Johnny's memory. We still think about him today and, along with Tony and Chris, he is always in May's prayers.

1997 came rushing in, and after the usual glut of one-nighters we looked forward to the annual *Beatles Festival* in Liverpool at the end of August, when, on a temporary stage in North John Street, we rocked the boat to at least 5,000 people. It was estimated that more than 100,000 went to Liverpool that day. A local band called Up and Running were on before us and did a great job. Our set was very well received by the large crowd and they joined in with all the old favourites.

We packed our bags again in February 1998, to accompany the Merseybeats and the Swinging Blue Jeans on a tour of South Africa. We were all contracted to perform at venues in and around the Pretoria and Johannesburg areas with a bill made up of local expat performers, all of whom were originally from Liverpool and Rochdale. The gigs went well and we all enjoyed ourselves, often having a sing-song at the hotel after the shows, with the piano in the bar well-played by Les Braid of the Swinging Blue Jeans, and comedy provided by his bandmate Colin Manley and Allan Cosgrove of the Merseybeats.

We did have a few problems with the weather conditions. At one open-air performance near Pretoria, the Swinging Blue Jeans were hit by a torrential rain storm (apparently quite a regular occurrence in that part of the world), but carried on regardless without missing a note. The temperature onstage for us at our last open-air gig was well over 100 degrees Fahrenheit. At one point, I thought Steve Carlisle was going to faint from heat exhaustion.

That summer, Tony Sherwood announced he was going to retire from the agency business with effect from 1 July 1998. He had decided to go into consultancy work involving '60s music. This, of course, was not the end of the story, and Tony was to return to us in the fullness of time. I knew he would.

While touring with Joe Brown in April 1998, we dropped in a few new songs with 'Needles And Pins' as the encore: 'Tulsa Time', 'Sweets For My Sweet', 'Sugar And Spice', 'Hearts In Her Eyes', 'Don't Throw Your Love Away', 'To Love Somebody', 'City To City', 'Love Potion No. 9', 'Goodbye My Love', 'When You Walk In The Room', 'Heartbeat', 'Oh Boy!', and 'That'll Be The Day', which Joe remarked was in too high a key.

In addition to shows throughout the summer with Joe Brown & The Bruvvers, we also appeared at Scarborough's Futurist Theatre with Mike Berry & The Outlaws on Wednesdays from mid-July through to the beginning of September. We played many of the major resorts with both line-ups.

The original, classic Searchers line-up was featured in the BBC2 television series, *Rock Family Trees*, compiled by Pete Frame, following on from his well-known publications. I was delighted to be selected by the BBC as the representative of the '60s Searchers. The programme covered Mersey beat in general and also included interviews with Gerry Marsden and Billy J. Kramer. The Beatles also got a mention.

In April, May and June 1999, we were on the *Sixties Gold*

tour with Gerry & The Pacemakers, the Fortunes and the Merseybeats. The tour's 38-date itinerary covered most areas of the UK, but halfway through Paul Jackson left the group to concentrate on his work as a guitar tutor and Kevin Healey joined us. Kevin had also been with Brian Poole & Electrix and, most recently, in a Status Quo tribute band. The tour was a great success – up to a point.

I was not happy with a lot of things. Although it was Derek Franks who booked the acts, it was actually Mark Howes and my former manager Robert Pratt who put on the tour. From experience, I know for sure that, if you tour or do any show with Gerry Marsden, he will more than likely want to be top of the bill. That's because he will probably have it written into his contract that he must top the bill. Or else his manager – who at that time was Derek Franks – will make sure he will. So, I knew before the tour started that I wouldn't be topping on this tour, but I did expect to be second on the bill. As it happened, we were bottom! Does it matter?

The Beat Goes On magazine sponsored a major gig – the *Millennium Festival of the '60s* – at the Brighton Centre on 21 and 22 August 1999, to celebrate the new Millennium. MPS were invited to appear alongside many great bands and artists of the era including the Tremeloes, the Fortunes, Dave Berry & The Cruisers, Marmalade, the Merseybeats, the Tornados, the Nashville Teens, Freddie & The Dreamers, Jet Harris, the Four Pennies, Brian Poole, Cliff Bennett & The Rebel Rousers, and Dave Dee. Apologies if I've left anyone out.

The winter issue of *MPS News* announced the very welcome news that Tony Sherwood was back, returning as MPS' sole representation after a well-earned 18-month break. Tony had stage-managed the Brighton Centre show, which was a great success...except nobody got paid.

The Beat Goes On (no connection to *The Beat*) was a monthly magazine, and, like today's *The Beat* mag, was for lovers of '60s music. Edited and run by Mike and Christine Bones, it was probably the best mag of its kind at the time. Mike and Christine were lovely people and I met them both many times.

When the idea for the *Millennium Festival* came up, they both agreed to sponsor and publicise the event, and even helped to sell tickets, which went on sale well in advance. As they were the sponsors, most of the tickets were sold through their magazine – probably 75% of the gross, which they held in their account. The remaining 25% was taken at the Brighton Centre box office. After the event, nothing more was heard from Mike and Christine. They suddenly disappeared, as did the 75% ticket proceeds. All the acts who appeared on the show – including MPS –were notified of the situation and were told they wouldn't get paid for appearing. As it happened, MPS did eventually get a share of the box office receipts.

We jetted off to the States in July to perform on the *British Invasion 2000* show, which was to be recorded live for broadcast in December. The venue was the Foxwoods Resort and Casino in Connecticut, the largest such complex in the USA. After being picked up at JFK, we were treated to a 'rock star' ride in a stretch limo with all the trimmings, TV and refreshments. When we arrived at Foxwoods, we were greeted by almost everyone who was on the show: Billy J. Kramer, the Troggs, Gerry & The Pacemakers, Eric Burdon & The New Animals, Herman's Hermits featuring Peter Noone, Clem Curtis & The Foundations, Freddie & The Dreamers and Wayne Fontana & The Mindbenders.

We all had to rehearse for sound-checking reasons, but also to allow the television crews to run through what they needed to do. Our practice went well and we felt comfortable. The performance itself, in front of a large audience, was very successful. Incredibly, each band was given only a 30-minute slot – which is really nothing when you've flown so far to be there – but the experience and the audience made it all worthwhile. The filming took up three nights of live performances at the Fox Theatre. The television broadcast was called *The British Invasion Returns*. They love all the hype in America: a 'reminder of bygone days' more than 200 years ago when the British fought America for that continent. Every tour I can remember being on over there always has a similar title.

On 15 September 2000, we travelled down to the Sussex coast to give the first performance of our new show, *The Two Sides of Mike Pender*, at the Shoreham-by-Sea Community Centre. We opened with 'He Thinks He'll Keep Her', with our harmonies working well. I explained to the near-capacity audience that we were going to do different songs for the first set and then play as many hits as possible in the second set. I then changed from my 12-string to acoustic for 'Big River', with its Eagles-type vocals. We then did another new song about the nineteenth-century potato famine in Ireland, 'The Fields Of Athenry'. I had some good-natured banter with some of the audience who were impatient to hear the hits. I talked about the privilege of working with Roy Orbison many times, and as a tribute we did 'You Got It' followed by 'Running Scared', with me still managing, after all those years, to reach that final, dramatic high note! The crowd sang along with the Bee Gees' 'To Love Somebody' and Dobie Gray's 'Free My Soul', which closed the first half.

What we had thought would be a 35-minute set, had stretched to an excellent 45 minutes. For the first half, I had worn a black-and-silver patterned shirt and trousers, changing for the second half into my '60s-style high-collared suit, with white shirt and black tie. 'When You Walk In The Room' got everyone going, followed by 'Sugar And Spice' and 'Don't Throw Your Love Away'. I talked a bit about how I took over on lead vocals from Tony Jackson, and how the Searchers had achieved their unique sound with my 12-string Rickenbacker.

Steve then did his usual great job on 'City To City', then launched into 'What Have They Done To The Rain' and 'Love Potion No. 9', followed by 'Hearts In Her Eyes' and 'Goodbye My Love'. I told the story about going to see Buddy Holly and the Crickets in Liverpool in 1958, after which I did a medley of 'Peggy Sue', 'Heartbeat', 'Oh Boy!' and 'That'll Be The Day' – all with excellent audience participation.

'Needles and Pins' followed 'Take Me For What I'm Worth', and then a requested reprise of 'When You Walk In The Room'. We finished off with 'Rockin' All Over The World' with

Kevin on lead vocal, plus an encore of Ronan Keating's 'When You Say Nothing At All'. I was very happy with what had been a really good two-hour show with a great, friendly audience.

At the end of 2000, Sanctuary/Castle released the Searchers' *Swedish Radio Sessions* CD, which features my vocals and lead guitar on all 25 tracks.

In 2001, we played at the Winter Gardens, Blackpool for a charity supported by the very popular Irish singer, Daniel O'Donnell: the Romanian Orphans. The huge audience was treated to about an hour and a half of Daniel singing with acoustic backing, then he made a speech, and we came onstage to join him the audience responded really well to the music and sang along and danced.

Daniel started a conga to 'When You Walk In the Room', stopping for photographs at every opportunity Before the show, Danny (as I called him) was in chat mode, telling me he'd always been a fan and his favourite Searchers song was that one – so I suggested he come on stage and sing it with me, which he did. His fans and everyone just loved it.

On 29 August 2001, Steve and Kevin were involved in a car accident on their way to a gig in Bournemouth. Fortunately they only suffered minor injuries, though Kevin's car was written off. Steve was taken to hospital, while Kevin recovered from shock at home. Though they both quickly returned to performing, they did have to miss a couple of gigs, so I drafted in Mike Junior to play drums and Brian Wood from Dave Berry's Cruisers on guitar.

My son Mike did a great job standing in for Steve – to the amazement of the audience, and probably Mike himself. This was only the third time he had performed live onstage since 1988, though he had been in five or six bands in and around Liverpool since the early 1980s. One of the first – the Bushfinders – nearly found fame when they were asked to do a demo for a Hofmeister beer advert. Sadly, that didn't work out for them and they carried on working the clubs and pubs. Mike was also in a band called Red, who wrote their own material and were very popular locally. He then joined Waterfront, but left them in 1988 to become MPS' sound engineer. He was ably assisted in those early days at the sound desk by his glamorous assistant, Eve, who happened to be Anne and Roger Askey's daughter.

In January 2002, we were given the tragic news that our fan club secretary, Anne Askey, had passed away after a long battle with cancer. Anne had worked very hard for eight years with her husband, Roger, running the fan club and producing and publishing *MPS News*. Everyone involved with MPS paid tribute to her. Roger agreed to carry on her outstanding work as secretary, and editor of *MPS News*, and I am delighted to say he is still our fan club secretary today.

Later that year, the *Searchers At The Star-Club* CD was released in Germany by the Bear Family record label, to coincide with the Star-Club's 40th anniversary. The CD featured all 19 tracks that we recorded in Hamburg for Philips in March 1963, before signing with Pye.

The death in August 2003 of my old friend and bandmate Tony Jackson was a shock. I knew he had been in very poor health, but didn't expect him to go quite so soon. I will always remember 'Tone' as I used to call him. Another of my original Searchers bandmates, Chris Curtis, died on 28 February 2005. I have devoted a later chapter to a tribute to both Tony and Chris.

CHAPTER 24

Keeping It in the Family

I was very sad to hear of the passing of two more greats from the '60s – Gene Pitney and Freddie Garrity.

When my drummer, Steve Carlisle, retired from MPS in 2003, he had come to a point, having moved to deepest Lincolnshire, where he realised he had become tired of all the travelling. He had other professional commitments closer to home and decided to concentrate on those. I then did some performances as MPS with Kevin Healey on guitar and the drummer and bass player from Electrix. However, this arrangement didn't work, and I quickly enlisted Mike Junior on drums and brought Baz back on bass. My son Mike had already stepped in previously on drums after Steve had the car accident back in August 2001.

2003 had been a very busy period during which I had made a record number of stage appearances. I couldn't remember being so busy since the '60s. Towards the end of the year, I stepped in to take Gerry Marsden's place on a national tour with the Troggs, Herman's Hermits, the Ivy League and P.J. Proby after Gerry was taken ill. The tour management gave me a 25-minute slot and decided there was no need for MPS to back me. Cost obviously came into this decision, but it was a bad decision from my point of view, for, although the backing band were all accomplished musicians in their own right, they were not right for me and I paid the price with poor reviews. The band consisted of Eric Wright on keyboards, Garth Watt-Roy on bass, Martin Wild on drums and guitarist Tim Rose – all great musos for *ReelinandaRockin*, but definitely not for MPS.

I had a business to run and sometimes commercial decisions have to be taken that don't – and can't – please everyone. The number of '60s shows had reduced and the costs associated in staging a single performance had become respectively more expensive. I needed to explore every avenue for potential work: the very nature of the business is to go on stage and get a 'buzz'.

I was continuing my performances with MPS, such as the show at the Adelphi Hotel, Liverpool on August Bank Holiday, as part of the annual *Beatles Convention*. I was very keen to reinstate the old MPS line-up, with Barrie Cowell on bass and Mike Junior on drums, but I needed to find a suitable guitarist/vocalist. Mike Junior is a very capable drummer, but I sometimes needed him on the sound desk too. In September, we had an MPS gig when Kevin was unavailable, so I needed to find a stand-in – which wasn't easy. Pete Brill, who had played with many top performers including Eric Clapton and P.J. Proby came in at short notice.

The great sadness of losing Tony Jackson in the summer was contrasted when May and I celebrated our 40th wedding anniversary in December. I was taken ill just before Christmas and was rushed into hospital with appendicitis. Fortunately, I was operated on immediately and I didn't miss my Christmas dinner at home! I was also fit and well for the MPS New Year's Eve show at Manchester's Piccadilly Hotel with Barrie, Mike Junior and new guitarist Garth Watt-Roy.

It turned out to be a great debut welcome to the band for Garth, although not all gigs end with parties like this one. The family also joined us for this well-attended gig, which featured comedian Stu Francis. Garth, who had previously been with Brian Poole's Electrix, rehearsed an updated set with us, which included 'Hold Me' and 'Games People Play'. Very regrettably, he left the band in the summer of 2004 to join Gerry Marsden's Pacemakers. It was a big loss, and I really missed his harmony vocal and superb guitar-playing. It was an ideal arrangement. Garth had also been on the *ReelinandaRockin* tours as bass player with the Big Beat Band. Fortunately, Kevin Healey and Pete Brill were both on call to help out at the limited number of MPS gigs for the rest of the year.

Live at the Marquee is an annual event held at Stockport Rugby Club. On 18 June, MPS headlined the 2005 event, which was attended by over 1,500 people. Kevin Healey was back with us for this gig. Also on the bill for that great night of entertainment were the Animals and the Fortunes. At £15 for a ticket, including a free barbecue meal, that had to be great value for anyone – though it did get a bit hot inside the marquee!

I knew that I would have to find another guitarist sooner or later – not that I wanted to, but Kevin was becoming unreliable. Very unreliable. I was delighted to appoint Keith Roberts as his permanent replacement. Keith had formerly been the bass player and vocalist for Herman's Hermits and is an accomplished guitarist, bass player and singer. He fitted into the band very well, and our harmonies were now seriously good and tight.

Another show which proved very popular was *'60s Night Out*, which toured in September and October 2006 with MPS and Dave Berry & The Cruisers. We covered a lot of venues from the north to the south of the UK, including two piers and a church.

The 'church' was Huntingdon Hall in Worcester, which has a pulpit on the stage and pews for the audience. After Dave Berry and his band had rocked through his hits from the '60s, we played a lot of Searchers hits and B-sides, plus other classics like P.J. Proby's 'Hold Me' and Roy Orbison's 'You Got It', closing with 'Games People Play'. I had a bit of fun earlier in the show, when I introduced former Hermit Keith Roberts, who started singing 'I'm Into Something Good', at which point I pretended to walk off the stage – which got a lot of laughs.

The idea for the show was put together by my good friend of more than forty years, Mr Brian Yeats, who, with the help of son Ashley, has toured the show now for almost ten years. Dave Berry and I did the very first tour backed by the Dakotas, since when I have done it three or four times with Dave and Tony Crane.

2006 saw the passing of two more greats of the '60s – Gene Pitney on 5 April and Freddie Garrity on 19 May. I first met

Gene back in the '60s at a party given by our manager, Tito Burns, at his house in London. Lots of well-known people were there, and I particularly remember meeting Bobby Vee and Roger Moore. Gene was a typical outgoing American and a considerable talent. He was writing songs even then, and also played the piano that night at Tito's. We were at No. 1 in the charts at the time, but I realised, listening to Gene play and sing, just how good you have to be to be called a superstar. He certainly was a superstar.

As for dear Freddie, I first met him on a *Thank Your Lucky Stars* show. I will always remember how chirpy he was, bouncing around everywhere like a little gnome – not at all the usual pop star. Freddie made people laugh, especially the children, but he had been seriously ill for several years prior to his death in May 2006. In February 2007, we played at a gig at the Willows in Salford – Freddie's home area – to celebrate his life and to raise money for his family. Many other '60s bands and artistes took part and everyone did the show for free.

In early June, we played at the ever-popular *Whitby Festival of the '60s* with our old friends the Fourmost, the Ivy League, the Dreamers and Herman's Hermits. Also featured that weekend were some good Buddy Holly, Shadows and Everly Brothers tribute bands.

On 15 December, we got the sad news that Margaret Brown, MPS' first fan club secretary from 1986, had died at the relatively young age of 63. She had worked very hard to establish the fan club and remained a dedicated fan for all of her life. She had written out the programme for her funeral, which included playing my rendering of 'Solitaire'.

In 2008, I was invited to appear at the *Number One Project Show* – a major national event scheduled to take place at the new Liverpool Echo Arena on 19 January. It was organised by the *Liverpool Echo* to mark the city's year as *European Capital of Culture 2008* with a celebration of the 56 No. 1 hits recorded by Liverpool artistes since the record charts began in 1953. The hits were performed on the night by the original artistes, wherever possible. All the money raised from the event went to charity.

Two more well-known '60s stars also passed on around

that time: Rod Allen of the Fortunes on 11 January, and Mike Smith from the Dave Clark Five on 28 February.

On 3 April 2008, MPS headlined the gig to celebrate the reopening of a famous '60s music venue: the Tower Ballroom in Edgbaston, Birmingham. The venue had been saved from demolition by a local businessman after lying derelict for several years. The Merseybeats and the Cuff-Links were also on the bill to entertain an audience of more than 1,000 revellers, who all enjoyed the complimentary champagne. Tony Crane of the Merseybeats remembered playing there in 1963, because the place had such an incredible atmosphere. It also had a famous revolving stage, which was back in action on the night.

In the summer, I was awarded a silver disc by Universal Music for sales of *The Very Best of the Searchers*, a compilation CD which had reached the Top 20 albums chart in the UK. It was probably the best collection of '60s and '70s Searchers material to date, as it included the songs that should have made the charts but didn't! Songs like 'Solitaire' (Andy Williams' version got the radio plays, so he had the big hit), 'I Don't Want To Be The One' and 'Hearts In Her Eyes'.

Comedian Jim Bowen of *Bullseye* fame presented the disc to me at the Vine Bar in Eccleston, Lancashire, a small but famous music venue in the '60s and '70s owned by Ian Boasman. Among the invited guests were Tony Sherwood and cattle breeder Bill Fidler, who turned out to be a cousin of Joe Walsh of the Eagles! I returned the favour to Jim later that month, when MPS appeared at a special show organised by him at the Hornby Institute, near his home in the Lake District.

The following March, MPS played to an enthusiastic capacity crowd in Holland, where we met up with the great Searchers fan Bert Bossink, who manages a fantastic website and also publishes a music magazine called *The Fabulous Sound of the Sixties*. He had produced a 78-page issue entirely dedicated to the Searchers – a fascinating, comprehensive collection of material, which he sent to our fan club secretary, Roger Askey, at *MPS News*. I first met Bert after a Searchers gig in Maastricht in December 1979.

In September 2009, MPS were back for three days for the ever-popular *Whitby Festival of the '60s* on a very impressive bill including Love Affair, the Fortunes, Jet Harris, the Mindbenders, Union Gap and Billie Davis. There was also, as always, a great line-up of excellent tribute bands.

This year was extra-special for MPS – well, almost (only joking): a reunion with Chris Black. I didn't waste much time before inviting Chris join us on stage. We made sure his guitar was unplugged – just like old times – but there were a few of his fans in the packed audience, so he got a great welcome.

Dave Dee, a guy I had first got to know really well when we both did *ReelinandaRockin*, died on 16 January 2009 at the age of 65, after a long and courageous fight against cancer. In later years, he had been appointed a magistrate, and was still playing gigs with former band members Dozy, Beaky, Mick and Tich until just a few weeks before he died. Dave has been added to the prayers list.

Having met me at the *Solid Silver '60s Show* in Hull in March 2010, local MP Greg Knight also came to the MPS gig at the *Withernsea Festival* in August. He invited May and me to visit the Palace of Westminster for a tour. The former Home Secretary, Alan Johnson MP, is apparently also a Searchers fan. I read somewhere that he had been in a band in his youth. Greg is a member of the All Party Parliamentary Group at Westminster. It exists to provide a discussion forum between the music industry and parliamentarians. They bring together Lords and MPs from across the political divide and act as a point of dialogue amongst decision makers on issues of concern (think I'll give it a miss).

After a hectic but very successful *Solid Silver '60s* UK tour in the first half of 2010, we had some great gigs lined up for MPS in July, August, September and December in Germany, Belgium and Holland. In August, we played at two festivals – one in Belgium and the other in Germany, on consecutive days. Now, you would think that the two agents who booked these – and who were in touch with each other – would have organised travel to minimise time and exhaustion, but no. We had to fly back from Belgium to Heathrow, and then straight back out again to

Germany!

We were in really good company at those gigs. In Hildesheim on 4 December, we were joined by Smokie, Spencer Davis, the Animals, Herman's Hermits, Sailor and Dozy, Beaky, Mick & Tich. On 8 December in Bremen, Bill Hurd's Rubettes were on the bill with us, as well as Sailor and DBM&T again.

At our gig at the Locomotion Club in Zoetermeer on 19 November, we met up with many of our devoted fans in Holland, including Bert Bossink and his wife and friends. We included 'Take It Or Leave It', which Bert told me was the Searchers' biggest hit in Holland. A great Searchers and MPS devotee, Bert runs a very active '60s music website and magazine, and does a great job promoting Searchers and MPS music to radio and TV stations in Holland.

I also managed to fit in two P&O cruises in November and December: the Virgin Islands to Madeira on the *Aurora*, and Valencia to Southampton on the *Artemis*. Keith Roberts accompanied me on guitar and vocals and acted as my musical director.

In January 2011, the Nottingham newspapers reported in that former MPS member Chris Black was facing devastating floods at his home outside Brisbane. He and his neighbours had been warned that the flood water could reach as high as 22 metres, and, although their houses were built on stilts, thousands of people were being evacuated. Thankfully, Chris managed to get through the crisis without serious problems. (Thank you Tony Sherwood.)

The following March, we were back at Butlins, Skegness for a '60s weekender sponsored by *Yours* magazine. Various events were on offer including live shows by Buddy Holly, Everly Brothers and other tribute acts, as well as original bands. The acts were split between two theatres, with shows going on simultaneously. We appeared at the Reds' theatre, named after the hard-working Butlins redcoats. It reminded me of a very plush working men's club – an excellent venue, seating about 200 people.

Irish veterans the Bachelors went on before us. We kept

the packed audience waiting for about 30 minutes because our sound system hadn't arrived and in the end we had to use the house PA. After that hitch, the gig itself went really well. We included 'Ain't Gonna Kiss Ya', 'Hearts In Her Eyes' and 'Hold Me'. I heard some compliments after the show about Mike Junior's drumming, and how he had followed the original drum patterns played by Chris Curtis on the original Searchers recordings.

I had a really busy day on 17 September 2011: I stood in at the last minute for an indisposed Dave Berry to perform with the Dakotas, who were backing everyone at a garden party in Henley-on-Thames. Then, after tea, I had to dash to London to perform with MPS at a birthday party.

A great Searchers and MPS fan, Dave Metcalf, published a book called *Celebrity Gatecrasher*. I was very happy to be featured in his book and to write the foreword and a piece for the back cover, in which I described Dave as 'the epitome of a true music fan – he knows his subject and has studied it like a degree student'. The book describes Dave's adventures in the world of music, the people he has met, fascinating anecdotes and lots of photographs and memorabilia.

Over the years, we have been regulars at the Savoy Hotel's '60s music weekends in Blackpool, where we always go down well – and 3 December 2011 was no exception. We were the headline act at this three-day event organised by CW Promotions, who also stage the brilliant Whitby festivals. They also organise '60s weekends in nearby Southport. As always, there was a great bunch of people there – including a lady from Newcastle upon Tyne who had last seen me 46 years ago!

We got on stage at about 11.00 p.m. and launched into an extended version of 'Sweets For My Sweet', complete with audience participation. I even got down from the stage to get some assistance on the vocals for 'Games People Play'. Keith and I also really enjoyed some solo guitar duelling on 'Hold Me'.

In March 2012, we were part of an incredible line-up of '60s bands at the *Super Sixties* weekend festival at a holiday park in Ilfracombe. This event was one of the Yesterday Once More music-themed weekends and holidays, and featured an almost-complete set of '60s acts: apart from MPS, there were Herman's Hermits, New Amen Corner, Dave Berry & The Cruisers, the Merseybeats, the Fortunes, Union Gap and the New Dreamers, plus the 'Legends of the '60s Show' with Mick Avory (Kinks), Eric Haydock (Hollies) and Martin Lyon (Love Affair).

On 11 May 2012, MPS played their second gig in twelve months at the Green Room cabaret club in Duke Street, Liverpool. The venue is co-owned by actor and comedian Ricky Tomlinson, star of the *Royle Family* TV show, who is a self-confessed Searchers fan. As on the previous occasion, the gig was sold out well in advance and the audience was very lively. I joked about the effects of advancing age on my eyesight and held up our set list, written in large capital letters.

We played at three '60s events by the seaside during 2012. There were two shows in Blackpool – one in June at the Winter Gardens and the other in November at the Savoy Hotel, as part of their '60s weekend. The third one was at the Delmont Hotel in Scarborough in October, which was also part of a '60s weekend. I turned down a major gig in Germany to do this show, because we were already committed to doing it and I did not want to let down the sell-out audience. Our open-air show for the *Mathew Street Festival* on August Bank Holiday Monday was cancelled by the organisers due to high winds and torrential rain – part of a typical British summer!

After a run of 50 issues over 17 years, our fan club magazine, *MPS News*, went online in the summer of 2012 and was incorporated into our website, www.mikependersearchers.co.uk. Searchers fan Sylvia Beaumont expertly looks after the site, which has been completely revamped and is now regularly updated with news, views and gig dates. Photos, articles and messages for the *Guest Book* are always welcomed by both Sylvia and our fan club secretary, Roger Askey. The *MPS News* tab carries all fan club matters and contributions from our fans. Contact details are also included for Roger. We have also set up a feedback page.

Just for the record, it is an almost incredible fact that MPS has only featured a total of nine musicians over the past 28 years. I have always been very loyal to my bandmates, and they have returned the compliment.

The original 1986 line-up included drummer Steve Carlisle, guitarist/keyboards player Chris Black, and Barrie Cowell on bass guitar – all of whom also helped out on vocals. Amazingly, that line-up remained unchanged until Chris emigrated to Australia in 1996. Paul Jackson from Brian Poole & Electrix replaced him and stayed until 1999, when Kevin Healey – also from Electrix – joined. Kevin stayed until 2005, but his place was sometimes taken by Garth Watt-Roy when he had other commitments.

Keith Roberts joined the band in 2005 – he was previously with Herman's Hermits as lead vocalist (so he told me), but seriously, I have to say Keith's harmony vocals do add to our sound. When Steve Carlisle left the band in 2003 to take up a solo career, my eldest son, Mike Junior, took over on drums. Michael had been the band's sound engineer for many years and had also been a drummer with several bands on Merseyside.

Barrie Cowell, my bass man, is up for a pension! After 28 years there is no doubt that the original MPS line-up was the best group of musicians I ever worked with, musically speaking – and this includes the 'classic' Searchers line-up of Tony Jackson, Chris Curtis, John McNally and myself. For vocal and musical ability, Chris Black and Steve Carlisle take some beating. Barrie Cowell must also be included as, although limited vocally, his bass-playing style is unique.

These guys never got the recognition they deserved, especially Chris and Steve, so I hope that this small tribute from someone very limited in musical ability goes some way to letting them know just how much they were/are appreciated. Chris, Steve, Baz – you were/are all brilliant with a capital B!

CHAPTER 25

Solo Reeling and Rocking

Life on the road can be very tiring, but we also have lots of laughs and share many jokes with our audiences.

It's always good to meet up again with my contemporaries from the '60s – sadly sometimes for the last time – and, of course, we are all much older now. I have my own theory about why so many artistes have not lived out their full cycle. Many a heart has been broken in the world of the recording artiste. It seems to me that the more famous you are, the chances of living to a ripe old age become less.

Over the past 25 years or so, I've had a great time playing in what we used to call in the '60s 'package tours'. With or without MPS, it has been a privilege to join many 'golden oldies' from the '60s, like myself, on major tours of the UK taking in America, Australia, South Africa and many other exotic places – especially with *ReelinandaRockin* and the *Solid Silver '60s* shows. I was honoured to be asked to headline the 25th anniversary tour of the *Solid Silver '60s* show in 2010, when we played for three months at more than 50 venues throughout the UK to big audiences who enjoyed themselves as much as we did.

On the road with me for that tour were several of my old friends from the good old days – my good friend Dave Berry (without his Cruisers), Reg Presley and the Troggs, Peter Sarstedt, the Swinging Blue Jeans and Brian Poole. Vanity Fare, featuring three original members, provided good backing for the solo singers. Every show ended with a real rave-up finale after I brought everyone back on stage.

We played many big venues on that tour, including Birmingham Symphony Hall, rated as one of the best concert halls in the world. Those tours are very well organised and presented by Derek Nicol of Flying Music, and my agent, great friend and trusted right-hand man, Tony Sherwood, always had me well organised for them.

The only things I don't enjoy about touring are the travelling and being away from home, even though May often travels with me. You will appreciate that I have done more than enough touring in the UK and overseas in my time, but it's always good to see the fans singing along with their favourite artists and bands, some still with original members.

I joined up once again with Dave Berry, Wayne Fontana, the Merseybeats and New Amen Corner for the *Solid Silver '60s* tour of the UK throughout March and April 2013. As with previous, highly successful *Solid Silver '60s* tours, it was promoted by Flying Music. The tour started at Sheffield City Hall on Thursday, 7 March, and included more than 40 dates. Other venues included Manchester Opera House, St. David's Hall in Cardiff, Glasgow's Royal Concert Hall, the Princess Theatre, Torquay, Wolverhampton's Grand Theatre and the Royal Centre in Nottingham.

'60s fans, or any music fans for that matter, always look forward to 'meeting and greeting' their favourites. This is to be expected. After all, many fans travel a fair distance to see their idols, and after buying tickets as well, we as the artists should at least sign an autograph for them. However, some of us don't – me included. I do sometimes have a valid excuse, but a pretty lame one: when you come off stage after closing the show, as I have done most of the time, you find your clothes are soaked with sweat. If you have to go outside to get to the front of the theatre, some of us (we are old now!) can end up with a chest infection, as I did on the 2013 *Solid Silver* tour. Even so, one should make the effort, and I will next year on the 30th Anniversary *Solid Silver* tour. That's if anyone is interested.

As you can imagine, life on the road can be very tiring, but

Together again.
Tony Jackson on stage with me at Birmingham Town Hall, 1992.

That's my boys! Michael and Nathan soundcheck for the show.
Nantwich Civic Hall, early '90s.

Plate 33

Celebrating my 30th anniversary gig,
Nottingham Commodore, 13 November 1993.
Left to right: Chris, me, Barrie and Steve.

Flanked by present and past MPS fan club secretaries
at the Commodore gig: Ann Askey *(left)* and Gill Westwood.

Plate 34

Lunch on the *QE2* – after we'd caught up with the ship!

Rickenbackers rule, OK?

Plate 35

With my agent and great friend of almost 30 years, Tony Sherwood.

Plate 36

ReelinandaRockin' in Australia. *Left to right:* Dave Dee, me, unknown fan, Dave Berry, Brian Poole and Wayne Fontana.

Daniel O'Donnell joins us on stage at Blackpool.

Plate 37

Entrepreneur and good friend Derek Franks helps out on vocals
at Wakefield Theatre Club.

Mr Bully himself, Jim Bowen, presents me with a silver disc
for sales of *The Very Best Of The Searchers* CD, October 2008.

Plate 38

Onstage with the Merseybeats.
My lovely Aria 12-string was later stolen.

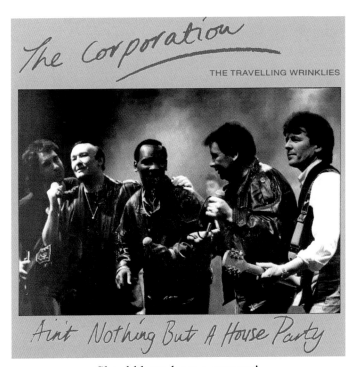

Should have been a success!
Left to right: Tony Crane, Brian Poole, Clem Curtis, Reg Presley and me.

Plate 39

Gone but not forgotten.
Left: Tony Jackson
(with Vibrations drummer Paul Francis).
Above: Chris Curtis.
Below: Joe West.

Plate 40

MPS fan club secretary
Roger Askey.

A Rickenbacker birthday cake
presented to me on my 70th by
MPS webmistress Sylvia Beaumont.

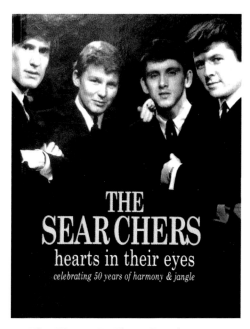

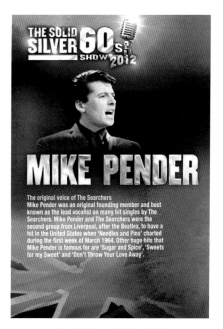

The *Hearts In Their Eyes* box set.

Solid Silver '60s, 2012.

Plate 41

MPS performing at the Star-Club's 50th anniversary celebration, 2012.

50th Anniversary of the British Invasion US tour, 2014.
Left to right: Chad & Jeremy, me, Terry Sylvester,
Denny Laine and Billy J. Kramer.

Plate 42

My mother
and father,
somewhere
on holiday.

May and me with May's mum – our resident babysitter!

Plate 43

Michael, Nathan (with monkey!) and Stephanie.

Kevin Clarkson gig at the Leyland Civic: me, Steph, Mike, Nathe and Mum.

Plate 44

Our 25th Wedding (that we never had) Anniversary, 2 January 1988.

Nathe with his best friend – his mum!

Plate 45

A couple of groupies. May and sister Veronica, Australian tour date, 1995.

Dancing with 'The Vision' – Alex Young – Tenerife , 1981.

Plate 46

Peckforton Castle, Cheshire.
Stephanie and Paul on their big day with May and me.

Steph with new baby.

Alexander with his grandad.

Plate 47

Alexander going to school!

Playing with Benjie at
Nanna and Grandad's.

The green green grass of home.

Plate 48

we also have lots of laughs and share many jokes with our audiences, mostly about subjects like our grey/white hair or our winter fuel allowance. We don't play the same practical jokes on each other like we did on the tours in the '60s – we don't have the energy any more.

I did experience one mysterious incident about three years ago on the *Solid Silver '60s* tour, although I'm not sure if you could call it a practical joke. I was at the Fairfield Halls, Croydon – a venue I know very well from way back. After the show, I did the usual 'meet and greet' (yes, I really did) and photo sessions in the foyer. As I went out of the stage door, several fans approached, so I put down my guitar and suit bag to sign autographs for them. Regrettably, one of them repaid my good manners by stealing my stage suit. Incredibly, my suit with its distinctive white piping on the lapels and pockets, was found hanging in my dressing room a few days later at a show on the tour, and in perfect condition with a note saying 'It didn't fit me'!

Old friends that MPS and I have met up with on tours over the last fifty years include Reg Presley (the Troggs), Gerry & The Pacemakers, Tony Crane and Billy Kinsley (the Merseybeats), Peter Noone, Herman's Hermits, and Billy Ashton, better known as Billy J. Kramer (with and without the Dakotas), Chip Hawkes (the Tremeloes), Terry Sylvester (the Hollies), the Four Pennies, Love Affair, Chris Farlowe, P.J. Proby, Bobby Vee, Cliff Bennett (without his Rebel Rousers), Paul Jones and Mike d'Abo from the Manfreds (minus Manfred), Marmalade, Dave Dee, Dozy, Beaky, Mick & Tich, Freddie & The Dreamers, Joe Brown (minus his Bruvvers) and the Easybeats' Ray Martin and his 'Dreamers'.

It is only right that we also remember the great performers who took part in those tours and are sadly no longer with us – Roy Orbison, Phil Everly, Reg Presley, Dave Dee, John Walker (the Walker Brothers), Rod Allen (the Fortunes), Les Braid (the Swinging Blue Jeans), Del Shannon, Freddie Garrity, Gene Pitney, Lonnie Donegan, Bert Weedon and others.

An American singer who I admired a lot, Joe South, died in September 2012, aged 72 – not a bad innings, but that is not old by today's standards. He was a great artiste and songwriter. His song, 'Games People Play', is a classic and will always be a firm favourite of mine. He was unlucky in love: his first marriage ended in divorce and his second wife died in the 1990s.

One of the nice things for me, nowadays, is being able to take my wife with me to faraway places like Australia, New Zealand and the USA. One of the really great trips was cruising from New Zealand to Australia on the *QE2* with Gerry Marsden, Mike d'Abo, Dave Berry and Brian Poole. We did two concerts on the ship. That 2002 tour was a great success for the five 'frontmen', all performing without our respective bands. I did, in fact, have to turn down the offer of a 40th anniversary tour with MPS for early 2003 because I was committed to *ReelinandaRockin* for most of that year.

This was all organised by Derek Franks, someone I got to know well. His company organised many world and UK tours, including *Oh Boy!* The *ReelinandaRockin* show went to the Far East, Asia, and on to Australia, taking in Hong Kong, the Philippines and China. That show was also very popular with UK audiences and ran for six years. Sadly, Derek died suddenly a few years ago, but I will always remember him with great affection.

One of the nice things about having your own band is that you can pick and choose what you want to do without having to explain yourself or pacify other members. So, I suppose it was inevitable that I would split from John and Frank to do this and have the freedom to experiment with new ventures – such as when Tony Sherwood telephoned to ask if I would be interested in recording a song with four of my contemporaries: Brian Poole, Reg Presley (the Troggs), Clem Curtis (the Foundations) and Tony Crane (the Merseybeats).

The recording was done in June 1988 at the former Pye studios at Marble Arch, a place I knew very well. It was there I had recorded my one and only solo single, 'It's Over'. I travelled down to London by train, as the recording session was only expected to last three or four hours, meaning I could be back home by evening. Ray Santilli, whose idea it was, was there with the other guys when I arrived, and the session was funny and fraught, but friendly. The plan was that each of us would record a vocal track individually, then Ray would pick what he thought were the best bits and do a final mix. This was a good idea, as, had it been left to us, the end result would have been messy.

The track was a cover of the old Showstoppers' hit, 'Ain't Nothing But A Houseparty'. Have a look at the video on my website: there is no doubt in my mind this recording would have made the charts and given us all a new lease of life. Sadly, it never happened. The powers that be at the BBC were not enamoured, apparently, by the fact that five 'wrinklies' from the past were trying to cash in and make a comeback, while young bands and young musicians were struggling to be heard (the story of my life). That was the way I saw it, anyway. Only one deejay, Mike Read, was complimentary and wanted to play it. However, one good thing was that television and the national press loved it because it was good showbiz news.

That period was one of the happiest of my career. We had a great time making the video to go with the single, and had a real bundle of laughs. Poor old Clem Curtis was so sure the record was going to be a success, he threw a big party at his wine bar with champagne flowing all night...or was it day? Anyway, it must have cost him dearly. Although we wanted to be known as 'the Travelling Wrinklies', the record company preferred 'the Corporation', and that's what appeared on the record sleeve. I still see the other guys, but not much of Clem. If you ever get to read this, Clem, please email me – I owe you at least a bottle of champagne!

A veritable galaxy of artistes from the '60s including yours truly was assembled by the *Mail on Sunday*'s magazine, *Night and Day*, for a photo shoot that was published on 9 March 1997. Splashed across two pages, the photo was taken by Trevor Ray Hart at the 100 Club at 100 Oxford Street, London. It was No. 23 in a 'Hall of Fame' series in the magazine. I was pictured at the front with my 456/12 Rick alongside Brian Poole, who was holding a microphone. Ex-Tornado Clem Cattini was seated behind his drum kit, while Tony Crane, Billy Kinsley and Mike Berry pretended to play their guitars. Dave Dee and Wayne Fontana brandished tambourines, and Clem Curtis, Reg Presley and Freddie Garrity were also seated on the stage.

The magazine also printed notes on all eleven of us with the photo. Under 'Most Admired', my entry listed Michael Bolton and the Mavericks. Several of my '60s colleagues said that Oasis was the band they most admired. Wayne Fontana said he most admired the Spice Girls, 'but I can't put my finger on why'. Brian Poole most admired Alisha's Attic because they had 'great songs' and 'look fantastic' – which is fair enough, they are his daughters!

None of us are getting any younger, and some guys have decided to bow out from performing for various reasons. Ray Ennis, an original member of the Swinging Blue Jeans retired after over fifty years. As I progress into my 70s, it will, at some point, be my turn to hang up my Rickenbacker and retire gracefully – but not yet! Touch wood, I have been very fortunate, even blessed, to have good health. I have always been careful about what I eat and drink, and never drink more than three bottles of Rioja a day! (I wish.) As I've said so often in this book, my family life has always been a major priority for me, but I will carry on performing with MPS, or as a solo artiste, as long you, the fans, want to hear the old songs – and some more recent ones.

It still hurts that old wounds, real or imagined, would not heal. May and I, and lots of '60s and '70s music fans in Australia and New Zealand were very disappointed when a 25-date *Solid Gold Hits* tour scheduled for October and November 2010 was cancelled at short notice. The reason given was that it was 'under threat of legal action taken by the Searchers and their legal representatives'. The tour promoter had been advised to bill me as 'The Original Voice of the Searchers', but, for reasons that are not entirely clear, he ignored that advice, which invited the inevitable challenge from John and Frank and their lawyers. This highly regrettable cancellation, of course, also affected all the other acts who were to be on the tour with me: Paper Lace, Edison Lighthouse, Brotherhood of Man and Wayne Fontana & The Mindbenders. You could say they put the frighteners on the promoter.

After a gig in Torremolinos in October 2012, I travelled to Malta later that month for a *Solid Silver '60s* show, which also featured Dave Berry, Wayne Fontana, Brian Poole and Vanity Fare. I really enjoyed that night. With an audience of more than 2,000 people, the place was rocking! Tony Crane was in the audience, on holiday with family and friends, and after we had all signed photos and CDs for what seemed like an hour, Tony and I shared a bottle of red before wishing each other all the best and getting off to our relative hotels.

I had turned down the offer of a gig at a major '60s music festival in Canada for the following weekend, because I wanted to fulfil an existing booking for a sold-out MPS show at the Delmont Hotel in Scarborough – it would have been very unfair to our UK fans to let them down, but I was sorry to miss meeting up with old mates Billy J. Kramer and Peter Noone, who were headlining the event in Ontario.

Going back to the gig in Malta: I had an unusual fellow passenger occupying the seat next to me on the Air Malta flight – my precious Rickenbacker 12-string guitar! It was actually more cost-effective for my guitar to travel as a 'passenger', than to go as excess baggage in the plane's hold. It also avoided the serious problem that I had on arrival in Australia a few years before. And my guitar didn't need a passport!

CHAPTER 26

Tony and Chris – The Twilight Years

It was tragic that Tony had let success go to his head in the '60s. Chris was obviously past the point of no return.

Tony Jackson

How many crossroads are there on the path of life? Looking back, happy memories are mixed with disappointment and loss for most of us.

After his music career with the Vibrations broke up in 1967, Tony Jackson had a succession of jobs including being a furniture salesman, a deejay, and managing a nightclub in Majorca and a golf club in Nuneaton. It was former Vibrations drummer Paul Francis who persuaded him to return to the music business, even if on a part-time basis.

Paul had a reunion with Tony in London in May 1990. It was agreed they would do some gigs, and a new line-up of the Vibrations was put together. They were all experienced musicians, who had worked with people like Steve Harley, Jack Bruce and Maggie Bell. Promoters in the Netherlands and Scandinavia showed interest in Tony's band reunion, but he was to do very few gigs over the following years. There were now three Searchers-related acts on the road: MPS, John and Frank's Searchers, and Tony's band.

Their first as the new Tony Jackson & The Vibrations was on 8 December 1990 in Enfield. In 1991, the Strange Things label issued a Tony Jackson Group compilation, *Just Like Me*, on both LP and CD.

Tony performed onstage with MPS on four occasions between 1992 and 1995. As already mentioned, he was in the audience for our *Swinging '60s* gig at Birmingham Town Hall on 2 May 1992, which also featured the Troggs, Cliff Bennett, Love Affair and Billie Davis. Tony's hair was now silver, but he looked good. I managed to persuade him to come up and sing a couple of numbers with me, 'Sweets For My Sweet' and 'Needles And Pins'. It was the first time we had performed together for many years – it certainly was an emotional reunion and the audience went wild.

I was delighted to meet up again with Tony and his new band at a *Mersey Reunion* show at the Civic Hall, Guildford on 1 November 1992. The Merseybeats and Mike McCartney from Scaffold were also on the bill. Tony and I sang 'Sweets For My Sweet', 'Sugar And Spice', 'Needles And Pins' and 'Love Potion No. 9'. Some weeks later, we did another show with them at the Parr Hall in Warrington.

I don't remember to much about that one, but the next gig when Tony and I would again come together on stage was on 9 September 1995, again at Birmingham Town Hall. It was another great nostalgic event in front of another packed audience of 1,300. The Merseybeats, the Four Pennies, Love Affair, Chip Hawkes and Twinkle were also on the bill that evening. We all had a great night and Tony sang four songs with me: 'Sweets For My Sweet', 'Sugar And Spice', 'Needles And Pins' and 'Farmer John'. It was to be last time that we performed onstage together.

In an in-depth feature about Tony in *Record Collector* magazine in 1992, Liverpool musician and Beatles biographer Alan Clayson attempted to explain how it was that one of Merseyside's most distinctive voices never won the fame he deserved. Tony talked about the early days and how he and I had practised a lot of Everly Brothers songs. 'Our voices suited each other,' he said, but I found the article flawed.

It quoted my theory on why Tony left in 1964: 'Individual egos came to the fore and started demanding a few things. The band becomes a prison in the end. You can't do anything without the others. Some bands today... do things outside the band and still re-form to tour. We couldn't do that. Someone asked me if they could use me on an album, and the rest of the lads didn't like it. There was the chance of doing the title song of a film, *Saturday Night Out*. Before that, we were promised parts in it and straight away Tony said: "You mean *acting*?" All it meant was appearing on a stage in a nightclub. Afterwards, Tony felt he wanted to express himself more. He half wanted to leave and half wanted to stay. Our manager, Tito Burns, told Tony he'd get a band together for him. Chris was quite happy because he and Tony weren't hitting it off about choosing material and the performance onstage. I could see something was going to give.' Regrettably, the rest of the Tony Jackson life story was not a happy one and included a 12-month prison sentence. I will not dwell on the details.

It was early on the morning of 18 August 2003 that I received a telephone call from Paul Francis to tell me that Tony had died just a few hours earlier in his tiny council flat on the outskirts of Nottingham. I was one of the first people that Paul rang, and I was obviously saddened by the passing of my old friend and former bandmate at the age of only 65. Tony had been in very poor health for many years, suffering from asthma, arthritis and cirrhosis of the liver, and had had two heart attacks. He had been living alone with his five cats, hardly able to walk. He had been married three times, but his personal and family life had often been turbulent and unhappy.

A few weeks earlier, Tony had called his former bandmates to say his last goodbyes. Paul Francis had been with him when he died, and we both attended his funeral at Wilford Hill Crematorium in Nottingham – Paul and I were among the pall-bearers. Frankie and John were also there. Frankie spoke briefly to May and myself, but John kept his distance. Tony 'Joe' West, our original Searchers bassist was also there, but Chris Curtis did not attend.

It was a lovely but lonely funeral (if there can be such a thing) to celebrate Tony's life. I didn't know if Tony's first wife,

Margaret, was still alive, and thought she might have been there. His only daughter was there – from which marriage I couldn't say. 'Sweets For My Sweet' and a Roy Orbison song were played, and a guitar made from white flowers was placed on the coffin. I had the honour of paying tribute to Tony at the service, and afterwards a TV crew did interviews. Many national newspapers covered the news of Tony's death. Frankie also placed a tribute to him on the Searchers' website. In some obituaries, John was quoted as saying that, as the Searchers had a very clean-cut image during the '60s, nobody ever really knew that Tony was the 'wild man' of the group.

It was tragic that Tony had let success go to his head in the '60s. While everyone enjoyed a drink from time to time, Tony did not know when to stop. But in his last years, and in failing health, the once-combative Tony's character had changed. As Paul Francis writes in his book, *Drumming Up Vibrations*, 'In his younger days, Tony would take on the world, but he mellowed as he got older and there was a lovely, soft side to him.' He had taken up painting and had become a proficient artist.

In 2004, Castle released a CD by the Tony Jackson Group, *The Complete Recordings: 1964-66*, and it is very appropriate that the Searchers box set released in July 2012, *Hearts In Their Eyes*, includes several of Tony's singles. Perhaps it would have been more appropriate for the group photo on the cover to have included Tony, rather than Frank, but to be fair, Frankie does pay tribute to Tony (and Chris) in the box set booklet.

Chris Curtis

When Chris returned to Liverpool in 1969 after his music career in London had collapsed, he went to work for the Inland Revenue at their head office in Bootle. Sometime in late 1978 or early 1979, just before our Sire sessions at Rockfield, he made a habit of telephoning me several times a day, almost to the point of becoming a pest. By that time, and certainly since moving back to Liverpool, he had become even more zany than when I first knew him. I had to change my telephone number – it got that bad.

He would call me and stay on the phone for maybe half an

hour, telling me about songs he had written. He would also invite me to come over to his house, which was falling down around him due to neglect. He couldn't grasp the fact that I had moved on from the heady days of the '60s, and that I wasn't interested in getting together with him to write or record songs. We had started down that road in 1963, but his ego had ended our collaboration and it was too late now to turn back the clock. When he didn't have my phone number, he would arrive at my house in a taxi, with flowers and strawberries and dressed in strange clothing, out of his head sometimes. I'm afraid I lost my temper a few times before he finally got the message. I didn't see him again for a long time.

When Chris found out that the Searchers were recording two albums for Sire at Rockfield, he phoned the studio and threatened to burn the place down. He shouted down the phone that the Searchers were 'nothing' without him – a bad case of 'eat your heart out'.

Chris was obviously past the point of no return. I often think about how good he was in those early days, when we were trying to make it. He was really the one who drove us on and caught the eye of many promoters and punters. As I remarked in my eulogy at Chris's funeral, we looked upon him as 'our own John Lennon'. I doubt very much if the Searchers would have made the world stage and sold all those millions of records, had it not been for Chris.

After he left the band in 1966, it was his idea and his brainchild to prepare for the formation of Deep Purple, although he was burned out long before that band eventually made it. Ritchie Blackmore has said that, without Chris, Deep Purple would not have happened. Chris had also worked with other recording artistes, including Paul & Barry Ryan.

In his last years in Liverpool, Chris's eccentric behaviour included giving away his record collection and items of Searchers memorabilia to complete strangers on a bus. He also had a habit of phoning people in the early hours of the morning, including well-known BBC Radio Merseyside deejay, Billy Butler.

Chris had returned to performing, but in a very low-key

Liverpool **ECHO**   Thursday, March 10, 2005

FINAL FAREWELL

60s stars pay respects to ex-Searcher Chris

THEY came to say goodbye to one of their own.

By GREG O'KEEFFE

With hair still touching their collars, leading lights of Liverpool's '60s Merseybeat scene said farewell to ex-Searchers drummer Chris Curtis, 63.

He had been suffering from diabetes and was found dead in his Aintree flat last month.

Yesterday his family, friends, and former band-mates attended a funeral service at Holy Rosary church, Aintree.

Among the congregation were fellow Searchers Mike Pender and John McNally, Kingsize Taylor, former Merseybeats star Tony Crane and Faron, from Faron's Flamingos.

Chris Curtis had been a member of the Searchers who topped the charts with classics such as Sweets For My Sweet, Don't Throw Your Love Away, and Needles And Pins between 1963 and 1964.

Born Chris Crummey, the drummer changed his surname to Curtis when he joined the group. His family moved to Liverpool from Oldham when he was a young child.

He left the Searchers in 1966 after a tour of Australia and spent time producing other musicians, before returning to Liverpool to work as a civil servant.

With church doors open to allow for standing room

at the back, mourners heard a eulogy from Mike Pender.

After the service, Mr Pender said: "I was really touched when his sister Rose phoned me and asked me to say a few words.

"We wrote a song together which reached number 12 in the charts and had a lot of success.

"It was Chris who gave me the conviction to give up my job in the Sixties and concentrate on making it big with the band."

Mr Pender attributed much of the band's success to his friend.

He said: "He had such charisma. Chris was always different - an individual. He was what set us apart from all those other bands at the time.

"He had a special confidence and I can vividly remember him standing up playing his drums on stage.

"He was like our John Lennon, the two were similar in a way.

"My favourite memories are rehearsing in Chris's living room and his sister making us cups of tea.

"But we had so many amazing times together, from those early days in Liverpool to gigging in Hamburg and then across the world."

gregokeeffe@liverpoolecho.co.uk
0151-472 2488

FOND GOODBYE: The funeral cortege and, clockwise from below left, John McNally, Faron, Kingsize Taylor, Tony Crane, and the Searchers in New York in 1964 with Chris Curtis second from left

EULOGY: Mike Pender of the Searchers
Pictures: TONY KENWRIGHT

way, singing with a karaoke machine at the Old Roan pub and at Cooper's Emporium. He was still very enthusiastic – almost hyperactive – just like in the old days.

He also made some classier appearances with the Merseycats at the Marconi Club in Huyton, taken there by my cousin, Michael Prendergast, from his house in Aintree. Merseycats consisted of current musicians and former members of Mersey beat bands who joined forces to raise money for sick and underprivileged children on Merseyside. Chris enjoyed singing at some of the shows and one night even took along an acoustic guitar to sing 'Love Potion No. 9'. It was, however, obvious to everyone that he was in very poor health. His last-ever public performance was to be with the Merseycats. He was found dead at home, alone, on 28 February 2005. He was only 63.

I was really touched when Chris's sister, Rose, phoned me to ask if I would say a few words at his funeral. It was Chris who had convinced me that I should give up my job and concentrate on making it big with the band, and much of our success should be attributed to him. He had such charisma – he was always different, an individual. He was what set us apart from all those other bands at the time. Chris had a special kind of confidence – I can vividly remember him standing up, playing his drums on stage. There is no doubt in my mind that, without Chris's genius and perception in those early days, the group would not have made it to the Star-Club. When Horst Fascher first saw us at the Cavern, although he never said it at the time, it was Chris who caught his eye with his unique style of drumming and singing. It also has to be said that, when we became established in the recording world, although Tony and I did the vocals, it was Chris's musical ability and understanding of the finished product that was all-important, with the harmonies that he would work out in advance.

One of my favourite memories is of the band rehearsing in Chris's living room and his sister making us cups of tea. We wrote a song together which got to No. 12 in the charts in 1965, and had a lot of success, 'He's Got No Love'. We had so many amazing times together, from the early days in Liverpool to gigging in Hamburg, and then across the world.

With hair still touching our collars, many of the leading lights of Liverpool's '60s Mersey beat scene came to the Holy Rosary Church in Aintree on Wednesday, 9 March 2005 to pay our respects and say a sad farewell to one of our own. Chris had been associated with that church in his later years and had encouraged the priest to include folk music and even rock'n'roll to attract young people to services.

Among the congregation at the funeral were many faces from those early days in Liverpool: John and Frankie, as well as Tony Crane from the Merseybeats, Kingsize Taylor, and Faron Ruffley of Faron's Flamingos. Afterwards, at the small reception in the nearby church hall, Frankie Allen and I shook hands, and we put aside our differences for the day. He was warm with May and gave her a hug when we said our goodbyes later.

Chris left the stage in style: the funeral cortège consisted of a carriage drawn by two black horses. The church was so full that the doors had to be left open to allow standing room at the back. The media paid their full respects too: the *Liverpool Echo* devoted half a page to its report, including a photo of the funeral procession. Our former bass player, Tony 'Joe' West, was quoted as saying that Chris had been 'the epitome of the group'.

It was a privilege, I suppose, for me to give the eulogy at Chris's funeral, just as I'd done at Tony Jackson's in Nottingham two years earlier. John McNally had known both of them quite well, and had actually spoken with Chris not long before his death. Even Frankie, having been very close to Chris at one time, probably felt he or McNally should have given the eulogy, but it was Chris's sister Rose who had the last word.

Chris was hugely talented, a true one-off, hyperactive character with boundless enthusiasm and confidence linked to a razor-sharp wit. He was not just our drummer – he was the singer-songwriter and musical inspiration behind our incredible success, helping to create the Mersey beat era's second most successful beat band. He wasn't wrong.

CHAPTER 27

Returning to Hamburg

Memories came flooding back – the nightclubs, seedy bars and hustling doormen with gnarled and toothless faces, making them look like hardened criminals, rather than bouncers.

Yes, thirty years on, it was still a great adventure. I have tried to describe my first two trips to Hamburg with John McNally, Tony Jackson and Chris Curtis in those far-off days of 1962-63, when it was the start of a great adventure for us, performing at the Star-Club and meeting all our rock'n'roll heroes. We really reckoned we had made it – and we did not long after. By the end of the '60s, by which time our hit recording career was over, the Searchers were still a name, especially in Hamburg, and even in Germany itself. We would find ourselves there many times throughout the 1970s and the early 1980s. I returned with MPS in early 1992, almost thirty years after my first visit, wondering how much had changed since then.

We were met by Thomas Helwig, a concert promoter living in Denmark who had been brought up on '60s music and was still booking 'oldies but goldies'. My agent, Tony Sherwood, had organised everything very carefully, as we had a show to do in Hamburg, and then another gig in Denmark.

Our hotel was only five minutes from the Reeperbahn, and we decided not to do a sound check, as the gig – a big festival – had been underway since midday. We could hardly do a sound check with 10,000 screaming music fans all wanting to get their rocks off. So, with plenty of time to spare, we all set off to get something to eat and do some sightseeing.

We all knew the Star-Club didn't exist any more. There wasn't even a plaque on the wall then, but we all wanted to see the former site. Our drummer, Steve Carlisle, was about to realise one of his ambitions, as was Mike Junior, my eldest son and our road manager at that time. Young Mike had heard so many stories about the place – and to think he was a mere twinkle in his dad's eye all those years ago!

When we got to Grosse Freiheit ('Grosse' for short), almost everything seemed to be as it used to be – maybe not as busy, but the old feeling was still there. Memories came flooding back to me: the nightclubs, the seedy bars and the hustling doormen with their gnarled and toothless faces, making them look like hardened criminals rather than bouncers. Even the smells were the same – 'Bockwurst' (large sausages), and 'Frikadels' (the equivalent of a 'Big Mac'), all frizzled and frazzled at every snack bar on the Grosse, mixing with the smell of stale beer. Music throbbed from every doorway, and many of the clubs were still there too – the Kaiserkeller, where the Beatles played in their very early days, the Regina, the Monika-Bar. Only the faces of the people had changed: a new generation had taken over. We walked on like five English tourists.

Suddenly, I stopped and said, 'Yes, that was where the Star-Club used to be.' We looked in disbelief at the black hole in the wall, where the entrance to the world-famous venue had once been. No sound was to be heard, no neon lights flashing now. Like an empty electric socket, the black hole stared back at us. Suddenly, I remembered why this time was different: the building had burned down since I had last been there. I looked at young Mike, Chris, Steve and Barrie, and said, 'Come on, let's go and eat before it gets too late. We've got a show to do tonight!'

One of the most important eras of pop history began with the opening on 13 April 1962 of the Star-Club, located at Grosse Freiheit 39, just off the Reeperbahn in Hamburg. It is hardly believable today, but for a few years this 'concert temple' in the St Pauli district was the most famous music club in the world. When the Beatles, the Searchers, and many other British bands were still learning their trade there in the early 1960s, shows were being headlined by legends such as Jerry Lee Lewis, Ray Charles, Chuck Berry, Bill Haley, Fats Domino and Brenda Lee, to name just a few. The Star-Club was more than just a rock'n'roll venue; it was a magical place. It had shaken off the austerity and drudgery following the Second World War and released a youth rebellion on both sides of the North Sea.

The two men who made it all possible were Hamburg businessman Manfred Weissleder, who owned the club, and the one and only Horst Fascher, who managed the venue with an iron fist and had a legendary reputation with all who performed there. Today, the original Star-Club, like the original Cavern in Liverpool, is no more. It closed in 1969 and the building was destroyed by fire in 1987. The world-famous club has gone, but its spirit lives on.

I was delighted when Tony Sherwood called me to say the organisers of the Star-Club's 50th anniversary celebrations in 2012 – including Horst Fascher – wanted to book Mike Pender's Searchers for the show in Hamburg. Like the 'new' Cavern in Liverpool, the 'new' Star-Club is in the same street as the original venue, at Grosse Freiheit 36, just opposite where the famous club used to be. I've met Horst a couple of times in the interim years when gigging around the Hamburg area, but it was a good feeling to meet up again on this most special occasion.

For me, there was one huge, significant difference from when I was there, fifty years before with John, Tony and Chris: the girl, who most nights I tried to phone (when I could find one) is now my wife, and along with our eldest son, Mike Junior, and the other members of my band – Barrie and Keith – we all had a great weekend.

The show took place on 13 April 2012 at the 'new' Star-Club. Now looking his years and with a fully-grown beard, Horst Fascher brought everyone on stage that night to rapturous applause from the capacity audience, who clapped and clapped when I inadvertently said into the microphone, 'Horst Fascher, almost as famous as the Beatles' – and in Hamburg he most certainly is. As well as MPS, many other acts associated with the

Tony Sherwood

From:	"Horst Fascher" <horstfascher@aol.com>
To:	<ts@tonysherwood.co.uk>
Sent:	10 May 2012 15:35
Subject:	thank you to Mike

Dear Mike and to your fantastic Band,

This is the first opportunity I have found since the Concert on the 13th of April to write and express my profound gratitude to you all for your contribution to making the 50th Anniversary of the opening of the Star Club such a resounding success. I have been overwhelmed with requests for interviews, personal appearances and so on and have had no time until now. I want to say that the atmosphere at the concert was absolutely super and this was due in no small part to the excellent quality of the music and the enthusiasm and skill with which it was played and sung.

I would like to say a big, personal â€œThank Youâ€ to each and every one of you for your part in this success and I shall remember it for the rest of my life. Maybe we shall have an opportunity to do something like this again if certain plans that I am now working on come to fruition. Meanwhile the DVD and the CD of the concert are in the process of being edited and produced and you will all receive a copy of the first cut.

Yours sincerely, Horst Fascher and his Team
****

× Horst Fascher Entertainment

BÃ¶hmkenstrasse 17
D-20459 Hamburg

Tel: +49 (0)40-36 75 93
Mobil:+49 (0)174 476 4510

club appeared that evening, including the Pete Best Band, the Undertakers, Lee Curtis, Jackie Lomax, the Mojos, Joe Fagin, Bobby Thompson and the Quarrymen (who were billed as 'The band that became the Beatles'). It was a real trip down memory lane, with many old friendships revisited. Some of the performances, including clips of our set, can be seen on YouTube.

More than two years have gone by now since that night. I

count myself lucky to have been there among those Liverpool legends, some of whom I will probably never meet again. Indeed, and inevitably, that probability became a reality on 15 September 2013, when Jackie Lomax, once of the Undertakers and later a star in his own right, passed away. He will be remembered on May's prayer list.

CHAPTER 28

The Wedding We Never Had

But the greatest day was yet to come.

Peter Dolan and I were very close friends from a very early age. We lived within a stone's throw of each other in Bootle and we were both football-mad, urchin-like trainspotters. We also attended the same school and were friends throughout that time. When it was time to leave and go into the big, wide world, we both went our separate ways. Peter became a draughtsman with the then-famous Dunlop Corporation. Me you are reading about.

Over the years, we would occasionally meet up. Later, when we both had grown-up children, we would start seeing each other a little more often, remembering our far-off trainspotting days. That's when my wife May came up with the 'train idea', and the four of us – Peter, his wife Maureen, May and I – all had a fantastic time on the 'Orient Express'.

During this trip, after a few bottles of shampoo(!) we all decided that, on our return, we would introduce our daughter, Stephanie, to their son, Paul, and hope for the best. It seemed a good idea, as they were both still single. The idea worked, and May and I decided to give them the wedding that we never had.

I remember the night well, in 2003, when Stephanie and Paul officially met. I say 'officially', as, although they had met each other as children at organised kiddies' parties, this was now a different ballgame: both were now grown-up people, but both were still single and unattached.

So there we all were. May and I had arranged to meet Peter

and Maureen at a restaurant in Southport, where they lived. They would make up some excuse to get their son Paul to go with them, and we would do the same with Stephanie. Hardly a 'romantic evening' for them, with both sets of parents listening in, but on reflection we all had a great night and Paul and Stephanie had finally met each other.

Over the next couple of weeks, we would ring Steph once in a while for an update, but Paul had not been in touch. But then we got the call that we'd been waiting for: Paul had rung and they were meeting up! Six months later, they were 'courting' (as we used to say), and eventually decided to marry on 20 August 2005.

May and I wanted to make our only daughter's wedding day really special, so the reception was held at the fairytale Peckforton Castle in Cheshire. What a great day that was!

But the greatest day was yet to come. On 28 February 2007, our only grandson (to date) was born at Ormskirk Hospital. Stephanie and Paul named him Alexander.

My old mate Peter and I got very drunk that night.

CHAPTER 29

The New Box Set – My Favourite Tracks

There will always be discrepancies in the text – even photos. In this text, there are many!

Back in 2010, a lot of people, myself included, looked forward to the release of a 4-CD retrospective dedicated to the Searchers mainly covering the 1963-1985 period. Sanctuary's new owners, Universal, were to bestow upon the band the lavish box set treatment. It was also to be released almost simultaneously in the US. The 120 tracks would include demos, BBC recordings, rarities, solo recordings by Tony and Chris, interviews, material from the Sire sessions, as well as all the classic hit singles.

I had been interviewed by Roger Dopson and had given him lots of quotes for the accompanying booklet, plus some rare photos from my personal collection. The actual release date and the final track listing had not been announced, but we had a working title: *Sweets, Spice, Sugar, Pins and Needles*. Favourable advance reviews even appeared in *Record Collector* and *Mojo*. In their August 2010 issue, *Mojo*'s reviewer, Jim Irvin, gave the box set three stars out of a possible five. He described it as 'an impressively exhaustive set' drawn from the band's 'picaresque career' as Mersey beat pioneers.

So far, so good. We waited for the box set to appear – then nothing happened. Explanatory information was very sparse – there may have been copyright problems with some tracks.

215

Rumoured release dates came and went. Then, almost exactly two years later, it appeared in July 2012 with a new (and in my opinion, much better) title: *Hearts In Their Eyes: Celebrating 50 Years of Harmony and Jangle*. The track listing appeared unchanged from what had previously been announced.

The box set kicks off with live tracks from the Iron Door Club and the Star-Club, both recorded early in 1963. It naturally includes both sides of all the band's hits originally recorded for Pye between 1963 and 1967, except for 'Lovers' (the flip side of 'Popcorn, Double Feature'). The set also features rare songs recorded at Liberty, RCA, Sire and Pye's successor, PRT, including the previously unissued 'In The Heat Of The Night'.

In addition to copious and very informative though inaccurate liner notes by Jon Savage and Bob Stanley, the 64-page booklet includes photographs, memorabilia and picture-sleeve reproductions. I'm delighted to say that the vast majority of the tracks feature my vocals and lead guitar-work, recorded before I left the band in December 1985.

It is probably the most definitive compilation of the Searchers' recorded legacy released to date. The song 'Hearts In Her Eyes', recorded in 1979 for Sire, should have been a big hit to relaunch the band. It is one of my favourites, and is much requested and rapturously received at MPS gigs. With all due respect to Frank, I would have preferred to have seen a photo of the band which included the late, great Tony Jackson on the cover. At least some of Tony's recordings with the Vibrations are included in the set.

Reviews in the national music press in July 2012 were very favourable. *Mojo* awarded it three stars out of five. Reviewer Mark Blake said the Searchers were 'Liverpool's second-greatest '60s band' and had 'invented folk rock, power pop and more'. He said the band's 'spotless harmonies' and 'pealing guitars' became 'foundation stones for folk rock, and had left a mark on the Byrds, Buffalo Springfield and Tom Petty'. He also highlighted lesser-known tracks like 'Don't Hide It Away' (the flip of 'Take It Or Leave It') and 1967's 'gorgeous psych-pop hits', 'Pussy Willow Dream' and 'Popcorn, Double Feature'. From the Sire sessions, he picked out 'Silver' and 'It's Too Late' for their 'pounding choruses and chiming Rickenbackers'.

Record Collector's reviewer awarded it four stars and said the box set was 'well deserved' and 'a worthy tribute to a half-century, of which three years were spent shaking up the hit parade and the rest riding the shockwaves'.

So now we have what every major recording artist or group aspires to at some time in their career: the much-awaited, fairly definitive box set. It is extra special to me because, as the subtitle says, it is 'celebrating 50 years of harmony and jangle'. Although it is now more than 25 years since I split to form Mike Pender's Searchers, it is only right that the bulk of the written history in the box set booklet is devoted to the original four Searchers. The majority of the tracks feature my lead guitar or lead vocals, or both.

There will always be discrepancies in any text when covering a span of fifty years or more – even photos. In this text there are many! But I will refer only to one, our earliest known photo. When this picture was taken, neither I, nor John McNally, nor Joe West, nor Joe Kennedy had ever heard of, or knew of, anyone named Johnny Sandon! Work that one out !

I don't know who chose the photos, which are mostly very good, but I would especially like to know who picked the ones of the Sire sessions at Rockfield Studios. I think I know really, so it comes as no surprise to me that there are no shots of the lead vocalist actually singing. I wonder why.

I don't usually go on about putting vocals down, but on this occasion I have to make an important point: the Sire sessions were the hardest I had ever done, not only instrumentally, but mostly because I was learning the lyrics as we went along, and also double-tracking vocals. It was the first time I can remember in my entire career that I actually lost my voice at a recording session.

Unfortunately, we will never get the proper version of events, as Pat Moran, that lovely man and brilliant producer, died a couple of years ago. So, we are left with Frank Allen's carefully-worded account of the Sire sessions – a narrative that tends to give the impression that John McNally was the main contributor to those recordings. Again, why am I not surprised? I rest my case.

On an entirely different note, an obituary, or even a tribute, should, wherever possible, be written by someone who was known to the deceased person, especially when those two people have spent much of their lives together.

This was the case with Tony Jackson and me: Tony and I became very close from the night that we first met at the Cross Keys pub. (I should mention here that Frankie gets it wrong in his tribute to Tony, when he states that John came with me to the Cross Keys on that fateful Saturday night. John was not with me. It was I who befriended Tony and later introduced him to John. This is another of the many myths that have been written over the years.) Frank didn't know Tony like I did, and, after reading the box set tribute, I feel it would not only have looked better, but the whole text would have been warmer, funnier and more sincere, coming from me. But I was not consulted about any of the tributes, or indeed any of the actual planning or compiling of the box set. Again I have to say: Why am I not surprised?

After listening to most of the tracks, I was transported back to the studio sessions of the '60s, '70s and '80s. I have to say they brought back some pleasant memories, though there were some unpleasant ones as well. But I will be philosophical about all that and will just talk about the songs.

One of my all-time favourites has to be 'Vahevala'. Listening to it again, I felt it is maybe a bit too long for anyone listening to it for the first time. But not for me – I still love the song. Definitely a collector's item.

'Switchboard Susan' is another good song and also one of my favourites. In fact, I keep saying that I will put that song back into the MPS set – we used to sing it on a regular basis.

As I've said many times, 'Hearts In Her Eyes' deserved to go the distance and was acclaimed by many reviewers, who predicted that it would be a hit. History unfortunately tells a different story. When the record didn't even make a dent in the charts, it really was a downer, as they say. But it was also a real motivator for me in that, for the first time, in all our charades with different record companies, I now knew in my heart that we, as the Searchers, would never have another success with a chartable record. My departure from John and Frankie was now imminent. I had given my all to those Sire sessions and had been totally convinced the breakthrough would come and we would now make some serious money for ourselves, instead of for other people.

The debate will go on about the influence the original Searchers had on other bands and, indeed, on new forms of popular music, such as folk rock and country rock. In his excellent book on Liverpool's musical heritage, Paul Du Noyer clearly states that the influence of the Beatles and the Searchers in the mid-'60s on American bands like the Byrds was very important, especially through the use of the 12-string electric Rickenbacker by George Harrison and myself. The Searchers' trademark harmonies were also copied by many British and American bands. Paul points out that 'the Searchers were rare [*among Mersey beat bands*] in keeping a folkish element in their music.' Roger McGuinn and fellow Byrd David Crosby 'were galvanised by the arrival of the Beatles [*in the US*], but they both admired the Searchers, too.' He goes on to claim that, 'in the musical evolution of rock, the Searchers' effect on the Byrds was key.'

Du Noyer and other music writers have identified the influence of the Searchers on bands such as the Hollies, Buffalo Springfield, Crosby, Stills & Nash, Tom Petty & The Heartbreakers, the Eagles, REM and the Smiths. He describes this legacy as 'a jangling, spacious style of guitar pop that recurs down the decades'. It's heart-warming to know that the great Bruce Springsteen also still performs the odd original Searchers song from time to time.

CHAPTER 30

Finale

And so here I am, almost at the end of my story. There will be lots that I have forgotten, and many bits and pieces that I have left out as they would be interesting only to myself and not to you, the reader. I am now in my 73rd year, but don't feel I've lived all that time. It has gone in a flash. (Cue for a song?)

America beckons again later this year, when I will tour with some of my contemporaries from those golden years of the '60s. This will be the 50th anniversary of when many familiar names conquered America in 1964. Next year, 2015, will be the 30th anniversary of the *Solid Silver '60s* tours, and I look forward to meeting and greeting and entertaining all those who still, after all these years, enjoy listening to those hit recordings of yesteryear.

The greatest gift in life is life itself. I am blessed with the love and support of Miss Doyle (my dear wife May) and my family and friends – especially my good friend Ron Musker and his wife Barbara, who keep May and me in touch with our Liverpool heritage when meet up with them at the wonderful Mr Ho's Chinese Restuarant – and, as I have explained in this biography, I have no regrets about the decision I took in 1985. I had many great years – even before we made it – with Tony, Chris and John, and not forgetting Frank, but I needed to find myself, and, as the song says, 'go my own way'. My No. 1 priority has always been my family and I am sure most Searchers fans will appreciate that sentiment. Most fans will also understand that it's too late to turn the clock back. There will be no reunion with John and Frankie, for, as Paul McCartney once said, you can't reheat a soufflé.

I always have things to do. The days go by so quickly, especially during the winter months. It seems that I started writing my autobiography years ago, but, in reality it's been about two years, on and off.

May and I like to take quite a few holidays through the year – when gigs allow, of course. We take all the family and go to our favourite place, Los Gigantes, a wondrous little town in the hills of Tenerife where the sun always shines – even in winter. We spend a lot of time with our grandson Alexander who, after losing Nathan, is a godsend, and our daughter Stephanie lets him stay with us at weekends and during the summer holidays. We live in lush countryside with sheep, cattle and racehorses from the nearby stud all around us and, yes, we have a very large fridge-freezer, although we do eat out quite a lot. I have many interests and hobbies, and I'll always remember the loyalty of our fans and the support they have given us throughout the long years in show business.

I am delighted to have had the opportunity to set the record straight and tell my story. I sincerely hope you've enjoyed the read – and that you will continue to enjoy the music that we, as the original Searchers, played and recorded in those golden years of the '60s. Looking back, I wouldn't have changed anything. Fifty years of performing and recording have given me much to rejoice in. My treasures. My pleasures. My investments. And most of all, my loved ones – my family.

Will I retire? I think I've covered this, but the short answer is 'Not this year', and when I do retire, I will know it's time to do so.

Mike Pender
Somewhere in Cheshire

APPENDIX I

Origins of the Searchers

1956 — Mike and John McNally.

1956-1957 — Mike and John McNally with Ron Woodbridge and friends.

1957 — Mike, John McNally, Joe West and Joe Kennedy.

1957-1958 — Group breaks up after amplifier is stolen and ceases to exist. Mike and John lose touch with each other until Mike hears that John is in Walton Hospital.

1958 — On 20 March, Mike sees his idol, Buddy Holly, perform at the Philharmonic Hall in Liverpool and gets the urge to start the group again. Still hasn't seen John McNally.

1958-1959 — Mike takes it upon himself to meet other hungry musicians and finds Tony Jackson at the Cross Keys pub in Liverpool city centre, after which he makes contact again with John McNally.

1959 — Mike, John and Tony rehearse together and play at least one gig as a trio, briefly bringing in Tony's friend Norman McGarry on drums. Shortly after, Mike meets up again with Chris Crummey (later Curtis).

1959-1960 — Mike Pender, John McNally, Tony Jackson and Chris Curtis become 'The Searchers'.

1960-1962 — Bill Beck (Johnny Sandon) joins as vocalist from September 1960 until February 1962. During this time the group are known as 'Johnny Sandon & The Searchers'.

Appendix I: Origins of the Searchers

1962-1964   Mike, John McNally, Tony Jackson and Chris Curtis.

1964-1966   Mike, John McNally, Chris Curtis and Frank Allen.

1966-1969   Mike, John McNally, Frank Allen and John Blunt.

1969-1985   Mike, John McNally, Frank Allen and Billy Adamson.

1986   Mike forms 'Mike Pender's Searchers'.

APPENDIX II

The Searchers' Performances at the Cavern (1961-63)

We made many appearances at the Iron Door club between 1961 and 1963, but we also performed the following gigs at the Cavern:

1961

9 February   *The Beatles' first gig at the Cavern.*

5 April   Our first gig at the Cavern: Johnny Sandon & The Searchers.

18 April   Swinging Blue Genes, Johnny Sandon & The Searchers, the Remo Four.

14 June   Johnny Sandon & The Searchers.

26 July   'Beatles Guest Night': Johnny Sandon & The Searchers, the Four Jays.

6 September   The Beatles, Johnny Sandon & The Searchers, Ian & The Zodiacs. I noticed a lovely blonde girl in the audience and we spoke after the show. Her name was May Doyle – she was a 17-year-old Swinging Blue Genes fan.

9 November   *Brian Epstein's first visit to the Cavern to see the Beatles.*

23 December   'All-Night Session': Johnny Sandon & The Searchers, the Beatles, Gerry & The Pacemakers, the Remo Four. One of my former teachers, Matt Rooney, was there that night – I took him to the Blue Angel after the gig, where he got very drunk I put him in a taxi – a lovely man.

24 December   Johnny Sandon & The Searchers, the Swinging Blue Genes.

31 December   Johnny Sandon & The Searchers, the Swinging Blue Genes.

1962

3 January   The Beatles, Johnny Sandon & The Searchers, Kingsize
              Taylor & The Dominoes.

9 January   Swinging Blue Genes, Johnny Sandon & The Searchers, the
              Remo Four.

27 January   Johnny Sandon & The Searchers, Gerry & The Pacemakers.

30 January   Johnny Sandon & The Searchers, the Swinging Blue Genes,
              Ian & The Zodiacs.

19 February   Johnny Sandon & The Searchers, the Swinging Blue Genes,
              the Four Jays.

28 February   The Beatles, Johnny Sandon & The Searchers, Gerry & The
              Pacemakers. This was Johnny Sandon's last appearance with
              the Searchers, as he was joining the Remo Four for bookings
              at Butlins holiday camps and at US military bases in France
              and Germany.

18 April	The Searchers, the Dakotas.
1 May	The Searchers, the Swinging Blue Genes, Group One, the Dennisons.
15 May	The Searchers, Johnny Kidd & The Pirates.
1 June	The Searchers, Group One, the Red River Jazzmen.
30 June	The Searchers, Group One, the Red River Jazzmen.
3 July	The Searchers, Freddie & The Dreamers, the Swinging Blue Genes.
17 October	*Johnny Sandon returns to the Cavern with the Remo Four. The bill also includes the Beatles and the Swinging Blue Jeans.*
1-31 October	*The Searchers at the Star-Club, Hamburg.*

1963

1 Feb–28 Mar	*The Searchers at the Star-Club, Hamburg.*
26 July	The Searchers' last appearance at the Cavern – a lunchtime show.
2 August	*The Searchers' first single, 'Sweets For My Sweet', reaches No.1 in the charts.*
3 August	*The Beatles make their last appearance at the Cavern.*
10 December	*Frank Allen plays the Cavern as the bass player with Cliff Bennett & The Rebel Rousers.*

The Cavern finally closed in March 1973 and was subsequently demolished. The 'new' Cavern was opened in Mathew Street in 1984.

I am grateful to Spencer Leigh for permission to quote these performance details from his book, 'The Cavern – The Most Famous Club in the World', published in 2008. I am also grateful to Horst Fascher for confirming the dates of our appearances at the Star-Club.

APPENDIX III

Mike Pender's Searchers Line-Ups

1986-1996   Mike Pender *(lead guitar/lead vocals)*
Chris Black *(guitar/keyboards/vocals)*
Barrie Cowell *(bass guitar/vocals)*
Steve Carlisle *(drums/vocals)*

1996-1999   Mike Pender *(lead guitar/lead vocals)*
Paul Jackson *(guitar/vocals)*
Barrie Cowell *(bass guitar/vocals)*
Steve Carlisle *(drums/vocals)*

1999-2003   Mike Pender *(lead guitar/lead vocals)*
Kevin Healey *(guitar/vocals)*
Barrie Cowell *(bass guitar/vocals)*
Steve Carlisle *(drums/vocals)*

2003-2005   Mike Pender *(lead guitar/lead vocals)*
Kevin Healey/Garth Watt-Roy *(guitar/vocals)*
Barrie Cowell *(bass guitar/vocals)*
Mike Pender Jr *(drums/vocals)*

2005-Present   Mike Pender *(lead guitar/lead vocals)*
Keith Roberts *(guitar/vocals)*
Barrie Cowell *(bass guitar/vocals)*
Mike Pender Jr *(drums/vocals)*

APPENDIX IV

Venues Played by Mike Pender/MPS

These are just some of the venues played by Mike Pender or Mike Pender's Searchers between 1986 and 2014, including national package tours, but excluding private and corporate bookings. Apologies if your venue has been omitted

Aberdare	Cwmaman Hall, Colisseum
Aberdeen	Moat House Hotel, Music Hall, Holiday Inn, Stakis Hotel
Aberystwyth	Arts Centre
Accrington	Brassington's, Martholme Grange Country Club
Airdrie	Town Hall, Workingmen's Social Club
Alloa	Tullibody WMC
Alnwick	Playhouse
Altrincham	Chequers
Andover	Cricklade Theatre
Arundel	Stakis Hotel
AUSTRALIA:	
Adelaide	Entertainment Centre
Albury	Cinema Centre
Ballarat	Her Majesty's Theatre
Brisbane	Festival Hall
Canberra	AIS Bruce Stadium
Hobart	Derwent Entertainment Centre
Launceston	Silverdome
Mackay	Entertainment Centre
Melbourne	Flinders Park
Newcastle	Entertainment Centre
Perth	Entertainment Centre

Rockhampton	Music Bowl
Shepparton	Town Hall
Sydney	Entertainment Centre
Toowoomba	Rumours Cabaret
Townsville	Entertainment Centre
Tweed Heads	Seagulls Rugby Club
Wollongong	Shellharbour Workers
AUSTRIA	
Axbridge	Webbington Country Club
Aylesbury	Civic Hall
Ayr	Butlins, Ayr Festival, Haven, Gaiety Theatre
Banbury	Trades Club
Barnsley	Trades Council Club, Kerisforth Hall, Gawber Road WMC
Barnstaple	Queen's Theatre
Basildon	Stifford Clays WMC, Towngate Theatre
Basingstoke	Blades Ice Rink, Carnival, Sports Centre, The Anvil, Club 2000
Bath	Royal Pavilion
Batley	Frontier Club
Bedworth	Civic Hall
Belfast	Opera House, Waterfront Hall
BELGIUM	
Berkswell	Nailcote Hall
Beverley	Racecourse
Bexleyheath	Swallow Hotel
Billingham	Forum Theatre
Bingley	Myrtle Park, Bradford & Bingley RFC
Birmingham	Town Hall, Cannon Hill Park, King's Cabaret Club, Symphony Hall, Villa Park, E57 Club, Tower Ballroom, Alexandra Theatre, The Barn, Small Heath Gardeners' Club, NEC Arena, Leyland Social Club
Blackburn	King George's Hall, British Aerospace Club, Furthergate WMC
Blackpool	Talk of the Coast, Cavern Club, Pembroke Hotel, Grand Theatre, Globe Theatre, Some Place Else, North Pier, Savoy Hotel, Winter Gardens, Pontins
Bodelwyddan	Warners
Bognor Regis	Southcoast World, Butlins, Pontins
Bolton	Derby Ward Club, West Horton Labour Club, British Aerospace, Albert Halls
Boston	The Gliderdrome, Boston United FC
Bournemouth	Pavilion Theatre, Pier, Bournemouth International Centre

Bradford	St. George's Hall, Pennington's, Field Sports Club
Bransford	Bank House Hotel
Braunton	Saunton Sands Hotel
BRAZIL	
Brean Sands	Pontins
Brentwood	Brentwood Centre
Bridgend	Flutes
Bridgwater	Carnival
Bridlington	South Shore Holiday Village, Spa Pavilion
Bridport	Freshwater Holiday Club
Brighouse	Ritz Ballroom
Brighton	Ocean Hotel, Dome, Brighton Centre, Butlins, Thistle Hotel
Bristol	Broadlands School, Horseshoe, Paulton Rovers FC, Grange School, Yate Leisure Centre, Colston Hall, Bawa Club, Gala Bingo
Brixton	Rugby Club
Bromborough	Stork Club
Broseley	Social Club
Burnham-on-Sea	Night Owl, Pontins, Sandy Glades, King Edward's School
Burnley	Le Grand
Burton upon Trent	Gladstone Hotel
Bury	Castle Leisure Centre, Longfield Suite
Bury St Edmunds	Corn Exchange, Reflex Club
Buxton	Opera House
Caister	Holiday Centre
Camber Sands	Leisure Park, Pontins
Camberley	Theatre
Cambridge	Chilford Hall, Corn Exchange, Spicer's Club, Wood Green Arena
CANADA	
Caneby	Lindsay Suite
Cannock	Prince of Wales Theatre
Cardiff	Newport Centre, Cedars Hotel, St David's Hall
Carlisle	Marchon Sports Centre, Sands Centre, Swallow Hotel
Carlton-in-Lindrick	Village Hall
Carluke	Carluke Social Club
Carrickfergus	Quality Hotel
Castle Douglas	Town Hall
Castleford	Woburn House
Catford	Broadway Theatre
Charnock Richard	Park Hall Hotel
Chatham	Central Hall, Suburban Club

Cheddar	Draycott Strawberry Fair
Chelmsford	Marconi, Sussex Beach Holiday Village, Springfields
Cheltenham	Town Hall
Chepstow	
Cherbourg-Bilbao	Cruise
Chester	Alvaston Hall
Chichester	Embassy Ballroom, West Sussex Holiday Centre, East Wittering School
Chigwell	David Lloyd Club
Chorley	Pines Hotel, Rivington Barn
Christchurch	Regent Centre
Clacton	Seawick Holiday Lido, Princess Theatre
Cleethorpes	Winter Gardens, Beachcomber
Coatbridge	Four Aces Club
Colchester	Mercury Theatre, Charter Hall, Woods Sports Club
Collingtree	Hilton Hotel
Consett	Civic Hall
Corby	Grampian Club
Cork	
Cosham	Crown Bingo Club
Coventry	Parkstone WMC, Jolly Colliers, Rugby Club, Windmill Country Club, Peugeot Club
Coxhoe	Leisure Centre
Cranford *(Middx)*	Concorde Club
Crawley	Hawth Theatre, Football Club
Crewe	Crew Hall
Crickhowell	Manor Hotel
Cricklewood	Beacon Social Club
Cromer	Pavilion Theatre
Croydon	Fairfield Halls
Cwmbran	Top Rank
CYPRUS	
Darlington	Civic Theatre
Dartford	Orchard Theatre
Dartmouth	Norton Park, Wonton Park
Deeside	Royal Naval Club
Denham	Licensed Victuallers Club
DENMARK	
Derby	Markeaton Park, Assembly Rooms, Rolls-Royce Social Club, Zanzibar, Blue Peter Lounge
Dereham	Coco's
Derry	Millennium Forum, Rialto
Desborough	Ritz Ballroom
Devizes	Corn Exchange

Devonport	Fleet Club
Doncaster	Slicks, Eggborough Power Station, Dome
Douglas *(IoM)*	Summerland, Gaiety Theatre
Driffield	White Horse Inn, Westfield Country Club, Far Grange Holiday Park
Dublin	Hilton
Dudley	Town Hall
Dundee	Angus Hotel, Caird Hall
Dunfermline	Carnegie Hall
Dunmow	
Durham	Abbey Sports Centre, Meadowfield Sports Centre
Dyffd	Carrick Holiday Park
Eastbourne	King's Country Club, Congress Theatre, Royal Hippodrome, Winter Gardens
Ebbw Vale	Beaufort Theatre
Edinburgh	Cavendish Club, Masonic Club, Liberton Rugby Club, Balmoral Hotel, Usher Hall, Festival Theatre
Edmonton	Millfield Theatre
Ellesmere Port	Shell Club
Eltham Hill	Top Rank
Enfield	Rifles
Epsom	Playhouse Theatre, Racecourse
Exeter	Kellerton House, Festival
Exmouth	Haven Holidays, Pavilion
Failsworth	Home Guard Club
Falkirk	Stakis Hotel
Farnborough	Leisure Centre
Felixstowe	Spa Pavilion
Fife	Ex-Servicemen's Club
Filey	Haven Holidays
FINLAND	
Fleetwood	Marine Hall
Folkestone	Hotel Burstin, Leas Cliff Hall
Forest of Dean	Dean Snooker Club
Frimley Green	Lakeside Country Club
Frodsham	Mersey View
Frome	Memorial Theatre
Gateshead	Lancastrian Suite, Civic Centre, Leisure Centre, Sage, National Garden Festival
Glasgow	Albany Hotel, Holiday Inn, Hospitality Inn, Mecca Social Club, Pavilions, St Brendan's Social Club, Fairfield WMC, Marriott Hotel, Royal Concert Hall, Hamilton FC, Edmiston Suite, Renfrew Ferry
Glenrothes	Rothes Hall

Gloucester	Oakdene
Gosport	Thorngate Hall, R&A Club, Festival
Govan	Fairfield Club
Grantham	South Kesteven Centre, Football Club
Gravesend	Scotts Social Club, Woodville Halls
Grays	Civic Hall
Great Yarmouth	Marine Centre, Seashore Holiday Centre, Wellington Pier Theatre, Vauxhall Park, Seacroft Theatre, Britannia Pier, Kessingland Holiday Village
Grimsby	Auditorium, Casablanca Club
Guernsey	Beau Sejour Centre
Guildford	Civic Hall
Halifax	Victoria Theatre
Halstead	Empire Theatre
Hamburg	Star-Club
Hamilton	Town House
Hanley	Royal Theatre
Harrogate	Majestic Hotel, Nidd Hall Hotel
Harrow	Football Club
Hastings	Camber Sands Leisure Park, White Rock Theatre
Havant	Crown Bingo Club
Hayling Island	Mill Rythe Holiday Village, Sinah Warren, Crest Club
Hay-on-Wye	Festival Showground
Helston	Mullion Holiday Centre
Hemel Hempstead	Pavilion, Royal British Legion
Hemsby	Seacroft Holiday Village
Hemswell	Lyndsey House
Hendon	Football Club
Hereford	Holme Lacey, Leisure Centre
Heywood	Civic Hall
High Wycombe	Hazlemere Community Centre, Swan Theatre
Hinckley	Concordia Theatre
Holywell	Springfield Hotel
HONG KONG	
Hopton-on-Sea	Potters Leisure
Hornsea	Floral Hall
Horwich	Leisure Centre, RMI
Houghton-le-Spring	McEwan's Centre
Hucknall	Titchfield Park
Hull	Hollywood Nights, Willoughby Manor Hotel, The Lodge, City Hall, New Theatre
Hungerford	British Legion, Littlecote House
ICELAND	
Ilfracombe	Victoria Pavilion

Ilkley	King's Hall
Ilminster	Donyatt Sports Club
Invergordon	Cromley Social Club
Inverness	Eden Court Theatre
Ipswich	Regent Theatre
Irvine	Magnum
Isle of Wight	Savoy Country Club, Gurnards Pines, Harcourt Sands, Ryde Theatre, Norton Grange, Bembridge Coast Hotel, Sandown Pavilion, Ponderosa
JAPAN	
Jarrow	Neon Social Club
Jersey	Inn on the Park, Opera House, Hotel de Normandie
Kenilworth	Chessford Grange Hotel
Keswick	Convention Centre
Kettering	Kingsley Park WMC
Kidderminster	Cookleigh Social Club
Kings Lynn	Festival, Top of the World, Corn Exchange
Kirkaldy	Jackie O's, Temple Hall
Kirkby-in-Ashfield	Festival Hall
Kirkcudbright	Town Hall
Kirkham	Ribby Hall
Kirkintillock	Canal Social Club
Langholm	Buccleuch Centre
Leamington Spa	Spa Pavilion, Cubbington Sports Club
Leeds	Horsforth Ex-Servicemen's Club, Fforde Green Hotel, Grand Theatre & Opera House
Leicester	Presley's, Cleaver's Club, De Montfort Hall, Belgrave Club, Railwaymen's Club
Leighton Buzzard	WMC
Leyland	Civic Hall, Leyland Motors
Lichfield	Garrick Theatre
Lincoln	The Lawn, Castle Grounds
Little Singleton	Great Hall At Mains
Liverpool	Cavern Club, Green Room, Latham Club, Gladstone Hotel, Adelphi Hotel, Empire Theatre, Mecca Club, Carnatic Hall (Liverpool University), Echo Arena, Metal Box Club, Olympia, Royal Court Theatre, Philharmonic Hall, Mathew Street Festival, Reigate Social Club
Llandudno	Venue Cymru, North Wales Theatre, Pontins
Llanelli	Diplomat Hotel, Bailey's
Llanerch-y-Mor	Kinsale Hall Hotel
London	Barbican, Royal Albert Hall, Hackney Empire, Stringfellow's, Palladium, Hilton Hotel, Shepherds

	Bush Empire, Royal Lancaster Hotel, Carlton Tower Hotel, Metropolitan Police Club (Lambeth), Wembley Arena
Long Eaton	West Park Leisure Centre
Loughborough	Stanford Hall, Lynroys
Louth	Town Hall
Lower Gornal	British Legion
Lowestoft	Marina Theatre, Gunton Hall
Ludlow	Castle, Assembly Rooms, Festival
Luton	Kent's Club
Lyme Bay	Holiday Centre
Mablethorpe	Haven Holidays
Maesteg	Town Hall
Maidenhead	Town Hall
MALTA	
Manchester	Chateau Jacques, Pembroke Hall, Talk of the North, Rusholme New Cabaret Club, Flixton Ex-Servicemen's Club, Bigwigs, Hotel Piccadilly, Longfield Suite, Jarvis Hotel, Granada TV Studios, Hough End Police Club, Opera House, Bridgewater Hall, Astley Bridge Conservative Club, Middleton Arena, Greater Manchester Sports Club, Rialto Ballroom, Bredbury Old Hall, Midland Hotel
Mansfield	Ashfield Show, Civic Theatre, Shirebrook Miners' Welfare
Margate	Winter Gardens
Maryport	Civic Hall
Merthyr	Football Club
Middlesbrough	Ladle Hotel, Town Hall, Festival
Middlewich	British Legion
Milton Keynes	Milton Keynes RFC, Stantonbury Leisure Centre
Minehead	Butlins
Mold	Tivoli
Morecambe	Unknown venue
Motherwell	Colville Park
Nantwich	Civic Hall
Neath	Glyn Clydach Hotel, Neath WMC
Nelson	Silverman Hall
THE NETHERLANDS	
New Mills	Stax Leisure
New Milton	Hoburn Naish Holiday Park
Newark	Palace Theatre, Castle Grounds
Newbury	Highclere House
Newcastle upon Tyne	Pineapple Club, Opera House, Racecourse, National

	Trust, Moat House Hotel
Newmarket	Cabaret Club
Newport Pagnell	WMC
Newport *(Mon.)*	Caldicot Sports Centre
Newquay	Trevelgue Holiday Park, Ocean Sounds, Key West Hotel
Newton Abbott	Plough & Harrow
Northampton	WMC, Royal & Derngate, Moat House Hotel, Billing Aquadome
Northamptonshire	Wickstead Park
Northwich	Lostock Social Club
NORWAY	
Norwich	Talk of the East, Theatre Royal, Horsford Social Club
Nottingham	Commodore International, Nottingham Show, Royal Moat House, Oakleigh Lodge Social Club, Royal Concert Hall, Catton Hall
Old Leigh	Boatyard
Oldham	St Herbert's Centre, Civic Hall (Royton)
Ollerton	Thoresby Hall
Onllwyn	Miners' Welfare
Ormskirk	Shaw Hall Caravan Park
Oxford	New Theatre, Apollo
Paignton	Torbay Chalets
Paribourne	Springfield Hotel
Peebles	Ex-Servicemen's Club
Pembroke	Festival
Peterborough	Truckfest, Hotpoint Club, Cross Fields Club, Cresse, East of England Showground
Peterhead	Waterside Inn
Peterlee	Leisure Centre
Petworth	Petworth Park
Pickering	Festival
Plymouth	The Glen, Shire Horse Centre, Plymouth Argyle FC, Royal Fleet Club
Polmont	Inchyra Grange Hotel
Polperro	Killigarth Manor
Pontefract	Kellingley Social Centre
Pontlottyn	British Legion Club
Poole	Arts Centre, Rockley Park Holiday Centre
Port Sunlight	Hulme Hall
Porthcawl	Trecco Bay Holiday Centre
Portsmouth	Guildhall
Poulton-le-Fylde	Lawdie Miss Clawdie's
Prestatyn	Talesloe Beach Club, Haven Holidays, Pontins

Preston	Guildhall, BAC, Grasshoppers Rugby Club, Preston Golf Club, St Catherine's Hospice, Greenlands Social Club
Pudsey	Bienvenue
Pwllheli	Butlins
Rawtenstall	Astoria
Reading	Hexagon, Rivermead Leisure Park
Redcar	Lakes Social Club, Rugby Club
Redhill	Harlequin
Retford	Majestic Theatre
Rhyl	Pavilion
Rochdale	Kirkhalt WMC, New Carlton Ballroom
Rockley Sands	Bourne Leisure Centre
Romford	Top Rank, United Services Club, Dolphin Centre
Rotherham	Consort Hotel
Roydon	Roydon Mill Leisure Centre
Royton	Civic Hall
Runcorn	F.C.
Rushdon	Diamonds FC
Rushton	Town Band Club
Rutherglen	'60s Festival
Saffron Walden	Audley End House
Salford	Willows
Salisbury	Town Hall, Dinton Village Hall
Sandown *(IoW)*	Norton Grange
Saundersfoot	Sunnyvale Holiday Park
Scarborough	Grand Hotel, Cayton Bay, Futurist Theatre, Delmont Hotel, Spa Theatre
Selby	Drax Power Station
Sheffield	City Hall, Arena, Richmond Club, Aston Hall Hotel, Embassy Club
Sherburn	Leisure Centre
Shoreham-by-Sea	Community Centre
Shrewsbury	Lord Hill Hotel, Music Hall
Singapore	
Skegness	Butlins, Richmond Caravan Club, Embassy Theatre, Vauxhall Holiday Park
Skipton	Black Horse
Solihull	Arts Complex
Somercotes	Lakeside
South Shields	Cleadon & District Social Club
SOUTH AFRICA	
Southampton	Guildhall, Dockers' Club, Mecca Club, Polygon Hotel, Bitterne Park Social Club, Mayflower Theatre

Southampton-Barcelona	*QE2* cruise
Southend	Cliffs Pavilion
Southery	Village Hall
Southport	Pontins, Southport Theatre
Southwoodham Ferrers	Queen Elizabeth Hall
SPAIN	
Spalding	South Holland Centre, Springfields, Willow Ball
Spennymoor	Leisure Centre
Spilsby	Aviation Heritage Centre
St Albans	Arena
St Helens	Beeches Country Club, Thatto Heath Labour Club, Moss Bank Club
St Ives	Holiday Village
St Leonards-on-Sea	Haven Holidays, Combe Haven Holiday Park
Stevenage	Gordon Craig Theatre, Concert Hall, Leisure Centre, Timbers
Stockport	Quaffers, Rugby Club
Stockton	Henry Afrika's, Portrack Conservative Club, The Mall
Stoke-on-Trent	Hem Heath Social Club, Victoria Hall, Kings Hall
Stoneleigh	National Agricultural Centre
Strichen	Festival
Sudbrook	Gala
Sudbury	Quay Theatre
Sunderland	Empire, Roker Hotel, Riverside Lodge
Sutton Coldfield	Town Hall
Sutton-in-Ashfield	St Joseph's Secondary School
Swansea	North Gower Hotel, Grand Theatre, Tower Hotel, Pewlan Social Club, Singleton Park
SWEDEN	
Swindon	Supermarine, Wyvern Theatre
SWITZERLAND	
Tamworth	Assembly Rooms
Tavistock	Town Hall
Telford	Forest Glen Pavilion, The Place, Shopping Centre, Oakengates Town Hall, Moat House Hotel
Tenby	Unknown venue
Tewkesbury	Puckrup Hall
Thameside	Hippodrome
Ton Pentre	Football Club
Torquay	Princess Theatre, Babbacombe Theatre
Treharris	Millennium Park
Truro	Showground, Hall for Cornwall

Tunbridge Wells	High Rocks Hotel, Assembly Rooms
Tynemouth	Park Hotel
UNITED ARAB EMIRATES	
USA	
Uxbridge	Yeading FC
Valencia –	
Southampton	Cruise
Virgin Islands –	
Madeira	Cruise
Wakefield	Samson's
Walkden	Pembroke Halls
Walsall	Walsall FC (Saddlers Club)
Waltham Abbey	Swallow Hotel
Warrington	Parr Hall, Greenalls Centre
Wavendon	Stables Theatre
Webbington	Country Club
Weston-super-Mare	Weston AFC, Winter Gardens, Playhouse Theatre, Sandbay Holiday Park
Weymouth	Pavilion Theatre, Warmwell Leisure Centre
Whitby	Pavilion Theatre, Royal Hotel, '60s Festival
Whitchurch	Civic Centre
Wick	Assembly Rooms
Widnes	Ford Social Club
Wigan	Riverside, Lowton Civic Hall, Standish High School, Aspull Civic Centre
Willoughby	Grange Park Hotel
Windsor	Theatre Royal
Wisbech	Empire Theatre
Wisley	RHS Gardens
Withensea	Teddy's Club
Woking	New Victoria Theatre
Wolverhampton	Civic Hall, Grand Theatre
Woodbridge	Angel Theatre
Worcester	Huntingdon Hall
Workington	New Westlands Hotel
Worksop	Clumber Park
Worthing	Assembly Hall, Pavilion Theatre
Wrexham	Plas Madoc Leisure Centre, Pllay British Legion
Wymondham	Central Hall
Yarmouth	Gunton Hall
Yeovil	The Gardens, Westlands Sports & Social Club
York	Grand Opera House, Barbican Centre

APPENDIX V

High Court Judgment (8 June 1988)

IN THE HIGH COURT OF JUSTICE
CHANCERY DIVISION

Royal Courts of Justice
London.
8th June 1988

Before :

MR JUSTICE WHITFORD

McNALLY and another
- v -
PRENDERGAST

(Transcribed from the official tape recording by Cater Walsh & Co,
6 Jelleyman Close, Blakebrook, Kidderminster DY11 6AD.
Official Court Reporters and Tape Transcribers.)

MR R MILLER, instructed by Paul Krempel, WC2, appeared for the Plaintiffs.

MR A PATERSON, QC and Mr M Kalipetis, instructed by Wright Webb Syrett, W1, appeared for the Defendant.

JUDGMENT – as revised

MR JUSTICE WHITFORD: I have to consider a motion brought by two plaintiffs, John McNally and Francis McNeice, in which an order is sought for the committal of the defendant, Michael Prendergast to prison, and for leave to issue writs of sequestration, the allegation being that there have been breaches of an undertaking that was given when this matter came before Peter Gibson J, in 1986. I can say at the outset that it stands accepted that there have been breaches of the undertaking. It is said in affidavits which have been sworn by Mr Prendergast and a Mr Wellbourne, professionally known as Tony Sherwood who has been acting as his agent, that these were inadvertent breaches and very full apologies have been offered.

I must, however, just go into a little bit of back history. The defendant, who is professionally known as Mike Pender, and the first plaintiff started playing together in a band in Liverpool a good many years ago, now over 30 years. They took up with two other musicians who have since dropped out of the picture, and with the second plaintiff Mr McNeice who joined Mr Prendergast and Mr McNally in 1964, and playing together they undoubtedly had some success. There might be some slight difference of opinion as to the extent of that success, but certainly anybody who has any familiarity at all with the pop field will have heard of The Searchers, the name under which as a group they were happily performing together at one time; and the defendant, as the lead singer to the group, which he was over a quite considerable period of years, must inevitably have become very well known to those who were interested in this particular field of music.

In 1985, and there is no dispute about this, the band split up. The defendant felt that he would like to take off and start off on his own. The two plaintiffs wanted to continue to work together; so the split took place and, on the evidence of the defendant, it took place on the basis that he was going to be allowed to continue to perform using the name Mike Pender's Searchers, or Mike Pender and his Searchers, the plaintiffs to continue using the name The Searchers. Insofar as there was any agreement in 1985, that was an oral agreement and its exact terms may yet hereafter be the subject of dispute. Undoubtedly in 1986 there were discussions ostensibly involving solicitors acting for the defendant on one side and solicitors undoubtedly acting for the plaintiffs on the other. There is an assertion that the terms of a written agreement which has been exhibited in the evidence were agreed, and the action in relation to which this motion is brought and in the course of which the undertaking was give was started on a claim by the plaintiffs that an agreement was entered into in the terms of a final draft exhibited in evidence, a question which is still at issue between the parties and which still remains to be decided.

It is to my mind unsatisfactory in the extreme that this proceeding, which was started by a writ dated 25th March 1986 should have proceeded quite as slowly as it has, and I entirely concur in the view expressed by Mr Bateson, who has appeared on behalf of the defendant, that the sooner the action is heard and disposed of the better. Until that is done it is all too likely that accusations and counter-accusations of the kind which have already been made, may be continued.

The proceedings have been instituted, there was an application before Peter Gibson J. in the course of which a consent order was made embodying an undertaking in part in the terms set out in the Notice of Motion. The entirety of the undertaking dealt with two matters, one an undertaking by Mr Prendergast that he would not promote or publicise himself or cause anybody else to promote him under or by reference to any name incorporating the word 'Searchers' other than Mike Pender's Searchers with a possibility of a change to the use of the style Mike Pender and his Searchers, an option which does not appear ever to have been exercised; but the second undertaking which was given, which is the one material to the present proceeding, was an undertaking that Mr Prendergast or his manager would include in any contract for his appearance anywhere in the world as an artiste or as part of a group appearing under the name Mike Pender's Searchers, a provision instructing the other party thereto to call, promote or publicise him only under the name Mike Pender's Searchers, and in the case of written material in a form in which, save for *de minimis* differences, each word was given equal prominence as to size, colour, type of lettering, and that he or his manager would forthwith notify all parties to whom he was presently contracted that he might henceforth only be called, promoted or publicised under the name Mike Pender's Searchers, and in the case of written material in the form in which, save for *de minimis* differences, each word was given equal prominence as to size, colour and type of lettering. Nothing arises in relation to persons with whom he was at the date of this undertaking presently contracted so far as anything in the evidence goes, but questions have arisen with regard to contracts which have been entered into with various parties, and it is said, and in my judgement rightly said, by the plaintiffs that there has been a failure to comply with the terms of these undertakings and at least I think in two respects so much is accepted on the defendant's side.

If one goes to the evidence in support of this application for committal, one has got to look at such evidence as may support the grounds taken by the plaintiffs and the breaches of which complaint is made are set out in paragraph 3 of the Notice of Motion in what can only be described as general terms. What I have got to consider, in the light of the relevant provisions of the Rules relating to contempt proceedings, are the particular grounds specified in paragraph 4. Five heads are set out of contracts which it is said did not meet the requirements of the undertaking.

The first head was: 'All those contracts drawn up or entered into by Tony Sherwood Ltd. prior to the beginning of April 1986.' When the matter was opened there was apparently no notice of this given to the defendant before the matter was opened. I was told that there was a typing error and it should have been 1987. Certainly the date 1986 would have made the complaint meaningless having regard to the time at which Tony Sherwood Ltd. became the defendant's agent. I do not propose to pay any attention of the complaint under 4(i). It is not, in my judgment, sufficiently particularised and in any event this alteration of the date is not something which at this stage ought to be permitted. If one takes it, as I think one must, in the form in which it was served on the defendant, obviously the case cannot be made out.

There are then references to four specific contracts, the first being a contract dated 8th January 1987 between Royston Jones for an on behalf of RKO, and Mike Pender's Searchers. Now this contract, and indeed all the other contracts in relation to which specific complaint is made, is to be found exhibited to the principal affidavit in support of the application for committal, being an affidavit of Mr Paul Kempel, a solicitor having the conduct of the case, and the first of the exhibits which we have to turn to is exhibit 4, the relevant contract being at page 21. The contract contains a lot of details with which we are in no way concerned, but in the box in which the details of days and dates of engagement are set out there is a notification of these terms: 'It is essential that this artist is billed as follows: "Mike Pender's Searchers".'

Now there is nothing in the notice which to my mind makes it sufficiently clear that the words 'Mike Pender's Searchers' in billing are to be given equal prominence, though Mr Bateson was quite right in pointing out that they are given equal prominence at the bottom of the notice, and certainly there is nothing about equal prominence as to colour and type of lettering though there again it can be said that in all strictness I suppose one might come to the conclusion that so much could be inferred, but that is what I regard as a lawyer's point. The point of giving the undertaking was to make sure that when contracts were entered into, the persons with whom the contracts were being made would know exactly what they could or cold not do, and it was in my view necessary to make it plain that the words to be used were 'Mike Pender's Searchers' and that they, as words, should be given equal prominence as to size, colour and type of lettering. That was not done in this particular contract.

The contract in question is one dating back to January 1987 and that is a matter of significance and importance.

The next contract to which specific reference is made is one to be found forming part of the exhibit PK6. It is a Mr Neil Hook for and on behalf of a club called The Meadow Club and there again the endorsement on the contract is in similar terms: 'The act to be billed only as Mike Pender's Searchers', but no express words making it clear that when it was so billed those words should be given equal prominence as to size, colour and type of lettering. That was a contract back in February 1987.

Then next, and it is (iv) in the particulars under paragraph 4, a contract of 12th May 1987, to be found as part of exhibit PK11, the relevant contract being at page 2 of that particular exhibit. It does not say anything about billing only Mike Pender's Searchers, and it was in fact signed by the defendant personally using his professional name, Mike Pender. He accepts that he did this and that he should not have done it, and he explained that it was inadvertent and he deals with the circumstances in which he signed. Since he set up on his own he has been doing gigs here and there about the country, arriving just in time to go on, so he said, and leaving as soon as he can when he has done his act, and the result of that is that he did not really look sufficiently closely at this contract, so he signed it and he accepts that he should not have signed it.

There is one other matter, however, connected with this particular contract to which Mr Bateson drew my especial attention and it is an aspect of the matter which applies with equal force to the last of the contracts to which I shall be turning. That is that when this case came to the attention of the plaintiffs, their immediate reaction was to enter into correspondence with Lakeside which they did on the 8th June 1987, as we can see by turning to page 7 of the exhibit, the contract it will be recalled having been entered into on the 12th May. In this letter there are references made to the order of Gibson J. and complaint is being made as against Lakeside going to this, that what they have done gives the plaintiffs ground for complaint in passing-off proceedings. In the course of this correspondence undertakings were sought in the letter of 8th June and eventually a writ was served, and I was informed on instructions that that action was subsequently settled; but it is I think of importance to note what immediate reaction of the plaintiffs was, for the immediate reaction was to make a complaint against Lakeside on the documents in this particular exhibit.

The final contract is a contract relating to an appearance at the Granby Hotel which was going to take place in the Christmas period of 1987. The contract in this case was the document which is to be found at page 3 of Mr Krempel's exhibit 12. It again is not in accordance with the terms of the undertaking. Once again the immediate complaint that was made was to the Granby Hotel who made apology for what was done and who in fact said that they would ensure that the form of the advertisement was changed, and I have no reason to believe that it was not changed so that by the time the performance actually took place what would have been advertised, would have been advertised in a form which would have complied with the undertaking that was given.

It was on the 18th September, page 2 of exhibit 12, that the Granby Hotel were writing to say that there were going to remove the advertising which is the subject of objection and that further advertising would clearly state Mike Pender's Searchers though it is not entirely clear from the correspondence whether it was accepted that this was going to be in strict compliance with the terms of the undertaking. However, nothing has appeared in the evidence to indicate that the fresh advertising material which went out was not in strict compliance, and Mr Bateson does, I think quite rightly, point out that it is a little strange that this motion seeking penal sanctions as against the defendant was not issued until November at a time, when, so far as the Granby Hotel incidence was concerned, that was all over and a time when the earlier incidents in May and February and January of this year were all matters of history. I regard it as regrettable in the extreme that this motion, concerned as it is with the liberty of the subject, which apparently came before Vinelott J. in the latter part of November should not be heard until today. That may in part have been explained, I think, by the fact not contested by Mr Bateson, spoken to by Mr Miller, that there have been negotiations. That there should have been negotiations is sensible enough. The form of the undertaking which was given was unlikely satisfactorily to protect the interests of the plaintiffs because whatever may be put on a contract, there can be no certainty that the conditions will be complied with and those who are responsible for producing advertisements or putting out posters or anything of that kind may, notwithstanding the express terms of the contract, be using a form of words which in trust if the interests of the plaintiffs are adequately to be protected, should not be used.

The only matter with which I am concerned, however, is Liability so far as the defendant is concerned in respect of the undertaking which he has given. The plaintiffs have established that there have been breaches of the undertaking. I should say at once that although in the notice of motion claims are made for a committal to prison and orders for sequestration, Mr Miller did, when opening the matter to me, make it clear that the plaintiffs were not intending to press the matter to this extreme I think quite rightly.

Mr Bateson submitted that this was not a case of what could be described as a deliberate or intentional contempt, and he did point out that these earlier incidents having been drawn to the attention of the defendant and the defendant's agent, steps have on the face of the evidence been taken to ensure that all the contracts that are now entered into carry a wording sufficient to alert the persons contracted with as to the requirements that have got to be met if the court order is to be complied with, and on the evidence I am satisfied that these contracts now all carry the wording 'To comply with court order this act must be billed, advertised or promoted only as Mike Pender's Searchers' and these words are all in block capitals, with the addition of the words: 'All wording must be of equal size, colour and prominence'. If that has been the practice and is going to continue to be the practice, then the undertaking given to the court is now being complied with. I should say that as I understood the argument on the plaintiff's side, it was being suggested that they are by no means satisfied that what has been sworn to is necessarily right; that is to say, that all contracts have, since complaints of this character have been made, borne the wording which I have just given, but that is the evidence.

I think Mr Bateson was right when he said that it would be wholly inappropriate in this proceeding to make any order to discovery of all the contracts. A very large number of them do in fact appear to have been disclosed, and so far as the contracts disclosed are concerned it is accepted that they do all carry the relevant wording.

So there it is, and I have to consider what must be done. There have been these breaches. It is, as I hope I have already indicated, a case in which I am entirely of the view expressed by Mr Miller that the making of an order for committal to prison or granting leave to issue writs of sequestration would be wholly inappropriate. There is, of course, the possibility of a fine but considering all the circumstances of the case, and the time which it has taken to bring even this motion on, and the dilatory way in which the action has been proceeding, and bearing in mind the very full apologies which have been offered, the only order which it is appropriate to make upon the motion is that the defendant should pay the plaintiff's costs on an indemnity basis.

APPENDIX VI

A History of My Guitars

1954	6-string battered acoustic (can't remember colour)
1955	6-string Zenith semi-acoustic, sunburst
1956	6-string Hofner Club 60, blonde
1959	6-string Burns Tri-Sonic, cherry red
1963	6-string Gibson ES-345 Stereo, sunburst
1964	12-string Rickenbacker Rose Morris 360, sunburst *(stolen 1969)*
1964	12-string Burns Double-Six, white
1964	6-string Burns Marvin, white *(stolen)*
1969	12-string Danelectro Belzouki, sunburst
1974	12-string Rickenbacker 456 6/12 converter, maple glow
1974	6-string Fender Stratocaster 1963 model still with original bridge cover, natural
Late '70s	12-string Aria Pro-11 Aquasound, sunburst and stripes *(stolen 1993)*
Late '70s	12-string Aria Pro acoustic, natural
Late '70s	6-string Aria Pro-11 PE-R80, sunburst
1993	12-string Aria Pro-11 Revsound, blue
2002	12-string Rickenbacker 660, jetglo (black)
2006	12-string Yamaha electric, sunburst
2007	12-string Ovation Applause acoustic, natural

APPENDIX VII

Mike Pender/MPS Discography

45s

Mike Pender

Sierra FED-23   It's Over / Brothers & Sisters   1986
(also 12" FEDT-23)

The Corporation (The Travelling Wrinklies)

Corporation KORP-1   Ain't Nothing But A House Party /   1989
(also 12" 12KORP-1)   Ain't Nothing But A House Party (Instrumental)
                       **Mike with Reg Presley, Tony Crane, Brian Poole
                       and Clem Curtis.**

Gulf Aid

Gulf Aid GULF-1   As Time Stood Still / As Time Stood Still   1991
                       **Charity record sponsored by *The Sun* featuring
                       Mike, Gerry Marsden, Sonia, Timmy Mallett,
                       Maria Whittaker, Hazell Dean, Frank Bruno,
                       Tessa Sanderson, John Payne, Rose-Marie,
                       Brotherhood of Man, the Grant Twins, Mark
                       Peters, David O'Leary, Donna Ewin, Suzanne
                       Mizzi, David Rocastle, Pat Sharp, Tracey Elvik,
                       Kathy Taylor, Paul Davis, John Conteh, Mandy
                       Sharp, Andy Frampton, Russell Carline, Charles
                       Shirvell, Derrick Evans, Sandra Jones, David
                       Taylor and Chris 'Snake' Davis (sax solo).**

LPs

Class of '64

Holly BUDDY-001   *Class of '64*   1989

Mike appears as guest vocalist/lead guitarist on
'Falling Apart At The Seams'.
**Class of '64 is a group formed in 1989 by Frankie
Connor (Hideaways), Alan Crowley (Tuxedos)
and Billy Kinsley (Merseybeats). This was their
first release. It was reissued in 1995 on CD *Cavern
Days* [Holly FAB-1964].**

Cassette Tapes

Mike Pender's Searchers

MP-001   *Mike Penders Searchers*   1989

Sweets For My Sweet / Take It Or Leave It /
Goodbye My Love / When You Walk In The
Room / Don't Throw Your Love Away / Take
Me For What I'm Worth / Needles And Pins /
Sugar And Spice / What Have They Done To
The Rain / Someday We're Gonna Love Again /
Love Potion Number Nine
**New versions of Searchers' hits recorded by MPS
at Dave Williams Music Works, Nottingham.
This cassette tape was available only from the
MPS Fan Club/at gigs. These and other MPS
recordings have since been licensed to various
labels. Many of these releases have been
incorrectly credited to 'The Searchers' rather
than 'Mike Pender's Searchers' and/or have
used a photo of the Searchers, rather than MPS,
on the cover.**

Mike Pender's Searchers

MP-002   *Mike Penders Searchers*   1996

Same as the 1989 cassette plus seven additional
tracks: 'It's Over' *(1986 Sierra single),* 'Falling
Apart At The Seams' *(1989 Holly recording),*
'Blue Mondays', 'Broken Hearts', 'Red Ferrari'
and 'Needles & Pins (Version 2)' *(1990 recordings
originally released on 1991 Karussell CD)* and
'Two Hearts'.
**This cassette tape was available only from the
MPS Fan Club/at gigs. Also released on CD
MPCD-002 (1996).**

CDs

Mike Pender's Searchers

Karussell
847 551-2

Sweets For My Sweet   Germany, 1991
Sweets For My Sweet / Love Potion
Number 9 / Broken Hearts / Goodbye My
Love / Needles & Pins '90 / Take It Or
Leave It / Take Me For What I'm Worth /
What Have They Done To The Rain /
Someday We're Gonna Love Again / Red
Ferrari / Blue Mondays / Sugar And Spice /
Don't Throw Your Love Away / When You
Walk In The Room
**This was the first appearance of 'Blue Mondays',
'Broken Hearts', 'Red Ferrari' and 'Needles &
Pins '90' (aka 'Needles & Pins (Version 2)').**

Class of '64

Holly FAB-1964

Cavern Days   1995
Mike appears as guest vocalist/lead guitarist on
'Falling Apart At The Seams'.
**Reissue of 1989 LP *Class of '64* [Holly BUDDY-001]
with six bonus tracks.**

Mike Pender's Searchers

MCPD-002

Mike Penders Searchers   1996
Same tracks as 1996 cassette MP-002.
**This CD was available only from the MPS Fan
Club/at gigs.**

Various Artists

Harry
no catalogue no.

Sixties Sing Nineties   1999
Mike performs Crowded House's 1992 hit,
'Weather With You'.
**Produced by Chip Hawkes. Reissued in 2003 on
Various Artists CD *Back To The Future* [Delicious
DEL-120]**

No label or   ***Various Artists*** [2-CD]
catalogue no.   *ReelinandaRockin*   2002
Mike performs 'Dont Throw Your Love Away',
'Needles And Pins' and 'When You Walk In
The Room', and also sings and plays on various
tracks featuring other artists.
**New versions specially recorded at 1079 Studios,
York for the Derek Franks Organisation.**

Delicious   ***Various Artists***
DEL-120   *Back To The Future*   2003
Mike performs 'Weather With You'.
**Produced by Chip Hawkes. Reissue of 1999 Various
Artists CD *Sixties Sing Nineties* [Harry, no cat no].**

No label or   ***Various Artists*** [2-CD]
catalogue no.   *ReelinandaRockin (Volume II)*   2004
Mike performs 'Love Potion No. 9' and 'Sweets
For My Sweet' and also sings and plays on
various tracks featuring other artists.
**New versions specially recorded at 1079 Studios,
York for the Derek Franks Organisation.**

MP25CD2010   ***Mike Pender***
The Original Voice of the Searchers   2010
Same tracks as 1996 CD MCPD-002 plus two
previously unissued live cuts recorded at the
Tivoli, Stockholm on 23 September 2010:
'My Girl' and 'You Got It'.
**This CD was available only from the MPS Fan
Club/at gigs.**

Bibliography

Allen, Frank - *The Searchers and Me* (Aureus, 2009)

Allen, Frank - *Travelling Man: On the Road with the Searchers*
            (Aureus, 1999)

Bacon, Tony - *Rickenbacker Electric 12-String: The Story of the Guitars,*
            the Music and the Great Players (Backbeat Books, 2010)

Du Noyer, Paul - *Liverpool: Wondrous Place – Music from Cavern to Cream*
            (Virgin Books: 2002)

Francis, Paul - *Drumming Up Vibrations* (Twizz Publications, 2011)

Harry, Bill - *Bigger Than the Beatles* (Trinity Mirror, 2009)

Kinsley, Billy - *It's Love That Really Counts* (Cavern City Tours, 2010)

Leach, Sam - *The Birth of the Beatles* (Seven Hills, 1999)

Leach, Sam - *The Rocking City* (Pharaoh, 1999)

Leigh, Spencer - *The Cavern – The Most Famous Club in the World*
            (SAF Publishing, 2008)

Lewisohn, Mark - *The Complete Beatles Chronicle* (Hamlyn, 2003)

Metcalf, Dave - *Celebrity Gatecrasher* (Bank House Books, 2011)

Roberts, David - *Rock Atlas* (Clarksdale/Red Planet, 2011)

Rogan, Johnny - *The Byrds: Timeless Flight Revisited – The Sequel*
            (Rogan House: 2001)

White, George R. - *British Hit EPs 1955-1989* (Music Mentor Books, 2014)

Index of People's Names

259

Index of Songs & Album Titles

265

Index of Films & Shows

Illustrations & Photo Credits

Box set cover on plate 41 (bottom left) from author's collection.

Documents on pages 21, 26, 54, 55, 81, 82, 149 and 210 from author's collection.

Flyers on page 144 and plate 41 (bottom right) from author's collection.

Leaflet on page 62 from author's collection.

Newspaper cutting on page 170 from author's collection, unknown newspaper; page 204 from author's collection, courtesy *Liverpool Echo*.

Photos on dust jacket, pages 1 and 9, and plates 1, 2 (top), 3, 4 (top), 5 (top and bottom left), 6, 7 (bottom), 8, 9 (bottom), 10 (top left and top right), 11 (bottom), 13 (bottom), 15 (top), 18 (bottom), 21, 22, 23, 24 (bottom), 26, 28, 29, 30 (top), 31, 32, 33, 34, 35, 36, 37, 38, 39 (top), 40 (top right and bottom), 41 (top left and right), 42 (top), 43, 44, 45, 46, 47 and 48 from author's collection; plate 2 (bottom) courtesy *Evening Express*; plate 4 (bottom) by and © Sylvia Beaumont; plate 5 (bottom right) by and © John Beer; plate 7 (top) by and © Richard Mahoney; plate 9 (top), 11 (top) and 15 (bottom) from author's collection, unknown newspapers; plate 10 (bottom) by and © Ben Brooksbank; plates 12-13 (top) courtesy Roger Dopson; plates 12 (bottom), 17 (bottom) and 19 (top) courtesy Pye Records; plate 14 courtesy ABC TV; plate 16 (top) courtesy Rediffusion; plate 16 (bottom) by Valerie Wilmer, copyright unknown; plate 17 (top) by Peter O. Stuart, courtesy *Disc*; plate 18 (top) by Marc Sharatt Photography, copyright unknown; plates 19 (bottom) and 20 (bottom) courtesy Granada TV; plate 20 (top) by and © Brian Bignell; plate 24 (top) by W.M. Ward Photography; plate 25 courtesy Sotheby's; plate 27 (top) by Steve Mason, copyright unknown; plate 27 (bottom) courtesy of Sire Records; plate 30 (bottom) by Tony Mottram, copyright unknown; plate 32 (top) by Linda Woods, copyright unknown; plate 40 (top left) by Ron Long, copyright unknown; plate 42 (bottom) by and © Steve Gardner/Digital Leaf Photographics.

Poster on page 226 from author's collection.

Programmes on pages 67, 69 and 139 from author's collection.

Record sleeve on plate 39 (bottom) courtesy Richard Mahoney.